The Cognitive Neuroscience of A

Fundamentals of Cognitive Neuroscience

General Editors: *Martha J. Farah* and *Mark H. Johnson*

The 'decade of the brain' has seen a growing rapprochement among cognitive scientists, specialists in artificial intelligence, neuropsychologists and brain scientists in their various efforts to understand human mental activity. New theoretical frameworks in cognitive science are being constructed while new technologies enable unprecedented observations of the live brain at work. Graduate and undergraduate syllabuses are advancing closely behind the research frontiers, but the task of synthesising the new knowledge being produced by such diverse enterprises is a daunting one not only for students but also for instructors.

Fundamentals of Cognitive Neuroscience will address this problem. Each book will constitute a concise, readable and up-to-date review of a particular problem area by a leading scientist. The aim will be both to provide balanced coverage, and to convey the excitement and challenge of new developments. Major emphasis will be placed on contrasting theoretical approaches to the masses of new data now being collected, though each author will be encouraged to express a point of view and to discuss the relative merits of these approaches as he or she sees them.

Developmental Cognitive Neuroscience	Mark H. Johnson
The Cognitive Neuroscience of Action	Marc Jeannerod

Forthcoming

Connectionist Models in Cognitive Neuroscience	
	James L. McClelland and David C. Plaut
The Cognitive Neuroscience of Perception	Martha J. Farah

•

The Cognitive Neuroscience of Action

Marc Jeannerod

INSERM Centre National de la Recherche Scientifique, Lyon

Copyright © Marc Jeannerod, 1997

The right of Marc Jeannerod to be identified as author of this work has been asserted in accordance with the Copyright, Designs and Patents Act 1988.

First published 1997
2 4 6 8 10 9 7 5 3 1

Blackwell Publishers Ltd
108 Cowley Road
Oxford OX4 1JF
UK

Blackwell Publishers Inc.
238 Main Street
Cambridge, Massachusetts 02142, USA

1001868056

British Library Cataloguing in Publication Data

A CIP catalogue record for this book is available from the British Library.

Library of Congress Cataloging-in-Publication Data

Jeannerod, Marc.
    The cognitive neuroscience of action / Marc Jeannerod.
      p. cm. — (Fundamentals of cognitive neuroscience)
    Includes bibliographical references and index.
    ISBN 0–631–19603–X (hbk.); ISBN 0–631–196048 (pbk.)
    1. Efferent pathways. 2. Cognitive neuroscience. I. Title.
  II. Series.
  QP383.15.J43 1997
  612.8—dc20   96–18462
                                   CIP

Typeset in 11 on $13\frac{1}{2}$ pt Palatino
by Graphicraft Typesetters Ltd, Hong Kong
Printed in Great Britain by Hartnolls Ltd, Bodmin, Cornwall

This book is printed on acid-free paper

Contents

Figures

Figures

Series Editors' Preface

Science often seems to proceed in an excruciatingly slow and incremental manner. Between initial grant submissions and renewals, between first-year projects and doctoral defenses, it is rare to see significant change in our theories or methods. For researchers in cognitive psychology and behavioral neuroscience, the 1970s and early 1980s were periods of this type of steady but not terribly exciting progress.

By the mid-eighties, however, something decidedly non-incremental happened: a new field, called cognitive neuroscience, was born. Those of us lucky enough to have been working in the parent disciplines of cognitive science and neuroscience at this time experienced a major change in our thinking about mind and brain. Before, they had seemed related in principle, but not in any way that was tractable in research practice. Now the relation between mind and brain seemed not only tractable, but essential for further progress in understanding mind and brain. By the end of the decade, cognitive scientists were using data from brain-damaged patients and functional neuroimaging to test theories of normal cognition, and neuroscientists were using cognitive theories and methods, including computational modeling, to interpret brain anatomy and physiology. A host of new meetings, societies, journals, and funding initiatives signaled that a new field had been established.

From the perspective of the late 1990s cognitive neuroscience continues to flourish, and to attract new researchers from the ranks of graduate students and senior scientists alike. Unfortunately, these individuals face a problem: the dearth of general, introductory reading in cognitive neuroscience. It was with this problem in mind that we undertook to edit the *Fundamentals of Cognitive Neuroscience* series. The books in this series are primers on the essential topics of cognitive neuroscience. Each volume provides a theory-oriented overview of the current state of the art in its area, drawing upon the results of multiple research techniques. In addition to the present volume, other volumes currently in press or in preparation will cover Attention, Development, Language, Memory, and Vision. Additional volumes are likely to be commissioned in the near future.

One of the domains in which the cognitive neuroscience approach has been most successfully applied is motor control. This volume by Marc Jeanerrod on the cognitive neuroscience of action focusses on the central question of the nature and role of different representations in the planning and execution of movements. The book explores in detail the contribution of different brain structures, and particularly the cerebral cortex, to various aspects of movement preparation and execution. Consistent with the aims of the series, a range of neuroscience evidence is related to cognitive and behavioral experiments in normal subjects and to clinical observations in brain-lesioned patients, resulting in provocative hypotheses about the cognitive structure of central representations and processes that subserve action.

Martha J. Farah
Mark H. Johnson

Philadelphia and London, 1996

Acknowledgements

I am indebted to the many friends and colleagues who took the time to read critically and comment on earlier versions of this book. The final outcome owes much to their efforts. I wish to acknowledge in particular the contributions of M. A. Arbib, S. Lederman, G. Rizzolatti, M. Wiesendanger and J. P. Joseph. The series co-editors, M. Farah and M. H. Johnson and an anonymous referee also provided excellent advice.

Many of the experiments reported in this book were performed in collaboration with J. Decety. I also thank L. Fadiga, M. Gentilucci, J. Proust, J. Requin, H. Sakata and S. Zeki for their suggestions and discussions.

The author and publishers gratefully acknowledge the following for permission to reproduce copyright material:

Figure 2.10 reprinted from Jeannerod et al. 1995, Grasping objects. The cortical mechanisms of visuomotor transformation, *Trends in Neuroscience*, **18**: 314–20, with permission of Elsevier Trends Journals, Cambridge, UK.

Figure 4.1 reprinted from Decety et al. 1989, The timing of mentally represented actions, *Behavioural Brain Research*, **34**: 35–42, with kind permission of Elsevier Science.

Figure 4.2 reprinted from Decety & Jeannerod 1996, Fitts' Law in mentally simulated movements, *Behavioural Brain Research*, **72**: 127–34, with kind permission of Elsevier Science.

Figure 4.6 reprinted from Dominey et al. 1995, Motor imagery of a lateralized sequential task is asymmetrically slowed in Hemi-Parkinson patients, *Neuropsychologia*, **33**: 727–41, with kind permission of Elsevier Science.

Figure 6.2 reprinted from Jeannerod 1995, Mental imagery in the motor context, *Neuropsychologia*, **33**: 1419–32, with kind permission of Elsevier Science.

Every effort has been made to trace copyright holders. The publishers apologize for any errors or omissions in the above list and would be grateful to be notified of any corrections that should be incoporated in the next edition or reprint of this book.

chapter one

General Introduction

The generation of actions by the central nervous system is a fascinating problem. More than in any other area of neuroscience, the function of the mechanisms under study is directly accessible, simply because the observation of an action reveals its goal and gives access to its biological significance. The aim of this introduction is to briefly review some of the early concepts which have structured our current thinking on the generation of actions.

The early researchers in this field had noticed (perhaps not innocently) that even the simplest movements that the nervous system could produce already appeared to be organized purposefully. E. Pflüger, for example, claimed that reflex movements elicited by cutaneous stimulation in the spinal frog were real 'intelligent' actions, as if the animal tried to escape or to protect itself against undesirable stimuli (Pflüger's 'Rückenmarkseele'; see Fearing, 1930). Similarly, D. Ferrier interpreted the muscular contractions he elicited by faradization of the excitable cortex as coordinated actions: 'Many of the movements such as those of the hands, the legs, the facial muscles and the mouth have the aspect of purpose or volition and are of the same nature as those which the animal makes in its ordinary intelligent action' (1876, p. 95). These impressions relied on the fact that muscular contractions in response to stimulation were not localized to single muscles, they were coordinated contractions of several muscles. The term coordination, to use P. Weiss's terms, 'refers to the fact that the central nervous system engages the muscles in such a definite order that . . . their combined activities result in orderly movements, which, in turn, yield acts of biological adequacy for the whole animal' (1941, quoted in Gallistel, 1980, p. 268). But, Weiss added, we ignore the principle in operation in the centres to make the appropriate selection. This is exactly what this book is about: to try to understand how actions are 'represented' in the brain, in other words, how the elementary mechanisms which ultimately control muscle contraction are selected and assembled; and what are the selection and assemblage 'principles'. Coordination and purpose are indeed the two major challenges faced by any study dealing with the mechanisms of action.

1.1   Action as a coordination problem

There is in fact a striking disproportion between our knowledge of the physiological properties of the elements and our understanding of the operation of the nervous system as the coordinator of these elemental activities. Sherrington had led the way in searching for the simplest behavioural unit where coordination would already be at work (what he called the 'unit of integration'). Simple spinal reflexes, like the extensor or the flexor reflexes, for example, fulfilled his criterion for behavioural elements, as they integrated, in an orderly way, the activity of several motor units. According to his famous keyboard analogy, Sherrington considered that motor units (the motoneuron and the muscle fibers to which it is connected) are played by different reflexes, but in a different order and to a different effect. Coordination, a 'co-adjustment' of simple reflexes into more complex ones, was based on mechanisms such as reciprocal facilitation of reflexes having complementary effects, reciprocal inhibition of antagonist reflexes, irradiation for recruiting new reflexes as stimulus strength increased, etc.

Another Sherringtonian concept, sequential combination, accounted for the chaining of reflexes into behavioural sequences. The tendency for considering complex behaviour as a concatenation of simpler elements (reflexes, schemas, etc.) is still a very influential one, as some of the forthcoming analyses will reveal. This may be a survival of classical empiricist theories whereby behaviour depended upon external events: in the chaining hypothesis, the next movement in a sequence is triggered by proprioceptive discharges arising from the previous one. In fact, it now appears that even the most automatized motor sequences, like swallowing or locomoting, are not organized on the chaining model, but rather depend on built-in 'programs' (see Gallistel, 1980). In addition, the introduction in neuroscience of new concepts (in part derived from cognitive psychology) such as the concept of representation, has changed the views on coordination of complex actions. Although the notion of behavioural elements is still considered as valid, the way these elements are selected and assembled to produce a coordinated action is radically different.

1.2   Internal models and the purpose of actions

A major step in changing views on coordination is the notion of internal models. Organisms are not only reacting to external perturbations or events, they also actively initiate these interactions. This means that representations that account for behaviour must not only be reactive, they must be predictive. They must carry internal models of how the external world is, how it will be modified by the action of the organism, and how the organism will be modified by that action. To account for these notions, it is important to review in some detail an early predecessor to the modern internal models, that of homeostatic regulation. Let us first concentrate on the concept itself, by trying to define the notion of a representation as an 'internal model'. This notion progressively emerged during the nineteenth century when engineers felt the need of controlling the motion of machines. Special devices ('governors' and 'moderators') were used for keeping the velocity of the machine as uniform as possible, in spite of variations in the driving force or the resistance (Maxwell, 1867–68). The general principle was to determine a reference value of the parameter to be controlled and to automatically activate the moderator when its value exceeded the reference. Biological systems also appeared to be liable to the same mode of functioning. Claude Bernard discovered that systemic regulations were circular mechanisms aimed at maintaining 'constancy' of the internal milieu. Regulation of blood glucose, for example, was based on constancy of glycemia at a level corresponding to tissular metabolic needs (the reference value). When glycemia dropped below the reference, processes were activated to restore it. Since Claude Bernard, this idea of self-regulation (homeostasis) has received a broad recognition among biologists, and was used for explaining many different physiological functions (Cannon, 1932). Motor reflexes such as pupillary responses to light, postural reactions, vestibulo-ocular reflex, etc., are among them.

Homeostatic systems, however, are closed-loop systems aimed at maintaining the constancy of a fixed inbuilt reference. Their activation depends on the detection of an 'error' between their input level, which monitors the current state of the controlled parameter, and their central level, where the reference value is stored. The important point here is that this notion of a stored reference implies the existence of a certain form of representation (be it neural or otherwise) of the regulated parameter to which incoming signals are compared. In other words, the reference gives an image of what a representation could be, even though the homeostatic mode of regulation can only account for crude interactions between the organism and the external environment. Craik (1943) was among the first to assume the existence of such internal models in the brain; this was a major break from the prevailing emphasis on purely stimulus-response mechanisms. This notion drew attention to the role of endogenous factors such as stored knowledge or mental content, which are now currently considered by cognitive psychologists as causal factors in behaviour. Craik's internal models were thought of as analogue representations (he died shortly before the first digital computers were built). Later developments in Artificial Intelligence emphasized digital representations, and hierarchical structures similar to those of computer programs were used to conceptualize representations, where actions were represented as sequences of steps involving tests and operations (Miller et al., 1960).

Internal models had antecedents in the psychological literature. An early example was Head's concept of 'schema' (Head, 1920). Although this concept was first used by its author to account for maintenance and regulation of posture, it was later developed by others as an internal model of the body in action, built from sensations and previous responses to external stimuli (for a critical account, see Oldfield and Zangwill, 1942; see also Schilder, 1935). Neisser (1976) used the same terminology to designate the schema as a structure internal to the perceiver, but modifiable by experience. 'The schema accepts information ... and is changed by that information; it directs movements and exploratory activities that make more information available, by which it is further modified' (1976, p. 54). Neisser adds: '... a schema is a part of the nervous system ... an entire system that includes receptors and afferents and feedforward units and efferents' (p. 54). 'By constructing an anticipatory schema, the perceiver engages in an act that involves information from the environment as well as his own cognitive mechanisms. He is changed by the information he picks up' (p. 57). The important point is that schemas as they are conceived here are clearly distinct from the static, genetically coded references of the type involved in homeostatic regulations. Schemas can be acquired through experience and learning, they can be improved, changed, destroyed, etc., and, most importantly, they are available as building blocks for creating dynamic representations.

1.3   Motor engrams

Detailed neurophysiological studies in invertebrates or in lower vertebrates have demonstrated the existence of central discharges which may account for automatic behaviour (for example, Grillner, 1985). In the context of ethology, behavioural sequences have been described, which develop blindly and eventually reach their goal after they have been triggered by external cues (the so-called 'trigger features'). Localized brain stimulations can also trigger similarly complex actions which outlast for a considerable amount of time the duration of the stimulus (for a review see Bandler, 1988).

In the domain of human action, Bernstein (1967) also expressed the same idea of internal models of action. 'There exist in the central nervous system, exact formulae of movement or their engrams'. 'The existence of such engrams is proved ... by the very fact of the existence of habits of movements and of automatized movements' (1967, p. 37). According to Bernstein, the engram of an action must contain, 'like an embryo in an egg or a track on a gramophone record, the entire scheme of the movement as it is expanded in time. It must also guarantee the order and the rhythm of the realisation of this scheme; that is to say, the gramophone record ... must have some sort of motor to turn it' (p. 39).

The content of these models (the embryo in the egg) is still a matter of intense debate. Several important issues will be explored. The first one is that the neural structures which are involved in motor representation are organized as a functional hierarchy, a 'system of systems' (Weiss, 1941), where each level consists of an ensemble of subsystems, themselves decomposed into smaller units, etc. This notion of recursivity (which is now applied to several current models of action programming) offers a solution for the problem of the selection of motor elements that will compose the representation. The selection would be effected across levels by activating smaller and smaller elements. This mode of functioning is easily transferable to the neural organization.

A second issue is that of parallel processing in the motor system. The classical model of a serial organization inherited from the structure of computer programs is seriously questioned. Important new data suggest that activation is distributed simultaneously to several levels. This notion reflects in the concepts of parallel channels for visuomotor functions, parallel descending cortico-spinal pathways, etc. Experimentally, unit activity in cortical areas thought to represent levels of organization for the different steps of action occurs synchronously, and the existence of a sequence can only be detected statistically. Similarly, bidirectional connections between these areas account for this wide distribution of activity.

Finally, a third issue is that of the existence of a central coordinator which determines the temporal structure of the motor output and, ultimately, the sequence of the action. The concept of a hierarchically higher mechanism is not in contradiction with that of parallel processing. A hierarchy between levels, although it implies degrees of specialization for each of these levels, does not imply a sequential order of activation. Neuropsychological data clearly suggest that the prefrontal areas might play the role of such a central coordinator for structuring the pattern of action plans.

NO SUCH THING

1.4   Outline

The aim of this book is thus to investigate the main aspects of representations for actions. It explores in detail the contribution of cerebral structures, particularly that of cerebral cortex, to the various aspects of movement preparation and execution. This approach involves the study of anatomical connections between areas, as well as the recording of single neuron activity in animals. It also involves brain stimulation and brain mapping studies in human subjects. Finally, it attempts to describe the cognitive structure of central representations and processes which subserve actions by making inferences from behavioural experiments in normal subjects and clinical observations in brain-lesioned subjects.

Chapters 2 and 3 deal with an esssential aspect of motor behaviour, object-oriented action. This aspect has evolved as part of technological and cultural adaptation in man, though it has precursors in other species, for feeding or tool use behaviour, for example. As objects are part of the visual world, the description of the mechanisms of object-oriented actions first concerns visuomotor transformations. Chapter 2 summarizes the concepts of specialized visual pathways and reviews in detail those which underlie visuomotor transformation. The actions of reaching and grasping are analyzed using behavioural and neurophysiological approaches. Whereas behavioural data are mostly drawn from experiments in humans, cortical mechanisms are analyzed in non-human primates, where grasping and manipulative movements (still to be fully analysed experimentally) comparable to humans can be observed. The study of visually directed grasping will reveal the existence of a cortical network composed of areas with highly coherent and complementary properties. Neurons in these areas are specialized operators for controlling hand-object interactions and for transferring the visual code into a motor code. A computational approach using similar operators (the motor schemas) which account for object-oriented actions will be described. This model is a good image of a specialized motor representation.

Chapter 3 contributes to the study of object-oriented behaviour by identifying different modes of interaction with objects. Clinical cases with cortical lesions offer striking examples of dissociation between these modes of processing. An object can be correctly reached and grasped without being identified, and conversely. The same attribute of an object (for example, its size) can be correctly processed or not, according to whether a perceptual judgement or an adjustment of the finger grip is requested from the patient. These dissociations raise questions on the respective contributions of different neural pathways to perception or action. They also raise the point of a specific processing mode for dealing with objects as goals for actions.

The main point of chapter 3 is thus that the mode of processing to which an object is submitted and the corresponding representation that is created for acting on that object, depend on the task in which the subject is involved. If the task refers to the semantic content of the object, in the context of an explicit operation like naming, describing, evaluating, etc., the processing mode will involve mechanisms for perceptual recognition, verbalization, semantic memory. If, on the other hand, the object is an element in an action as a tool or an instrument, the processing mode will involve mechanisms for visuomotor transformation, kinematics, procedural memory. Obviously, these two modes are hardly separable from each other in ordinary life. There may even be a continuum between them, starting from the most pragmatic aspects of object-oriented action, like using an object as a tool, through situations like observing and imitating somebody using that same object, demonstrating its use to somebody else, mentally simulating the action, up to the most semantic modalities like recognizing a pantomime of that object or describing its use verbally. It will be argued that brain lesions can, within limits, specifically disorganize each of these levels of representation.

In chapter 4, the classical psychological paradigm of mental imagery is used to answer new questions on motor representations. The general idea is that motor imagery gives access to the structure and content of representations for action. Motor rules, constraints and potentialities which shape the pattern of motor behaviour can actually be described in simulated movements as well. In spite of being conscious, however, motor images retain one of the principal characteristics of pragmatic processing, that of being poorly verbalizable. For this reason, they are more easily studied through their physiological correlates, like the changes in excitability at different levels of the motor system, the activation of autonomic effectors or the local changes in brain metabolism. The fact that neural structures devoted to motor planning and execution are activated during mental simulation of movement, explains the effects of mental training, as well as the difficulties met by patients with motor impairment of central origin to simulate actions mentally.

Action involves steps which evolve over time, where each step contributes to the final goal. Chapter 5 describes the neural mechanisms for the organization of action plans. The discovery of set-related neuronal discharges in several cortical areas supports the notion, gained from the mental chronometry paradigms, that action plans are built as hierarchical structures. These neurons function as domain-specific working memories, for storing the spatial and temporal contingencies of the action or the significance of the external cues, or for signalling the completion of the intermediate steps. The study of the effects of lesions of prefrontal cortex in monkeys and man confirm the interpretations of classical neurology, whereby frontal lobes were the organ for coordination of actions. The mapping of brain activity in normal subjects, when combined with adequate cognitive experimental paradigms, reveals itself as a powerful tool for giving substance to concepts like willed action, for example.

Finally, chapter 6 aims to describe the internal structure (neural as well as cognitive) of the motor representation. Particular emphasis is placed on the notion of a comparison, within the representation, between the desired and the current states of the action. This choice is justified, not only by the ample historical validation of the concept of comparator, but also, and mainly by the recognition of the importance of interaction between the self and the environment. Although the notion of a control of behaviour by external events is rejected (a prerequisite for introducing the notion of representation), it remains that a pure feedforward model of the generation of action seems equally inapropriate. Action implies interaction with external objects and with other organisms. The role of internal neural signals which reflect the content of the representation will be considered as critical for detecting the degree of match between the content of the representation and its effects on the external environment.

chapter two

Neural Substrates for Object-oriented Actions

Many human actions are directed toward objects. Fundamental aspects of our behaviour, like the ability to use tools, for example, originate from neural specialization for perceiving, grasping, recognizing and categorizing objects. These operations correspond to adaptive acquisitions in primates and some are unique to man. In this chapter, we begin the description of an ensemble of mechanisms for behaving with objects. In the first part the emphasis will be placed on the anatomical and physiological arguments that allow us to delineate a specific neural system devoted to object-oriented movements. In this context we will try to define vision for action, as the basis for visuomotor transformations.

2.1 Visuomotor transformation as a dissociable visual function

Visuomotor transformation requires specific processing for mapping visual information into motor commands. In this section, the neural systems which account for this transformation will be described, starting with an analysis of the relevant aspects of the anatomy of the visual system (see Jeannerod and Rossetti, 1993).

2.1.1   The two-visual-systems hypothesis: early contributions

The notion that retinofugal fibres are distributed along several central visual pathways has a long history in neuroscience. Early anatomical studies first suggested the existence of three visual pathways by which the retina was connected to the cortex. Apart from the main route through the lateral geniculate body, von Monakow identified one pathway through the pulvinar and another one through the superior colliculus. These pathways terminated in cortical areas outside the striate area (see Polyak, 1957). The visuomotor function of the subcortical pathway relaying in the superior colliculus was particularly advocated by Cajal (1909). He described a 'descending' or 'motor' pathway arising from the fourth layer of the superior colliculus and terminating in the ocular motor nuclei and in the adjacent reticular formation. This anatomical description, which is still largely valid, became the substrate for orienting and pupillary reflexes. Subcortical vision was thus considered by Cajal as a pure 'motor' vision. Later on, Hess et al. (1946) and Apter (1946), based on stimulation experiments in cats, concluded that the visual orienting reflexes were organized in the superior colliculi. Accordingly, extensive lesions of this structure (Sprague and Meikle, 1965) were shown to produce severe impairment in eye movements and visuomotor behaviour.

The modern version of this hypothesis re-emerged in the late 1960s. The distribution of retinofugal fibers between retinogeniculate and retinotectal pathways was thus interpreted within the framework of a dichotomy between two visual systems endowed with complementary functions. Schneider (1969) proposed that the geniculostriate pathway was a system essential to the learning of pattern discrimination, and the retinotectal pathway, a system for mediating spatial orientation. Using hamsters (a species with a large and easily accessible tectum) to demonstrate his point, Schneider clearly dissociated 'cortical blindness' from 'tectal blindness'. Following ablation of visual areas 17 and 18 animals became unable to learn simple pattern discrimination (for example, vertical versus horizontal stripes), although they remained able to orient toward stimuli (for example, sunflower seeds) presented across their visual field. By contrast, following large undercuttings through the midbrain tectum, the spatial orientation ability was lost, whereas pattern discrimination was still possible. This anatomical and functional duality became known as the now classical opposition between a system specialized for answering the question 'What is it?', and another one specialized for answering the question 'Where is it?' (Schneider, 1969).

A slightly different version of the parallel visual functions model was used for explaining the mechanisms of visuomotor coordination. Hein and Held (1967) showed that kittens reared without sight of their forelimbs presented a defective placing reaction when moved towards the edge of a table. Whereas they were still able to extend their forelimbs prior to contact with the table, their response was inaccurate: if the edge was made discontinuous to render the task more difficult, they were unable to guide their forelimbs at the appropriate location, and contacted the table at random. Hein and Held thus concluded that the placing reaction was in fact dissociable into components, one of which, elicited extension, developed without sight of the forelimbs, and the other, guided placing, required a prolonged viewing of the forelimbs to be present. This dissociation of visuomotor behaviour into components implicitly suggested separate substrates for the visual control of each of them. Indeed, a similar dissociation was observed in kittens reared in complete darkness (a condition known to severely affect the functioning of visual cortex): these animals were able to avoid obstacles or to follow moving lights, but they could not reach accurately for objects (Vital-Durand et al., 1974). Visually decorticated animals also present defective reaching, principally due to lack of terminal accuracy. Accordingly, accurate guidance would be preferentially controlled by the visual cortex, whereas elicited extension would be a more primitive response arising from stimulation of the peripheral retina and processed outside visual cortex.

A model of visuomotor coordination built on the notion of two visual channels for movement control was also presented by Trevarthen (1968). This author, studying visuomotor behaviour in split-brain monkeys, came to the conclusion that the subcortical visual system subserved 'ambient' vision, while the cortical system subserved 'focal' vision. Ambient vision, which was supported by peripheral retina, referred to visuomotor interactions between the self and objects in space occurring during locomotion or orienting movements. Focal vision referred to interactions with objects requested by identification, manipulation or use. Paillard (1971) suggested that mechanisms related to the peripheral retina were responsible for localizing visual targets in space and for triggering a ballistic motor program carrying the limb within target vicinity. A terminal adjustment was effected under control of the central retina for guiding the limb at the target. In addition, Paillard suggested that the visuomotor mechanisms responsible for terminal adjustment were carried out by way of the corticospinal control of the distal limb segments (Paillard and Beaubaton, 1974).

The introduction of primates in visuomotor research led to one of the most striking outcomes of the two-visual-system hypothesis, namely the (re)discovery of residual visual function following lesion of visual cortex. Pathological destruction of visual cortex in man was classically thought to produce total blindness, except for pupillar response to light and very crude visual perception limited to sudden changes in illumination. This conventional opinion, however, was called into question on the basis of experimental findings in monkeys. Although destriated monkeys also appeared to be profoundly impaired in their ordinary visual behaviour, they were still able to avoid obstacles and to generate motor responses for reaching objects appearing in, or moving across their visual field (Humphrey and Weiskrantz, 1967). These residual visual abilities were attributed to retinal ganglion cells surviving ablation of visual cortex and projecting subcortically (see Dineen and Hendrickson, 1981). These anatomical findings represented a strong argument for the role of subcortical structures in mediating residual visual function in destriated monkeys. Mohler and Wurtz (1977) showed that partially destriated monkeys, which were able to orient visually toward stimuli presented within their scotoma, lost this ability after subsequent destruction of the retinotopically corresponding zones of the superior colliculi. Thus in monkeys, superior colliculi, and possibly other subcortical areas receiving input from the retina, might play a critical role either in mediating pure 'subcortical vision', or in relaying visual input to other structures on which they project, including extra-striate cortex. The role of extrastriate visual cortex in residual vision is also demonstrated by experiments with transient inactivation of striate cortex. In this condition, normal visual responses can still be recorded from neurons in other visual areas (Girard et al., 1991; see section 2.2.1).

In human subjects, clinical obervations suggestive of incomplete or 'relative' blindness within scotomata of cortical origin had been mentioned previously by several authors (see Weiskrantz, 1986 for review). However, systematic experimental evidence for residual visual abilities following lesions of the striate cortex was first reported by Pöppel et al. (1973), followed by Weiskrantz et al. (1974) and Perenin and Jeannerod (1975). All these experiments used a new methodological approach derived from the monkey studies and based on forced choice responses. Cortically lesioned subjects were requested to turn their eyes, or point their hand, each time a stimulus was presented. Responses were obtained, the amplitude and the direction of which definitely correlated with target positions, although they had a general trend toward undershooting. Similar results were obtained by Perenin and Jeannerod (1978) and Ptito et al. (1991) in hemidecorticated subjects.

In such cases, the complete loss of cortex on one side stresses the role of subcortical vision. The fact that subjects who present 'blindsight' remain unaware of the stimuli, and usually experience 'guessing' rather than 'seeing', is in accordance with the classical idea that sub-cortical vision is 'unconscious'. As will be discussed later on (e.g. in section 3.2), this may not be a property of subcortical pathways per se, but rather a characteristic of the mode of processing of visual stimuli used by the subjects to give the response. Indeed, Cowey and Stoerig (1995) replicated the human blindsight findings in monkeys with unilateral ablation of striate cortex. These animals were found to be able to accurately point at targets briefly presented in their hemianopic field when targets appeared alternatively in either field. However, when trials with no visual stimulus (blank trials) were randomly introduced among the normal trials with a visual stimulus, the monkeys shifted to a different strategy: they classified the trials with visual stimuli presented in the hemianopic field as blank trials, and failed to respond. Thus, when visual stimuli appeared each time and the animals had no choice, they responded, using extrastriate vision, whereas when they had to decide whether a stimulus was present or not, they did not. This is an example of a paradigm-dependent response where the same stimulus is treated differently according to the situation.

2.1.2   *The two-visual-systems hypothesis: its status in primates*

The two-visual-systems model as it was heralded by Schneider (1969) was rapidly considered as unsatisfactory. Lesions limited to the superficial layers of the superior colliculus in the tree shrew, sparing the deep layers and the adjacent midbrain, were shown to produce little or no visuomotor deficit (Casagrande et al., 1972). In rodents, lesions of striate cortex appeared to affect orientation toward targets located within the rostral visual field, whereas this ability was spared after collicular lesion. Superior colliculus, by constrast, was necessary for orienting toward targets placed in the far peripheral visual field (see Goodale, 1983). Thus, orientation seems a more complex function than suggested by the early Schneider's results: it cannot be completely dissociated from pattern discrimination, specially for what concerns the most central parts of the visual field.

Another school of thought, more influenced by human neuropsychology than by phylogenetic considerations, and using monkeys (rather than rodents) as subjects, came to the conclusion that the subcortical route was of less importance for spatial vision than initially thought. Instead, it was postulated that both modes of vision were mediated by two diverging corticocortical pathways (Ungerleider and Mishkin, 1982; Mishkin et al., 1983; Van Essen and Maunsell, 1983; Boussaoud et al., 1990; Merigan and Maunsell, 1993). One pathway was the ventral occipitotemporal route linking striate cortex to prestriate areas and from there, reaching inferotemporal cortex on both sides via callosal connections. Interruption of this pathway abolished object discrimination without affecting perception of spatial relations between objects. The other, dorsal, pathway diverged from the previous one by linking the prestriate areas to the posterior part of the parietal lobe. Interruption of this pathway produced visual spatial disorientation characterized, not only by misperception of the relative positions of spatial landmarks, but also by localization deficits during object-oriented action (for review, see Ungerleider and Mishkin, 1982). The two pathways are illustrated in figure 2.1 for one of their most recent versions.

These 'cortical' systems in fact expand to subcortical structures: Baleydier and Morel (1992) showed that groups of neurons in the posterior pulvinar complex projecting to cortical areas belonging to the ventral and the dorsal routes, respectively, are entirely segregated. In spite of both receiving separate subcortical inputs, however, the two systems seem to have different degrees of dependence with respect to these inputs. This was demonstrated in experiments with functional exclusion (by cooling) or lesion of area V1, at the origin of the two corticocortical pathways. We should expect that this exclusion will abolish, or greatly diminish, visual responsiveness in areas downstream to V1 in both systems. In fact, visual responses are completely abolished only in the occipito-inferotemporal pathway, whereas altered responses can still be recorded in the occipitoparietal areas (Rocha-Miranda et al., 1975; Rodman et al., 1989; Girard et al., 1991, 1992). Bullier et al.'s (1994) conclusion is that subcortical pathways responsible for visual responses in parietal cortex in the absence of V1 are part of a primitive organization of the visual system, common to primate and non-primate species. These pathways would be responsible for fast and unconscious processing of visual signals. By contrast, the more 'recently' acquired ventral system would be more dependent on V1 input. These data are summarized in figure 2.2.

In order to account for these different functional properties, it has been suggested that the two corticocortical systems relay

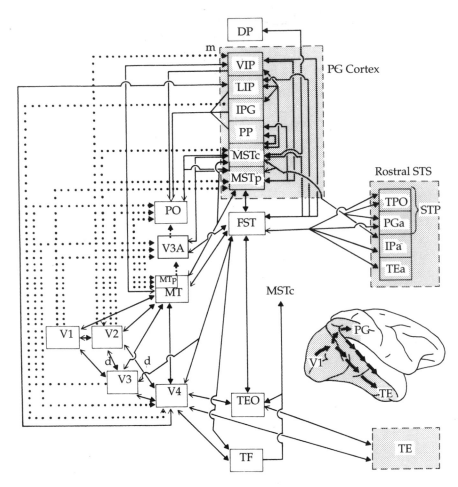

Figure 2.1 Corticocortical connections between visual areas in the macaque monkey

The pathways outlined on the right hemisphere of a monkey brain (on lower right), are detailed in the block diagram, together with some of the connections between areas. Note relatively divergent connections for the ventral pathway through areas V3, V4, TEO, TF, TE, and the dorsal pathway through MT and MST to posterior parietal cortex. *From Boussaoud et al., 1990*

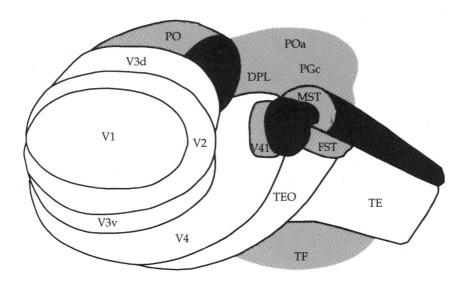

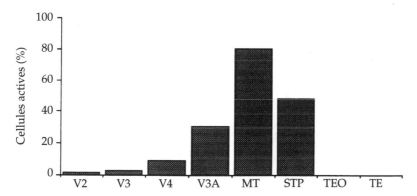

Figure 2.2   Visual areas containing visually responsive neurons in the absence of input from V1

Upper diagram: map of cortical areas. Areas in dark grey are those which remain responsive after cooling of V1. Areas in white contain only a few responsive neurons. Areas in light grey: not tested.

Histogram in lower part shows the proportion of active cells for some of the areas on the map.

From Bullier et al., 1994

different types of visual input. The ventral system would relay input from the P retino-geniculate pathway (which originates from the P retinal ganglion cells and projects on the parvocellular layers of the lateral geniculate), a pathway specialized for processing colour and form; the dorsal system would relay input from the M pathway (from M ganglion cells through magnocellular geniculate layers), specialized for processing motion (see Merigan and Maunsell, 1993 for review). This dichotomy, in spite of its obvious heuristic value, now seems far too simplistic, as will be illustrated by human experiments to be described in chapter 3. First, many of the cortical areas pertaining to the ventral or the dorsal system appear to be strongly interconnected, as it indeed appears on figure 2.1 (see also Morel and Bullier, 1990). Second, there are probably more than two pathways originating from V1. Finally, some areas, like V3 receive inputs from both P and M pathways. This same area V3, where most cells are orientation selective and which should be classified as a 'form' area, in fact projects mostly to parietal cortex (for a review of these points, see Zeki, 1993). Based on these arguments, it would seem more appropriate to draw a functional separation, not between a 'form' (or 'object') system (the ventral system) and a 'space' system (the dorsal system), but rather between two 'form' systems, the ventral one more concerned with form in association to color and the dorsal one with 'dynamic' form in relation to motion (Zeki, 1993). These points will become highly relevant in the discussion about form processing in relation to object-oriented action (see below, and chapter 3).

The dorsal system thus appears as the place wherein to look for the neural correlates of visuomotor transformations, for at least two reasons. First, the aspects of visual information processed in this system, like motion, are implicitly more relevant to motor control than static form or colour; second, as will be emphasized below, parietal lesions, not inferotemporal lesions, produce visuomotor impairments. Accordingly, the dorsal system will be considered here as a visuomotor system specialized for dealing with all aspects of object-oriented actions, which includes, not only directing action in the proper direction, but also interacting locally with objects.

2.1.3   Visuomotor channels

This renewed conception of parallel visual systems coincided with the formulation of another visuomotor model, no longer based on the modalities of visual coding of the movement, but rather on the modes of representation of the goal of the movement. Objects in space afford two main types of interactions, reaching and grasping, which correspond to two different visuomotor channels (Jeannerod, 1981). One channel deals with extrinsic properties of these objects (their location in space with respect to the body, their velocity of motion, etc.). Its function is to transport the hand to a desired location within extrapersonal action space. It must include mechanisms for computing distance and direction of the point in space where to move. The other channel deals with intrinsic object properties (like shape or size). Its function is to shape the hand with the purpose of manipulating, identifying, or transforming objects. The difference in biological significance between the two behaviours should be reflected at the level of their neural substrates and modes of control. Reaching is mostly effected by the proximal joints of the arm, it operates within a body-centred system of coordinates. By contrast, grasping relates to the specialization of the hand in primates and man (see section 2.3). The location in space where the interaction between the hand and the object takes place is therefore immaterial, at least within the limits imposed by biomechanical constraints. This suggests that, in principle, the finger movement patterns generated under visual and haptic control during object manipulation should be uninfluenced by spatial factors. This point will be rediscussed in section 2.3.1.

These concepts of parallel visual systems and of visuomotor channels in fact raise three distinct, though interrelated, issues.

1   As both reaching and grasping imply visuomotor transformations, they are both likely to rely on 'dorsal' functions. The descriptions below will indeed provide ample evidence that they correspond to two distinct and identifiable subsystems linking posterior parietal areas and premotor cortex.
2   Although the visuomotor channels for reaching and grasping

are distinct from one another, they must share a common mechanism for achieving coordination with each other. This is essential, due to the high accuracy requirements of prehension (as opposed to other visuomotor performances, like pointing, for example), and also due to the vastly different kinematic properties of the hand and the arm segments. This mechanism, however, is beyond the scope of this review. It will be briefly mentioned in section 2.4.

3   The fact that grasping clearly involves some type of form processing implies that the dorsal system should be able to process form, as was indeed suggested by Zeki (1993) on anatomical grounds. This prediction in turn implies that the classical dichotomy between a dorsal 'space' system and a ventral 'object' system should be abandoned and replaced by a more distributed version. The description of neurophysiological mechanisms underlying grasping will provide further arguments in this direction.

2.2 Neural coding in the visuomotor (dorsal) pathway: reaching movements

The action of reaching toward a location in extrapersonal space (be it pointing to a spot of light or transporting the hand for grasping an object) has been extensively studied, both in animals and man. The point here is not to review the kinematic aspects of reaching, nor the intermediate stages whereby the position of an object in space is transferred from an extrinsic (visual) into an intrinsic (proprioceptive) system of coordinates: these aspects have been extensively treated in several reviews (for example, Jeannerod, 1988; Flanders et al., 1992). The present description will concentrate on the cortical mechanisms for coding the direction of reaching movements.

2.2.1   *Reaching neurons in the parietal cortex*

The first arguments as to a role of parietal cortex in coding the direction of reaching were drawn from lesion experiments.

Studies focusing on the effects of inferior parietal lobule lesions on visuomotor behaviour in monkeys have revealed highly specific impairments, including a reaching deficit, first mentioned by Peele (1944). The reaching deficit following this lesion in monkey is characterized by the fact that the animals misreach with their arm contralateral to the lesion in either part of the visual field (the so-called 'hand effect') (Hartje and Ettlinger, 1973; Lamotte and Acuna, 1978; Faugier-Grimaud et al., 1978, 1985). Their ipsilesional arm is usually not affected, though a 'visual field effect' (involving also misreaching with the ipsilesional arm within the contralesional field) has been observed by Stein (1978). Misreaching following parietal lesion consistently involves a systematic bias towards the side of the lesion, a fact that was reported by all the above mentioned authors. Finally, the reaching deficit is more severe in the absence of visual feedback from the limb than under visual guidance.

Neurons related to reaching were first described by Hyvarinen and Poranen (1974) and by Mountcastle et al. (1975) within areas 5 and 7 (see figure 2.3 for a map of parietal cortical areas). These neurons belong to a broader category of neurons selectively activated during various aspects of visuomotor behaviour, also including manipulation, visual fixation or eye movement. The cells described by Mountcastle and his colleagues in both areas have no receptive field or other sensory properties in the visual or somatosensory modalities: instead, they discharge during active reach toward objects of motivational interest (a piece of food for example), or during active manipulation of these objects. Hence the terminology of 'projection neurons' and of 'command functions' used by these authors to designate an unspecified reaching system. By contrast, Hyvarinen and Poranen (1974) considered that the cells responding to arm movements in area 7 had directional properties, in specifying reaching in a given direction of extrapersonal space. In their experiments, activation of such neurons required association of a visual stimulus and of a movement toward it. Neither presentation of the visual stimulus, nor execution of the movement alone were sufficient for firing these neurons. A population of neurons

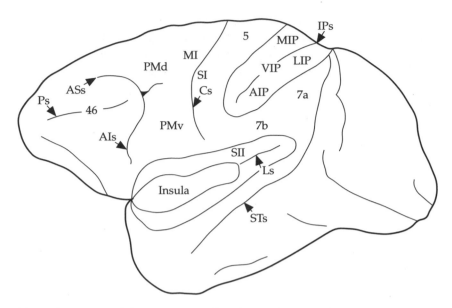

Figure 2.3   Map of the main parietal and frontal areas relevant to visuomotor transformation

Areas are shown on the lateral aspect of a left hemisphere of the macaque brain. The intraparietal sulcus (IPs) and the lateral sulcus (Ls) have been unfolded to show areas buried in the sulci.

MIP, LIP, VIP, AIP: medial, lateral, ventral, anterior intraparietal areas, respectively. SI, SII: primary and secondary somatosensory areas, respectively. MI: primary motor cortex (corresponds to area 4). PMd, PMv: dorsal and ventral premotor cortex, respectively. PMd and PMv are subdivisions of area 6. The Matelli et al. (1985) subfields F4 and F5 are not reported on this figure. They correspond to subdivisions of the ventral premotor cortex in area 6. Arabic numbers correspond to Brodmann areas.

Ps, principal sulcus; ASs, AIs, arcuate sulcus; Cs, central sulcus; STs, superior temporal sulcus.

coding for movement direction was also found in parietal area 5 (Kalaska et al., 1983).

Hyvarinen and Poranen (1974) and Mountcastle et al. (1975; see also Mountcastle, 1995) both tended to assign the parietal cortex a role in generating neural commands for movements directed at extrapersonal space. Other authors (for example, Robinson et al., 1978), however, considered that properties of the visuomotor neurons (specially a category of eye movement-related cells, the visual-fixation cells) could well be explained by 'passive' responses to visual stimuli. Accordingly, they proposed that area 7 is specialized in high-order sensory (visual) processing and has a predominant role in visual and visuospatial functions. In order to account for the fact that discharges of neurons in area 7 do increase when movements are actively produced by the animal during presentation of the stimuli, they proposed the intervention of an additional 'attentional' mechanism. The cells fulfilling these criteria are concentrated in subarea 7a. It remains, as Lynch (1980) argued, that the fact that a given cell receives a sensory input does not preclude its participation to sensorimotor or even motor processes: quite the reverse, it is indeed critical that these parietal 'reaching neurons' receive the relevant inputs (visual, tactile, kinesthetic) for elaborating the representation of the movement and controlling its execution. More recently, MacKay (1992) showed that 'reach' neurons in area 7a were activated during arm movements towards targets located in specific parts of the workspace, including when the movements were performed in the dark. In some cases, this directional preference held for movements performed with either arm.

MacKay's reach neurons were not influenced by eye movements and position, which suggests that they did not receive eye position signals, and could not encode the position of visual stimuli in space relative to the body. This result contrasts with those obtained in other posterior parietal areas. In area LIP (an area buried into the intraparietal sulcus at the rostral edge of area 7a, figure 2.3), Andersen et al. (1985) found a population of cells with distinct receptive fields, the response of which was influenced by the position of the eyes in the orbits. In area PO (see figure 2.4) in the superior parietal lobule also, neurons respond to visual stimuli placed at a given spatial location, regardless of eye position (Galetti et al., 1993). These neuronal ensembles would thus be well suited for detecting the position of visual targets in head or body-centred coordinates.

In area 5, where many neurons respond preferentially to somatosensory stimuli, responses to visuospatial stimuli were

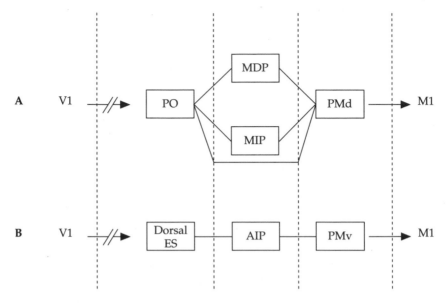

Figure 2.4   Pathways involved in visuomotor transformation

Within the dorsal visual stream, two main lines of processing can be identified from the primary visual cortex (V1) to the primary motor cortex (M1). The upper line (A) represents the connections between the parieto-occipital extrastriate area (PO) and dorsal premotor cortex (PMd) in area 6. Part of these connections reach PMd directly, whereas another part relays in areas within the intraparietal sulcus. This system is responsible for directional coding of movements (reaching) toward objects within the extrapersonal space.

The lower line (B) represents the connections between dorsal extrastriate cortex and ventral premotor cortex (PMv) in area 6. These connections relay in the anterior intraparietal area (AIP). This system is responsible for transforming visual intrinsic attributes of objects into motor commands.

also observed, specially in area MIP. During active arm movements, this neuronal activity is tuned in a body-centred frame of reference (possibly centred on the shoulder, Lacquaniti et al., 1995). Thus, a given cell in area 5 is not activated in the same way if the animal makes movements along the same trajectory but with different arm postures, indicating that area 5 codes the geometry of the arm and not the metrics of the hand trajectory.

The precise role of reach neurons in posterior parietal cortex still remains uncertain. The initial idea that these cells do not directly participate in motor output (for example, MacKay, 1992) is now challenged by several experimental arguments. First, on the anatomical side, most of these areas project directly on premotor cortex. Matelli et al. (1986) found that the rostralmost part of area 7a, in the intraparietal sulcus, does project to the dorsal area 6. Johnson et al. (1993) also found direct connections between area MIP and the dorsal premotor area, where they recorded reaching neurons. Finally, a connection linking area PO (see figure 2.4) to dorsal premotor cortex, either directly (Tanné et al., 1995) or via the superior parietal lobule (Caminiti et al., 1996), was disclosed. This connection, which provides a link between area PO, where the location of visual targets is coded in head-centred coordinates, and the premotor cortex, where directional output is generated, altogether reinforces the notion of an independent visuomotor subsystem for reaching movements (figure 2.4A).

The second set of arguments comes from electrophysiological experiments. Directional anticipatory activities, similar to those recorded in premotor cortex (see section 2.2.2) are commonly observed in area 5 (Crammond and Kalaska, 1989; Kalaska and Crammond, 1995), which also seems to be the case in area 7. Reach neurons could thus have a prominent role in monitoring on-going movements, and in providing signals for the generation of corrections, a suggestion which would account for the lesion effects. Correction signals might arise from movement execution, but also from central representations of static limb parameters relevant to the intended movement. This hypothesis of a feed-forward regulation exerted by posterior parietal cortex has been addressed by Sakata expressly (see below). Finally, as proposed by MacKay (1992), the parietal output to frontal cortex could also exert a role in coordinating reach and grasp. This explanation would be consistent with the fact that area 5 and 7a neurons receive both visual and somatosensory inputs. Disruption of somatosensory input at lower levels of the nervous system (for example, brainstem or spinal cord) is known to affect the coordination of reach and grasp movements (Jeannerod, 1986; Glendinning et al., 1992).

2.2.2   The role of premotor and motor cortex

Neurons coding for the direction of movements were also found in the monkey cortical premotor and motor areas. Concerning the premotor areas, Gentilucci et al. (1988) described a population of neurons located in the lower part of area 6 (subfield F4) that fired in relation to movements affecting the proximal joints, particularly during reaching at visual objects (refer to figure 2.3 for a map of premotor areas). These neurons were 'passively' activated by visual stimuli located within reaching distance and fired during arm movements directed to a particular space sector, congruent with the location of the visual receptive field. Most of them also had cutaneous receptive fields, the position of which corresponded to the projection of the visual receptive fields. The authors suggested that F4 neurons play a role in specifying the end-point area for reaching movements. Other experiments on this topic by Boussaoud (1995) showed that neurons in a more dorsal part of area 6 present gaze related modulation of their activity. Boussaoud used a paradigm similar to that used for parietal neurons by Andersen et al. (1985). The target stimulus for the hand movement was presented at a constant retinal location, but the spatial position of the fixation point (and therefore the eye position in the orbit) changed from trial to trial. The new finding, however, was that this modulation affected the preparatory activity of the neuron, after the monkey had selected the proper movement to make, but before the signal to make it (the go signal) was given. These neurons clearly concern the neural representation of directional movements (figure 2.5) (see also Kalaska and Crammond, 1995).

The mechanism for coding movement direction in premotor cortex also involves another type of neurons, in which the spatial position of the visual receptive field with respect to the body remains invariant. Fogassi et al. (1992) reported such neurons in ventral premotor cortex, which encoded the same spatial position with respect to the monkey despite changes in eye position in the orbit. More recently, Graziano et al. (1994), in focusing on premotor 'bimodal' neurons (those with both a visual and a

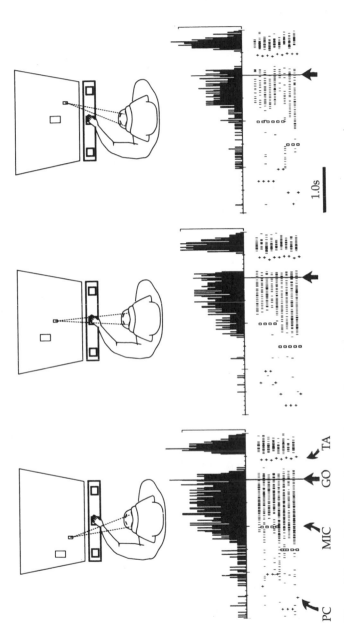

Figure 2.5 Spatial coding in dorsal premotor cortex

The monkey is trained to reach one of the targets (right or left) according to the colour of the cue presented on the screen. The location of the cue is kept constant in retinal coordinates, but can be varied in head coordinates (by changing the location of the fixation point). In this example, the same cue, yielding to the same reaching movement (hit the target on the right), is encoded by different levels of neuronal activity during the preparatory period, according to its position on the screen. PC indicates presentation of a precue, MIC, presentation of the motor instruction cue (for example, hit target on the right); GO is the signal to start the movement; TA indicates target acquisition.

Redrawn from Boussaoud, 1995

cutaneous receptive field), further demonstrated that the spatial position of the visual receptive field was anchored to the arm position in space and moved with it. For a given position of the arm, however, in accordance with Fogassi et al.'s findings, the position of the receptive field was unaffected by eye position in orbit. These neurons provide the 'missing link' in the sequence of events coding for visually goal-directed movements. These movements require mechanisms for coding target position on the retina, eye/head position, head/body position, arm/body position, and arm position with respect to the target (see Jeannerod and Prablanc, 1983; Jeannerod, 1988). Whereas neural substrates for the first four mechanisms had been identified, the latter remained hypothetical until now.

On the motor side, there are neurons in the motor cortex that correlate with the direction of reaching movements. In the primary motor area itself, Georgopoulos et al. (1982) found that the activity of single neurons changed in an orderly fashion with the direction of arm movements. Each of these neurons discharged most strongly prior to movements in a given direction and was therefore characterized by a preferred vector along which its discharge was maximum. Assuming that a movement in a particular direction involves the activation of a whole population of neurons, Georgopoulos et al. (1986) summated a large number of individual vectors measured during a reaching task. They found that the resulting population vector was a good predictor of the direction of movements. Caminiti et al. (1990, 1991), however, showed that activity of cells in both areas 4 and 6 varied for the same movement performed along parallel directions but starting from different initial positions. This result suggests that these cells do not encode a movement vector, but that their directional preference 'rotates' as a function of the position of the shoulder joint. This indeed seems logical: because motor cortical cells code movements in intrinsic (proprioceptive) coordinates, their preferred direction has to rotate to match the extrinsic (visual) coordinates which define the target position. Thus, the proper set of neurons for coding a reach in a given direction must be selected on the basis of visual information on

[handwritten margin note:] FALSE BECAUSE CODES DO NOT EXIST IN US. THIS IS ALL TAKING PLACE IN A CONCEPTUAL FRAMEWORK ENTRENCHED IN SYSTEM BUILDING, ALBEIT IN AN IDEALISTI WAY, BASED ON DETERMINISM WHICH DOES NOT EXIST.

target location, but also on the basis of proprioceptive information on initial arm position.

Finally, another 'motor' area with direct cortico-motoneuronal
connections, SMA, also seems to be involved in visuomotor
functions. Many neurons in this area are preferentially activated
during bimanual reaching movements directed at a visual goal
(Chen et al., 1991). The role of SMA is to be understood within
the framework of a parallelism of pathways controlling goal-
directed actions. Parietal, premotor and motor cortical mechanisms combine for selecting the proper movement direction as
a function of the visual goal. The timing of movement-related
neuronal discharges in these cortical areas suggests that motor
and premotor cortex areas (including SMA) relate to initiation
of goal-directed movements, whereas parietal neurons relate to
their monitoring during execution.

2.3   Neural coding in the visuomotor (dorsal) pathway: grasping movements

Hand movements have been the focus of an increasing number
of studies in the last fifteen years. Their description, however, is
mostly available in human subjects. This section will first provide
a review of the motor patterns of grasping in humans and will
include the monkey data whenever possible.

The hand is one of the highest achievements of motor function in primates and man. By using the criterion of stability of
the grasp as a prerequisite for handling objects, Napier (1956)
considered that human prehensile movements can be described
along only two main motor patterns. Napier stated 'If prehensile
activities are to be regarded as the application of a system of
forces in a given direction then the nature of prehensile activity
can be resolved into two concepts – that of precision and that of
power' (p. 906). The precision and the power grip patterns can
be used alternatively or in combination for almost every object.
In other words the pattern of the grip is not determined (solely)
by the shape or the size of the object (for example, a rod can be

held with a precision grip, as in writing, or a power grip, as in hammering); it is the intended activity that is the main determinant of the type of grip for each given action.

The two grips differ anatomically by the relative postures of the thumb and the other fingers. Precision grip is mostly characterized by opposition of the thumb to one or more fingers. Opposition means that the thumb is abducted and rotated at the metacarpo-phalangeal and at the carpo-metacarpal joints, so that its pulpar surface is diametrically opposed to the pulpar surface of the other fingers. In power grip, the fingers are flexed to form a clamp against the palm, the thumb is adducted at the two joints, and there is no opposition between the thumb and the other fingers. The two types of grip have clearly different degrees of involvement in manipulative actions. Only precision handling allows movements of the object relative to the hand and movements of the object within the hand, because of opposition of the thumb to the other fingers (Elliott and Connolly, 1984).

The problem is whether precision grip with true opposition of the pulpar surfaces of the thumb and the index finger is specific to the human hand or not. The human hand is the only one to combine the two major attributes that result in dexterity: an opposable thumb and independent fingers. The Heffner and Masterton scale for ranking digital dexterity (Heffner and Masterton, 1975), based on anatomy of the hand, includes only man in the topmost category (see also Napier, 1961). Recent work, based on fossil anatomical evidence, indicates that this category should be extended to remote predecessors of modern humans (for example, Paranthropus robustus, 1.8 million years), which are credited with dextrous tool use behaviour (Susman, 1988). The relative ratio of index finger and thumb length, as well as the position of the articulation of the thumb, have changed from a chimpanzee-like hand in Australopithecus afarensis (4 million years) to a modern human-like arrangement in Homo erectus (1.5 million years). It remains that the classification based on anatomy of the hand is probably under-inclusive, and should be counterbalanced by a classification based on behavioural observation with emphasis on the capability for independent finger movements and for the use of tools. Tool use behaviour is well known in apes like the chimpanzee and orang-utan (for example, McGrew, 1989). Others, like the gibbon for instance, due to the small size of their thumb relative to their other fingers, perform handling of small objects by means of the pulp of the thumb and the side of the middle phalanx of the index finger. It should not be concluded from this difference that these animals are not capable of opposition: they can abduct their thumb and rotate it in front of their other fingers, but the shortness of the thumb prevents contact between the pulpar surfaces (Napier, 1960).

Christel (1993), in describing the areas of the hand which come in contact with each other during grasping tasks, has made an extensive study of prehensile hands in a variety of primates. Many species are capable of opposing the thumb with the pulpar surface of the index and the side of the third finger. This is the most frequent type of precision grip in chimpanzees, humans, gorillas and orang-utans, in descending order. In addition, side opposition between the pulp of the thumb and the side of the middle or the terminal phalanx of the index finger, or between the side of the thumb and the side of the middle phalanx, is also commonly observed, specially in bonobos and orang-utans (figure 2.6). By contrast, according to Christel, the opposition (pulpar or otherwise) of the thumb with the fourth and the fifth fingers is never observed in any of these animals.

Animals like rhesus monkeys or baboons, or even new-world monkeys like cebus monkeys, are also capable of accurate precision grips (see Jouffroy, 1993 for review). Other still more primitive animals use whole hand prehension with a non-opposable thumb, a good example of which is given by behavioural observation of the squirrel monkey. In this animal, objects are reached with all the fingers in a slightly curved convergent position; in the later stage of the reach, the fingers diverge and straighten, closing in a scooping motion on contact with the object; the fingers frequently close to the palm with the distal and medial phalanges parallel to the palm, rather than curled

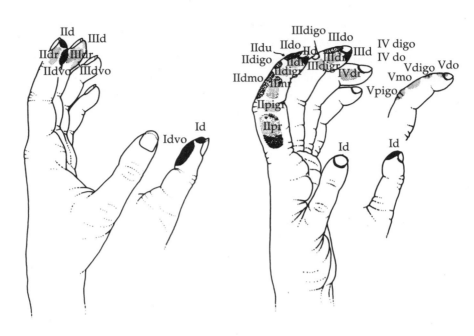

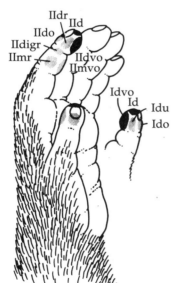

Figure 2.6 Areas of contact between fingers durng precision grip

These areas are shown for the human hand (left), a chimpanzee hand (middle) and a macaque hand (right). Note prominence of thumb/index pulpar contacts in man.

From Christel, 1993

around the objects as human fingers do (Fragaszy, 1983). Interestingly, this description of a primitive prehensile behaviour can
be applied almost without change to pathological prehension in
higher primates following motor cortical lesions (Tower, 1940;
Passingham et al., 1978). This observation predicts that the various types of grasps displayed by infra-human species relate to
different degrees of cortical control of the hand muscles. This
was indeed nicely demonstrated in a recent paper by Bortoff
and Strick (1993). They found that the corticospinal terminations on the motoneurons controlling the finger muscles differed markedly in two of the above mentioned monkey species
with different grasping capabilities: although dense terminations
were observed in the cebus, they were practically absent in
squirrel monkeys.

2.3.1   The pattern of grip formation

The type of grip that is formed by the hand in contact with the
object represents the end result of a motor sequence which starts
well ahead of the action of grasping itself. The fingers begin to
shape during transportation of the hand at the object location.
This process of grip formation is therefore important to consider,
because it shows dynamically how the static posture of the hand
is finally achieved. No systematic investigation of this aspect of
grasping (preshaping) seems to have been made until the film
study by Jeannerod (1981).

Preshaping first involves a progressive opening of the grip
with straightening of the fingers, followed by a closure of the
grip until its matches object size. The point in time where grip
size is the largest (maximum grip size) is a clearly identifiable
landmark which occurs within about 60 per cent to 70 per cent
of the duration of the reach, that is, well before the fingers
come in contact with the object (figure 2.7A) (Jeannerod, 1981,
1984; Wing et al., 1986; Wallace and Weeks, 1988). This biphasic
opening-closure motor pattern is not unique to man: obervations
based on films during prehension in rhesus monkeys have

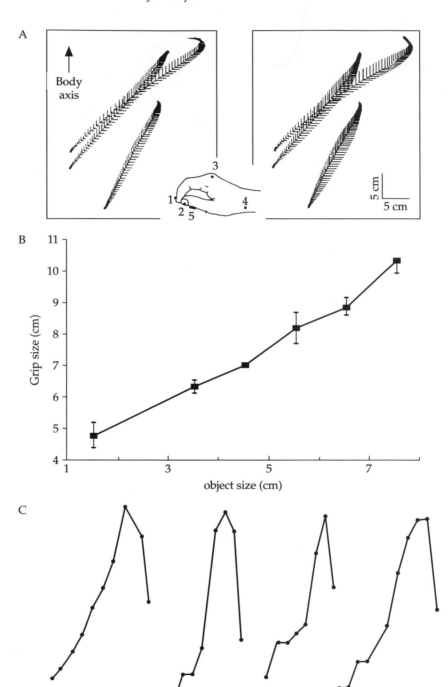

revealed a closely similar opening of the grip followed by closure before contact with the object (figure 2.7C).

One possible explanation for the biphasic opening-closure pattern of grip formation relates to the thumb-index finger geometry. Because the index finger is longer than the thumb, the finger grip has to open wider than required by object size, in order for the index finger to turn around the object and to achieve the proper orientation of the grip. Indeed, the movement of the index contributes the most to grip formation, whereas the position of the thumb with respect to the wrist tends to remain invariant (Wing and Fraser, 1983). The extra-opening of the grip during preshaping might also represent a safety margin for compensating the effects of the variability of the reach. Indeed, maximum grip size tends to become larger than required by object size in a number of conditions where the variability of the reach is likely to be increased (for example, lack of visual control, movements directed at targets in the peripheral visual field, etc.).

The pattern of grip formation, however, should not be reduced to biomechanical factors. The pattern of finger movements that arises prior to, and during grasping reflects the activity of higher order visuomotor mechanisms for detecting the shape of the object and generating appropriate motor commands. This is demonstrated by the fact that the amplitude of grip aperture during grip formation covaries with object size (Jeannerod, 1984; Wing et al., 1986; Wallace and Weeks, 1988). Marteniuk et al.

Figure 2.7 Pattern of preshaping during prehension movements

Upper row A: two-dimensional analysis of relative movements of wrist, tip of index finger and tip of thumb during prehension directed at vertical cylindrical objects. On the left, object diameter is 1.5 cm; on the right, 6 cm. Note curved pattern of index path. The represented movements are averaged over ten trials. The bars on the paths indicate one standard deviation from the mean trajectory in x and y dimensions.

Middle row B: mean value of maximum grip size (distance between tip of thumb and tip of index) plotted against object size in one normal subject.

Lower row C: plot of grip size during four grasping movement in one normal monkey. Note sharp increase in grip size followed by closure prior to contact with object. Reconstructed from film taken at 25 frames per second.

(1990) found that for an increase of 1 cm in object size, the maximum grip size increases by 0.77 cm (figure 2.7B). The problem is thus for the motor system of the hand to build an 'opposition space' which would take into account both the shape of the object and the biomechanics of the hand (Arbib, 1985; Iberall et al., 1986; Iberall and Arbib, 1990). Observations like those of Stelmach et al. (1994), for example, show that different positions of the same object in the workspace may yield different types of grips or different position of the fingers on the object. This strongly suggests the existence of a higher order coordination mechanism which couples the different components of prehension. This problem will be discussed in chapter 6.

These findings demonstrate that hand movements and postures during object-oriented behaviour are largely determined at a level of the system where representations are formed about the object. Indeed, visual feedback signals seem of very little importance during the movement itself, as both the pattern of grip formation and the coordination of the reaching and grasping components are correctly achieved in situations where the hand remains invisible to the subject. Similarly, the size of the maximum grip aperture correlates with the size of the object in the absence of visual feedback from the hand (Jeannerod, 1984). This is not to say that the correct representation of object properties must not be calibrated and updated by visual input arising from the central retina. Prehension movements directed at objects presented within the peripheral visual field are not only slower and less accurate; the grip formation is incomplete, the fingers do not shape properly (Sivak and MacKenzie, 1992). Similarly, grasping directed at memorized objects involve larger grip apertures than grasping directed at visible objects (for example, Wing et al., 1986).

Grasping cannot be reduced to its visuomotor aspects. It is the motor counterpart of a broader function. During handling and manipulation, for which grasping is a pre-condition, signals for object identification arising from sight and touch are co-processed. The fingerpads have been considered by some authors (for example, Sherrington) as the somatosensory 'macula'. Thus, the hand brings objects to be manipulated within the central field of vision, so that 'the finest movements of the fingers must be under simultaneous control from the very centers of the visual and tactual maculae' (see Phillips, 1985). Berkeley in his famous treatise on 'A new theory of vision', emphasized the fact that objects can only be known by touch, which he considered as the ultimate means of exploration and knowledge of the world (Berkeley, 1734). Vision is subject to illusions, which arise from the distance-size problem (size must be extracted from apparent distance) or the 3-D reconstruction problem (the visual third dimension is extracted from a two-dimensional map using indirect cues from perspective). Touch, and particularly active touch, is not subject to these constraints, as it involves direct assessment of size and volume. In addition, touch is critical for perceiving object properties like hardness, compliance, texture, temperature, weight, etc., which can hardly be accessed by sight alone. This is one of the reasons why reaching and grasping must be functionally interrelated. Reaching is a precondition for grasping, its finality is to bring the specialized area of the hand into contact with objects, for acquiring and using object-related information. Reaching is therefore a mere transition between visual processing prior to contact and haptic processing during manipulation.

Finally, another aspect of grip accuracy is specification of grip force. This parameter also has to be, at least partly, specified in advance, during the preshaping phase, in order for an adequate force to be applied on the object at the onset of the grasp. Lifting an object implies a sequence of coordinated events where the grip force (to grasp the object) and the load force (to lift the object) vary in parallel. The grip force/load force ratio must exceed the slip ratio, itself determined by the coefficient of friction between the skin and the object surface. Changing the coefficient of friction (by using an object coated with sandpaper, suede or silk, for instance) changes the grip force, so that the load force remains invariant and the grip force/load force ratio increases when frictional forces decrease. By contrast, increasing the weight of the object results in an increase of both grip force and load force and an invariant grip force/load force ratio (Johansson and Westling, 1987).

The respective contributions of anticipatory mechanisms and of reflex adjustments to the accuracy of grip force have been extensively studied. It appears that the adaptive changes in grip force are strongly dependent on tactile afferent signals. A demonstration of this point is that adaptation of the grip force to friction disappears if the fingertips are anaesthetized. The duration of the initial, isometric, phase of lifting movements (the preload phase, about 100 ms) is sufficient for tactile afferents from the fast adapting receptors to come into play, the latency between the onset of the slip and the change in the force ratio being in the range of 75 ms. In addition, these fast adapting receptors are very sensitive to slip signals (Westling and Johansson, 1984; Johansson and Westling, 1987). These signals may be used for updating the coding of initial forces based on internal representation of object properties, and for sensorimotor learning. It is likely that visual cues related to object size will also be used for building this representation (see Johansson and Westling, 1988). Several experiments have shown that available information about object weight, compliance, texture can accurately determine grip and load forces in advance with respect to the grasp itself (Gordon et al., 1991).

These data are critical for accessing the content of the representation that the subject has formed about the object, which expresses itself during the initial stage of the grasp (the preshape that occurs during the reach). Fingers shape in anticipation to object size and shape, the wrist rotates in anticipation to object orientation to give the optimal stability to the grasp, forces are generated which will be applied immediately at the time of contact, in order to grasp and lift the object.

2.3.2   Neural mechanisms involved in the control of visually guided grasping

The mechanism whereby finger movements are coordinated for producing an anticipatory hand configuration corresponding to the shape of an object is a fascinating one, as it directly impinges upon the mechanisms of neural representation of object-oriented action. The discovery of this mechanism, mostly through the efforts of the groups of G. Rizzolatti and H. Sakata in recent years, yielded to a detailed description of a cortical subsystem specialized for visuomotor transformation for hand and finger movements (for a review of this work, see Jeannerod et al., 1995).

2.3.2.1 *Motor cortex*

Only the data concerning the generation of isolated finger movements, which are relevant to hand movements during grasping, will be reviewed here. Sherrington, in his experiments on electrical stimulation of motor cortex in different animal species, had noticed that the more a species 'ascended' in the phylogenetic scale, the more movements triggered by the stimulation were localized in a small portion of musculature. It was only in apes that movements limited to one finger could be obtained (see Grunbaum and Sherrington, 1903). This property reflects the degree of selectivity of cortico-motoneuronal connections in higher primates.

Stimulation experiments, however, may give a false idea of cortico-motoneuronal connectivity. Instead, recent results suggest a large degree of flexibility of the relations between motor cortex and distal muscles. It can be shown, for example, that a monkey corticospinal neuron which fires during a movement of a given type (for example, a precision grip) will not fire during a movement of another type (for example, a power grip), in spite of the fact that the same muscles are implied in both cases (Muir and Lemon, 1983; Lemon et al., 1986). This result indicates that a given motoneuron can be connected to several sets of cortical cells, and that each set becomes activated in relation to a certain type of movement, not to the contraction of a certain muscle. The logical consequence of these findings is that there are several cortical representations for the same muscle, each representation coming into play as a function of the type of movement to be performed. Microstimulation experiments in motor cortex have in fact shown large overlaps between cortical zones which control individual motoneurons (see Wiesendanger, 1986).

The picture of cortical representation of finger movements gets even more complicated if we consider the fact that cortical pyramidal cells are usually connected to more than one moto-neuron (up to two or three, Buys et al., 1986). This divergence was directly demonstrated by intracellular labelling of cortico-spinal axons (Shinoda et al., 1981).

Experimental data in human subjects also confirm a 'task-dependent' mode of organization of cortical commands, rather than a somatotopical organization in the usual sense. Experiments using transcranial magnetic stimulation illustrate this point. The response of a given hand muscle (the first dorsal interosseus, for example) to a stimulus applied at the same cortical locus was tested during performance of different types of movements. The response was found to be different according to whether the muscle was contracted in isolation or in association with other muscles, during the performance of a precision grip, for example (Flament et al., 1993). Accordingly, each task would be characterized by a given pattern of activity of cortical cells, with the possibility of selecting populations limited to a small number of neurons. A normal human subject can, in certain conditions, activate selectively one motoneuron: this striking effect can be obtained in showing the subject the EMG recording of his own finger muscle, and instructing him to focus his attention on one of the motor units appearing on the record (Kato and Tanji, 1972).

These experiments make it difficult to conceive a simple model for the production of independent finger movements. It could be that the movements of each finger are controlled by a specific population of neurons. To obtain combined movements of several fingers, the corresponding populations would be activated. Alternatively, the coordination between fingers could be achieved by another type of neuronal populations, controlling the muscles of several fingers. According to Schieber (1990), however, these explanations are probably incorrect, for the reason that finger muscles are in fact not independent from each other (they are mechanically coupled at the level of their tendons). Thus the generation of independent movements of one finger would rely on inhibitory mechanisms preventing activation of muscles of other fingers, so that isolated finger movements would be 'extracted' from coarser synergies (like open or close the hand, for example). If this model revealed true, it would require more neurons to produce the movement of a single finger than those of several fingers.

2.3.2.2 Parietal cortical areas   Parietal cortex is known to be concerned with the visual control of hand movement, based on the effects of posterior parietal lesions in animals. Monkeys with lesions in the inferior parietal lobule, in addition to the typical misreaching with the contralesional arm already described in the previous section, fail to shape their contralesional hand and make awkward grasps (Faugier-Grimaud et al., 1978).

Neurons related to active arm movements were first recorded in the inferior parietal lobe by Mountcastle and his colleagues who identified, besides the 'arm projection' neurons related to reaching, a group of 'hand manipulation' neurons (Mountcastle et al., 1975). More recently, H. Sakata and his group found hand movement-related neurons to be concentrated in a small zone (which they called area the anterior intraparietal area, AIP) within the rostral part of the posterior bank of intraparietal sulcus (see figure 2.3). Neurons from this area were recorded in monkeys trained to manipulate various types of switches, which elicited from the animal different motor configurations of the hand. Most of them were selectively activated during grasping one or two of these objects among the four routinely used ones (Taira et al., 1990) (figure 2.8A). Neuron activity was not influenced by changing the position of the object in space, which shows that they were related to distal hand and finger movements rather than to proximal movements of the arm.

In order to determine, for each of these neurons, the role of visual factors in producing the increase in discharge rate, Sakata and his colleagues made two controls. First, they let the monkey perform the same task in the dark, guided only by a small spot of light on the object; second, they instructed the monkey to fixate the object without grasping it. Thus, the task-related

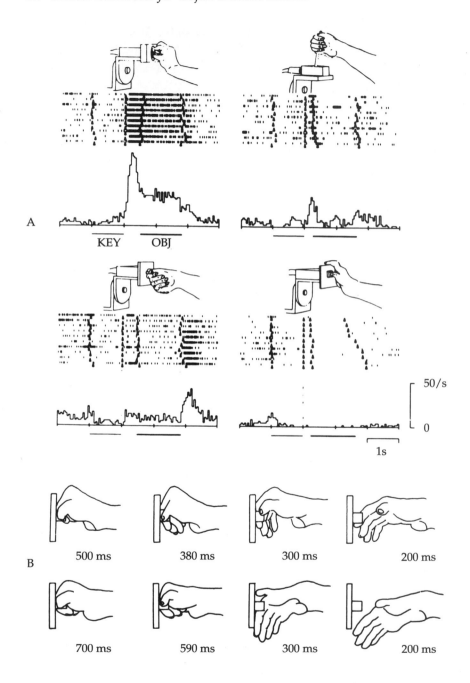

A

KEY   OBJ

50/s

0

1s

B

500 ms   380 ms   300 ms   200 ms

700 ms   590 ms   300 ms   200 ms

neurons were classified into three groups according to the difference between their activity in the light and in the dark: 'motor dominant' neurons did not show any significant difference in activity between grasping objects in the light or in the dark; 'visual and motor' neurons were less active during grasping in the dark than in the light; 'visual dominant' neurons were exclusively active during grasping the object in the light.

Many of these visually responsive neurons were also activated by the sight of objects during fixation without grasping. Using a broader variety of graspable objects, including primitive shapes such as spheres, cubes, cones, cylinders, rings and plates of different sizes, Sakata et al. (1992, 1995) found that AIP neurons which were activated during both grasping and fixation were selective for the same object whether the monkey looked at it or grasped it. Some of them were also sensitive to the size or the orientation of the objects. Finally, other neurons were not activated during the fixation of objects ('non-object' type) but seemed to require other visual stimuli, such as the view of the moving hand, to be activated. 'Non-object' type responses were usually elicited after the initiation of the hand movement, and were likely to be concerned with the interaction of the hand with the object.

The Sakata hand neurons cannot be dissociated from other groups of neurons, identified in close-by parietal areas, and which are related to processing complex visual stimuli. This is the case of neurons in the posterior part of area 7 (figure 2.3),

---

Figure 2.8 Parietal neuron involved in hand manipulation

A: discharge of an AIP neuron during object-oriented movement in monkey. The same neuron is recorded during presentation of four different manipulanda. Note strong preference for manipulandum on the upper left. This neuron corresponds to the 'motor dominant' type (see text).

From Taira et al., 1990

B: effect of transient inactivation of AIP on contralateral prehension movements in monkey. Prior to injection of muscimol (upper row), hand preshapes during approach toward target objet.

After injection (lower row), note lack of preshaping and tactile adjustment after contact.

From Gallese et al., 1994

specifically sensitive to rotation of a visual stimulus, regardless of its shape (Sakata et al., 1986). Another group of neurons sensitive to the 3-D orientation of the longitudinal axis of visual stimuli was recently found in the caudal part of the IPS posterior bank (Kusunoki et al., 1993, Sakata and Taira, 1994). It is therefore likely that the 3-D characteristics of the object are processed in parietal areas different from AIP and the output of such processing is then sent to AIP. Thus, the parietal visual neurons encode the 3-D features of objects in a way that is suitable to guide the movements for grasping them. 'Visual dominant' and 'visual and motor' neurons in this region are likely to be inter-connected both with the purely visual neurons where object properties are encoded, and with the premotor neurons where motor commands are asembled.

An interesting confirmation of the role of the hand neurons in representing grasping movements was provided by an ex-periment of Gallese et al. (1994). Transient inactivation of AIP, by injecting a GABA agonist (muscimol) in the rostral IPS pos-terior bank under electrophysiological control, produced a sub-tle change in the performance of visually-guided movements during grasping tasks. Grasping errors were observed in tasks requiring a precision grip or during sticking out the index finger to insert it in a groove. These errors were due to a lack of pre-shaping of the hand during the approach phase of the move-ment. In addition, there was a clear-cut dissociation of the muscimol effects on grasping and reaching. Whereas the altera-tion of preshaping was consistently obtained after injection in the rostral part of the posterior bank of the sulcus, misreaching occurred after injection within its more caudal part. This result provides the unambiguous demonstration that the hand-related parietal neurons play a specific role in the visuomotor trans-formation used for grasping objects. Indeed, the deficit is a visuo-motor one, not a motor one, as it can be corrected under tactile guidance: as soon as the monkey awkwardly touches the target-object, the hand shapes in accordance with object shape (figure 2.8B). Area AIP inactivated by Gallese et al. is only a couple of synapses ahead of executive areas in frontal cortex. This result confirms and expands those obtained by Faugier-Grimaud et al. (1978). Interestingly, the latter authors had observed, immediately following ablation of area 7, a transient 'paralysis' of the contralateral hand, which appeared to remain unused for several days.

2.3.2.3 Premotor cortex neurons Area AIP is directly connected with a limited zone of premotor cortex. This zone corresponds to one of the cytochrome-oxidase subfields (field F5) of area 6, identified by Matelli et al. (1985). In addition, F5, which forms the rostral part of inferior area 6, is itself directly connected with that part of area 4 (field F1) which corresponds to the hand primary motor field (refer to figure 2.3 for a map of premotor areas). Intracortical microstimulation and single neuron studies showed that F5 is specifically related to distal movements (Rizzolatti et al., 1988; Hepp-Reymond et al., 1994). It is thus particularly interesting to examine the properties of neurons in this cortical zone in relation to visually-guided grasping. Because F1 neurons have only very limited access to visual information (visually responsive neurons in this area are rare and have visual properties – brisk, transient responses to abrupt stimulus presentation (Wannier et al., 1989) – that hardly fit those we would expect for grip formation), the visuomotor transformations required for grasping movements have to occur upstream in motor control, in areas more closely connected to the visual system. The connections linking parietal areas like AIP to the 'distal' area of premotor cortex (F5) (Matelli et al., 1986) and then to F1 could thus represent another, parallel, specialized visuomotor system for encoding object primitives and generating the corresponding hand configurations. This system is outlined in figure 2.4B. It would be interesting to repeat the experiment of transient inactivation by injecting muscimol in the premotor neurons where AIP directly projects. The pattern of deficit observed during object-oriented behaviour should closely resemble that observed during AIP inactivation.

Rizzolatti and his colleagues recorded single neurons from F5 in behaving monkeys during object-oriented motor actions

(Rizzolatti et al., 1988). These experiments showed that most neurons located in the upper part of F5 are related to grasping and other object-related motor actions (holding, tearing, manipulating). 'Grasping' neurons discharge in relation with finger and hand movements during the action of grasping an object. The temporal relation of this discharge with grip movements changes from neuron to neuron. Some fire during the last part of grasping, that is, during finger flexion. Others start firing with finger extension and continue during finger flexion. Others are activated in advance of finger movements and often cease discharging only when the object is grasped. An interesting property of most F5 neurons is their selectivity for different types of hand prehension: 85 per cent of grasping neurons show selectivity for one of three basic types of grip – precision grip (the most represented type), finger prehension and whole hand prehension. There is specificity for different finger configurations, even within the same grip type. Thus, the prehension of a sphere, which requires the opposition of all fingers, is encoded by different neurons than the prehension of a cylinder, for which a palm opposition grip is used. Some of these properties are illustrated in figure 2.9.

Visual responses were observed in about 20–30 per cent of F5 neurons. Two types of responses can be distinguished. Neurons of the first class respond to presentation of graspable objects. Often, there is a relation between the type of prehension coded by the cell and the size of the stimulus effective in triggering the neurons. This is particularly clear for the precision grip neurons which are activated only by small visual objects. Neurons of the second class are of a particular relevance for the study of motor representations. These neurons (termed 'mirror neurons' by Di Pellegrino et al., 1992; see also Rizzolatti et al., 1995) respond when the monkey sees hand movements executed by the experimenter or another monkey. They also respond when the recorded monkey performs hand movements of a particular type. The important point is that, in order to fire a mirror neuron, the observed hand movement has to be the same as that which would activate that neuron if the monkey performed it. For

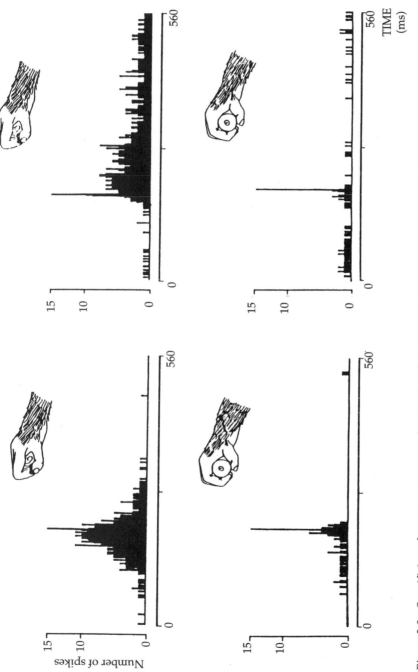

Figure 2.9 Specificity of premotor neurons' activation during grasping movements in monkeys

Two neurons are shown during two types of grasps: both discharge preferentially during precision grip (upper records) and very little during power grip (lower records). Neuron on left anticipates contact with object (indicated by high vertical bar) and discharge during preshape ('grasping' neuron, see text). Neuron on right discharges during holding the object ('holding' neuron).
Reconstructed from Rizzolatti et al., 1988

example, many mirror neurons fire when the monkey grasps a piece of food and also when the experimenter or the other monkey does so. They do not fire, however, when the experimenter makes a grasping movement without food, or when the food is grasped with a tool, etc. In other words, mirror neurons encode object-oriented actions, whether they are performed or they are observed by the recorded monkey, which suggests that they might be better defined as 'representation' neurons. These F5 neurons are somewhat complementary with those recorded in the superior temporal sulcus by Perrett et al. (1989), which are sensitive to observed hand and body movements, but have no motor counterpart. Thus, the F5 neurons can be activated visually in two ways: by objects and by events. In both cases the eliciting stimuli address specifically the F5 neurons coding the grip congruent with them.

If one compares the properties of parietal neurons with those of F5, striking similarities, but also clear differences, emerge. Visual responses to 3-D objects are found more frequently in parietal cortex than in F5. By contrast, 'mirror neurons' responding to the view of hand action of other individuals were not found in AIP. As for the motor properties, parietal 'motor dominant' neurons also code elementary motor acts, such as precision grip, whole hand prehension, wrist rotation, etc. However, most of the parietal neurons appear to represent the entire action, since they start to discharge with the hand shaping and continue to fire while the monkey is holding the object. This property contrasts with those of F5 neurons, which are commonly related to a particular segment of the action. Indeed, in primary motor cortex, on which F5 heavily projects, neurons code even more fragmentary movements.

Sakata et al. (1992) proposed an integrated view of the respective functions of hand neurons in parietal and premotor cortices. They assumed that the visual parietal neurons processed the visual information concerning the attributes of the object to be manipulated, and that this signal was sent to premotor neurons to prepare a command signal for grasping the object. They further assumed that this command signal was sent back to a different set of parietal neurons (the 'motor dominant' neurons) where it mixed with the visual signal. Finally, these neurons re-projected on the premotor neurons. This mechanism would be a highly efficient one for monitoring ongoing movements, matching the motor command with the visual signal, and providing corrections when necessary. This type of mechanism will be fully analyzed in chapter 6.

2.4   Predetermined motor patterns: the schema approach

The above behavioural and neurophysiological results suggest that actions are driven by implicit 'knowledge' of object attributes, such that stable and decomposable motor patterns arise to cope with external reality. In addition, these motor patterns appear to be encoded by identifiable neuronal subpopulations. It is therefore tempting to speculate that motor elements that are neurally precoded, can be assembled to form the motor representation responsible for a given action. This hypothesis, which is only briefly outlined in this section, will be further implemented in the subsequent parts of this book.

In the domain of motor control, this hypothesis arose from the classical concept of preorganized behavioural units used for producing a desired action. A new version of this simplified form of motor representation was proposed by M. Arbib (Arbib, 1981, 1985; Iberall et al., 1986; Arbib and Hesse, 1986; Iberall and Arbib, 1990). Arbib's view is that motor representations (which he calls 'coordinated control programs') are composed of elementary units (the 'motor schemas') which interact for controlling motor output. A motor schema is a predetermined set of commands (a micro-action), not an independent command: in that sense it already represents a certain degree of coordination of motor output for achieving a limited goal. When assembled with other schemas, a coordinated control program (in fact a higher order schema) arises, which in turn can be assembled with others, and so on. This recursive property of schemas is a convenient one for modelling their neural implementation at different levels of analysis (for example, neuronal populations, single neurons, etc.) of the nervous system.

Motor schemas are assumed by Arbib to be activated by perceptual schemas which serve encoding of visual input. Again, perceptual schemas do not deal with perceptual primitives, they encode configurations of the external environment which, in the visual domain, may correspond to one of the attributes of an object. During visually-guided prehension, perceptual schemas activate the corresponding motor schemas for the subactions of 'reach', 'preshape', 'enclose', 'rotate forearm', etc. They are the basis for 'visuomotor decisions' which are implicitly taken during actions towards visual objets, and which account for movement smoothness and accuracy.

The motor schemas are carried out by specific grasping units (the 'virtual fingers'). In a precision grip with pad opposition, for example, the thumb is one virtual finger (VF1), the finger(s) that oppose the thumb is another one (VF2), and the unused finger(s) a third one (VF3). In grasping a small object, VF2 will be composed of the index finger only. In whole hand prehension with palm opposition, VF1 will be the palm and VF2 will (usually) include the four fingers other than the thumb. The schemas acting on these functional units are assembled into appropriate hand postures: the posture selected during the pre-shape defines the configuration for applying the required forces to the object (Iberall et al., 1986). Accurate positioning of the fingerpads on the object surface is a prerequisite for subsequent handling and manipulation. This requires defining an opposition space corresponding to the grasp axis embedded in the object (see MacKenzie and Iberall, 1994). Then, the hand will be transported (the 'approach' schema) and the wrist will rotate it (the 'rotate' schema) in order to approximate the correct position.

The schema hypothesis thus explains how grasping interacts with other functions of the upper limb, such as reaching. Because the formation of the grip prior to contact with the object is the critical factor that governs the movements of the other segments

of the upper limb during the reach, studies of reaching in isolation from grasping ignore many of the key aspects of its
control. The kinematic redundancy of the whole limb, and not
only its distal segments, is exploited in building the appropriate
opposition space. This may seem in contradiction with the above
hypothesis of visuomotor channels: in fact this hypothesis had
to be modified according to new experimental data. The first
coordinated control program for reach and grasp, used by Arbib
(1981) to model the Jeannerod (1981) data, postulated that completion of the activity for grasping an object involved two motor
schemas, one for the slow phase of the reach and the second for
the enclose phase of the hand movement, both initiated by completion of the first phase of the reach (figure 2.10). However,
subsequent experiments contradicted this hypothesis, raising
the question of how schemas actuated by different limb segments were temporally coordinated by the program. In these
experiments, Paulignan et al. (1991a) suddenly displaced the
target-object at the onset of a reach-to-grasp movement. In this
condition, the untrained subject is perfectly able to correct for
this visual 'perturbation' and to accurately grasp the displaced
object. This correction, however, results in prolonging the duration of the reach by about 100 ms. Meanwhile, the opening of
the grip is interrupted, grip size decreases and increases again
until it reaches its peak aperture at a later time, when the hand
gets close to the displaced object. To address these data, Hoff
and Arbib (1993) proposed a model with a two-way interaction
between the transport and grasp schemas. They postulated the
existence of an additional, coordinating schema which receives
from each of the constituent schemas an estimate of the time it
needs to move from its current state to the desired final state.
Whichever schema is going to take longer (in this case, the reach)
is given the full time it needs, while the others will be slowed
down. The time needed by each schema is regulated by
optimality criteria which are embedded in feedback controllers
which respond to disturbances with some latency (figure 2.10).

Perceptual and motor schemas in the Arbib sense specifically
relate to visuomotor function. A similar concept, however, can

A

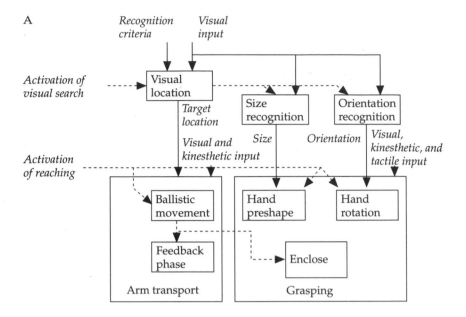

B

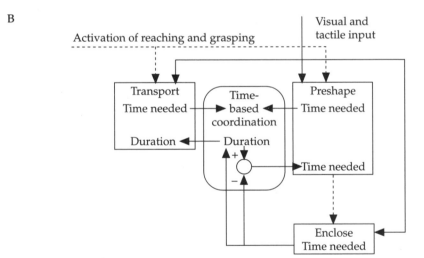

Figure 2.10 Coordinated-control program for prehension movements

A: visual processing of object attributes activate specific motor schemas for hand transport and for grasping. The grasping schema itself can be decomposed into simpler schemas such as hand preshape or enclose, etc.

Modified from Arbib, 1981

B: temporal coordination for reaching and grasping. The same coordinated-control program is shown with a device for time-based coordination between the different schemas that compose the program. The schemas provide the optimal arm or hand trajectories for the specified duration. For details, see text and chapter 6.

Adapted from Holf and Arbib, 1993

also be used for describing haptically driven movements. Lederman and Klatzky (1987) have described 'Exploratory Procedures' (EPs) as a repertoire of stereotyped patterns of contact and movement between skin and object. EPs spontaneously arise in relation to acquisition of a given haptic property during object manipulation (for example, tangential motion provides information on roughness, pressure on hardness, etc.). As EPs seem to be independent from vision (see Klatzky et al., 1993a), they must address a set of properties different from those addressed by the visuomotor schemas. EPs and schemas thus cooperate for organizing object-oriented actions.

Motor schemas provide a framework for segmenting grasping into elementary action units and for relating these units to the neural substrate. Still, the level at which motor schemas are implemented neurally remains hypothetical. The neurons recorded by the Sakata group in area 7 and the Rizzolatti group in area 6 would fulfill the requirements for 'schema neurons'. The presence of this motor vocabulary in F5 has several implications. First, since information is concentrated in relatively few elements, the number of variables to be controlled is much less than if the movements were described in terms of motoneurons or muscles. This solution for reducing the high number of degrees of freedom of hand movements comes close to that proposed theoretically with the virtual fingers. Second, the retrieval of the appropriate movement is simplified. Both for internally generated actions and for those emitted in response to an external stimulus, only one schema or a small ensemble of schemas have to be selected or coordinated.

chapter three

Task-dependent Representations for Action

In this chapter, we continue the exploration of motor representations in relation to object-oriented behaviour by adding a new perspective, drawn from studies in humans. The general idea will be that several processing modes, and therefore several types of representations, operate simultaneously. Experiments in normal subjects will reveal that representations associated with object-oriented actions have identifiable properties that are distinct from those of other representations used for other purposes, like object identification, for example. Observations in brain-lesioned subjects will allow, to some extent, dissociation between these representations and separate description of the underlying behavioural strategies.

3.1 Relevance of neural systems to task-dependent representations for action

3.1.1 *Effects of posterior parietal lesions on object-oriented actions*

In this section, the notion of task-dependent representations will be confronted with the neural mechanisms described in chapter 2. The point will be to determine to what extent the separation between neural systems (dorsal and ventral) is behaviourally relevant, and, more specifically, to what extent visuomotor mechanisms of the parietal cortex can be related to one of the object-oriented behavioural strategies.

Disclosing the homologies between human and monkey posterior parietal cortices is a difficult task. Obviously, this search
has had a long tradition in neurology and neuropsychology,
when attempts were made at replicating the effects of human
parietal lesions in monkeys. However, the renewal of the physiology of the parietal lobe in the domain of visuomotor functions, following Mountcastle's seminal work, has prompted new
experiments in normal subjects and new clinical descriptions in
brain-lesioned patients. The classical descriptions of the effects
of posterior parietal lobe lesions (the so-called 'optic ataxia'
syndrome, Balint, 1909; Garcin et al., 1967) were more recently
completed in groups of patients by Jeannerod (1986a) and Perenin
and Vighetto (1988). Visually-directed reaching movements made
by these patients are inaccurate, and often systematically err in
one direction (usually to the side of the lesion). In addition, the
movements are kinematically altered: their duration is increased,
their peak velocity is lower, and their deceleration phase is longer.
This alteration of movement kinematics becomes particularly
apparent in the condition where vision of the hand prior to and
during the movement is prevented. Restoration of visual feedback reduces the reaching errors, but the movements remain
slower than normal (Jeannerod, 1986a). Impairment in optic
ataxia is not limited to pointing. Patients fail to orient their
hand when they have to visually guide it to a slit (Perenin and
Vighetto, 1988). Grasping and manipulation are also altered:
during prehension of objects, patients open their finger grip too
wide with no or poor preshaping, and close it only when they
come in contact with the object (Jeannerod, 1986a; Jakobson
et al., 1991). The critical area for producing optic ataxia has been
located in the superior parietal lobule (Perenin and Vighetto,
1988) (figure 3.1), a result which must be interpreted with some
caution, as very similar effects can be obtained in conditions
where parietal areas remain intact, but are partly disconnected
from visual input. One of the cases reported in section 3.1.3 will
illustrate this point.

Patients with parietal lesions, with or without optic ataxia,
often present visuospatial impairments, such as difficulties for

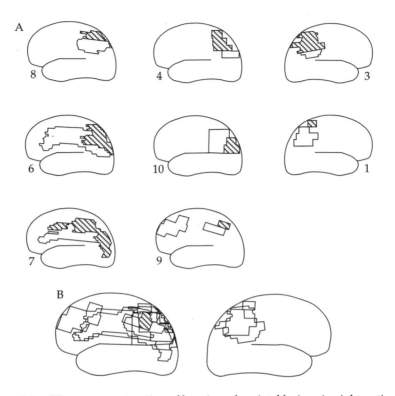

Figure 3.1 CT scan reconstruction of location of parietal lesions in eight patients with optic ataxia

The lower two diagrams represent the common locus of left-sided and right-sided lesions, respectively. Note common focus in the area of the intraparietal sulcus.
From Perenin and Vighetto, 1988

the perception of horizontal or vertical axes, length, distance or orientation (Von Cramon and Kerkhoff, 1993). In addition, they may present constructional apraxia, an inability to assemble object parts by drawing (we will come back later to the significance of constructional apraxia in this context). It remains, however, that they never have problems in recognizing objects: parietal lesion thus creates a clear dissociation between impaired object-oriented movements and preserved object recognition.

3.1.2 *Testing object-oriented responses*

To be entirely convincing, however, this dissociation must be observed in a situation where responses directed at the same object are compared and where the same effector is used to measure the performance. In other words, the automatic transformation of visual input into motor commands, which can be easily tested using object reaching and grasping tasks, must be compared with the transformation that occurs as a consequence of perceptual analysis. Jeannerod and Decety (1990) proposed to measure perceptual judgements about object properties by asking subjects to indicate their estimate by a gesture. This mode of perceptual testing was introduced in two experiments. In the first one, graspable objects (1.5–9.5 cm diameter plastic cylinders) were presented. The instruction to the subjects was not to reach toward nor to grasp the objects, only to *match* their apparent size by separating the thumb and the index finger from each other (the action of showing to someone how big is the object). The initial purpose of this experiment was to determine the accuracy of grip formation in a situation where it would not be contaminated by errors intervening at the level of the other segments of the arm during the reach. In fact, the experiment turned out to be an ideal situation for assessing a response strategy based on explicit processing of object physical properties. Feedback cues were excluded as much as possible, by preventing both vision of the performing hand and contact of that hand with the target objects. Thus, subjects had to match motorically the size of objects presented through a mirror precluding vision of their hand (the apparatus used in this experiment is illustrated in figure 3.2A). The distance between the tip of the index finger and the tip of the thumb was measured.

The results showed that, in spite of a general trend toward overestimation, the mean interfinger distance correlated positively and linearly with target size with high correlation coefficients (figure 3.2B). It is interesting to compare this result with

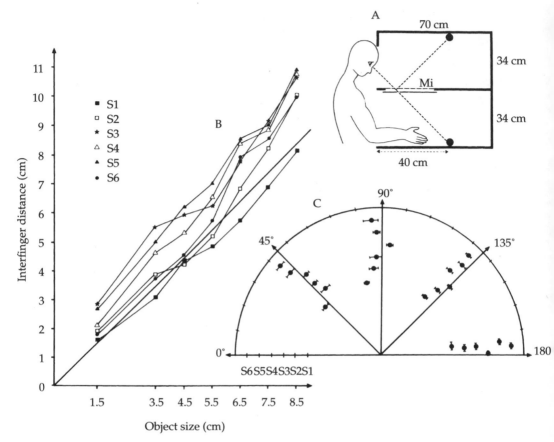

Figure 3.2 Perceptual judgement of object size and orientation in normal subjects

Two types of objects were presented, using the apparatus shown in A: Cylindrical objects of different diameters (1.5–8.5 cm) and a visual slit with different orientations (horizontal, vertical, 45°, 135°). Objects were presented as virtual images through a mirror (Mi). Subjects kept their hand out of sight and did not attempt to reach for the object: they used finger or wrist movements to indiciate their estimate of object size or orientation.

B: plot of perceptual estimate of object size, measured as the distance between thumb and index finger, in 6 normal subjects (S1–S6). Note linear relationship with overestimation in most subjects.

C: plot of estimates of orientation of visually presented slits, measured as the angle of a hand held card with the horizontal, in the same six subjects.

From Jeannerod and Decety, 1990

those obtained in psychophysical experiments testing the subjective scaling of visual length or size. Hering (quoted by Marks, 1978) had proposed that perceived length of a line should be proportional to its physical length, and should not follow a logarithmic function as is the case in the perception of other physical dimensions (the classical Fechner law). This contention proved to be true (Stevens and Guirao, 1963). The subjective scaling of area, however, has been found by several authors to be related to physical size by a power function with an exponent of 0.7–0.8 (Ekman and Junge, 1961; Stevens and Guirao, 1963). The discrepancy between subjective scaling of length and area might be related to the type of instructions given to the subjects. Teghtsoonian (1965) showed that, if subjects were requested to estimate the 'objective area' of circles (how large are the circles?), their judgements followed a linear relation to physical size, as was found for the lines. In contrast, if the task was to estimate the 'apparent size' of the same circles (how large do they look to you?), then their judgements followed a power function (exponent 0.76) with respect to physical size. In the Jeannerod and Decety task, the fact that the interfinger distance was linearly related to target size, indicates that subjects actually 'read' objective area rather than apparent size. Moreover, because the same type of relation with object size was found for maximum grip size during natural grasping (Marteniuk et al., 1990, see section 2.3.1), it can be concluded that explicit matching and implicit grasping use the same computation for determining object size. These considerations validate this size matching test as a way of testing perception of object size.

A second experiment based on the same principle explored the accuracy of matching orientations (Jeannerod and Decety, 1990). Subjects held a plastic card in their (invisible) hand. They were instructed to align its orientation with that of a slit presented in the mirror, as in the size experiment, without attempting to reach for the slit. Subjects responses were also quite accurate in spite of systematic underestimation of orientation by a few degrees (figure 3.2C).

3.1.3   Two illustrative clinical cases

Two recently described clinical cases will now be used to discuss the problem of posterior parietal functions in object-oriented behaviour. Patient AT was observed by Jeannerod et al. (1994) and patient RV by Goodale et al. (1994). In both cases the lesion was an infarction of a relatively large occipitoparietal zone on both sides. Areas 18 and 19 were destroyed in RV and AT, but whereas parietal areas 7 and 39 were destroyed in AT (figure 3.3), they were intact in RV. RV's lesion was thus likely to have produced a disconnection of parietal cortex from visual input rather than a parietal lesion per se.

Both AT and RV had presented a typical optic ataxia at the initial stage of their disease, but this particular symptom had largely disappeared when they were examined, several years later. Reaching accuracy was normal in AT and close to normal in RV. In addition, both patients were normal in recognizing, describing and naming visual forms and objects. AT still had difficulties estimating the length of lines and size of drawn figures and still presented a severe disorientation (she was hampered in her everyday life for actions like dressing, cooking, ironing, sewing or driving). Object-oriented actions were studied in both cases. The study in AT will be reported first.

AT was tested on two tasks, the grasping task, and the size matching task. In the grasping task, she was instructed to reach and grasp with a precision grip target objects (vertical plastic cylinders, 1.5–7.5 cm in diameter) with or without visual control of her hand. As these objects all had the same visual aspect, except for their size, they were considered as 'neutral' objects. During grasping neutral objects AT's movements offered a striking dissociation: whereas in all cases the reach was correctly oriented, the grasp was incorrect, particularly with the smaller objects. The patient ended the trial with the object in contact, not with the fingertips, but with the palmar surface of more proximal phalanges or even with the palmar surface of the hand itself. This behaviour (which was bilateral but more marked with the right hand) resulted in awkward and inaccurate grasps

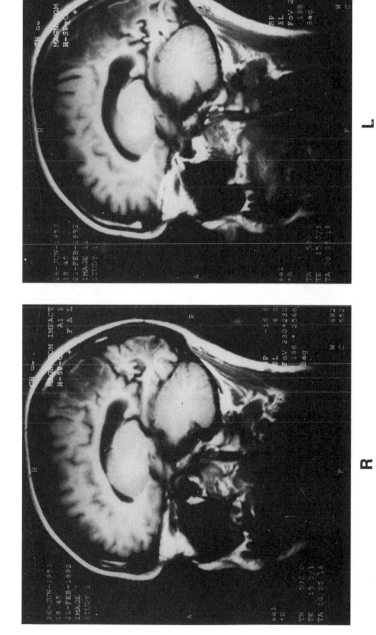

R   L

Figure 3.3   Posterior parietal lesion in subject AT

Parasagittal NMR scan sections through the right (R) and left (L) hemispheres in patient AT show bilateral involvement of parieto-occipital junction. Areas 19, 39 and 7 were affected. Primary visual area was spared.

with the thumb and index finger curled around the object. On a few occasions, the grasp was not possible, as the object was pushed down by the palm of the hand. Closer examination revealed an exaggerated aperture of the finger grip, such that the end of the finger closure, which should normally bring the fingertips in contact with the object at the time when the reach stops, was delayed and the reach tended to overshoot target position. Maximum grip size correlated poorly with object size, due to the fact that grip aperture was grossly exaggerated for the smaller objects, and this correlation was not improved by vision of the hand during the grasp. As a consequence, the rate of aperture (measured as the mean increase in grip aperture for 1 cm increase in object size) was much smaller in AT than in a normal subject. This value was 0.36 cm for AT, whereas it normally ranges between 0.7 and 0.8 cm (figure 3.4, upper left; for comparison with normal behaviour, refer to figure 2.7B in the chapter 2). The fact that the deficit was limited to grasping and that reaching was normal, although it is an unusual case, is consistent with the results obtained in the monkey, showing separate neural substrates for these two functions. In fact, as already mentioned, AT initially presented the two deficits, with the typical clinical picture of the optic ataxia syndrome. The reaching deficit recovered and the grasping deficit persisted. This finding reinforces the notion of distinct visuomotor channels for prehension movements, as explained in the chapter 2.

In the size matching task, AT's performance was closely similar to that of a normal subject (figure 3.4, upper and lower right).

Patient RV (Goodale et al., 1994) was tested on slightly different tasks which, however, explored the same functions. RV was presented with wooden shapes which she had either to grasp with a precision grip, or to compare with each other in pairs. The same dissociation as in AT was reported. During the action of grasping, RV was unable to use visual information about object shape to correctly place her fingers and to make accurate grasps. By contrast, she performed close to normal in the shape comparison task.

The dissociation, observed in the two patients following a

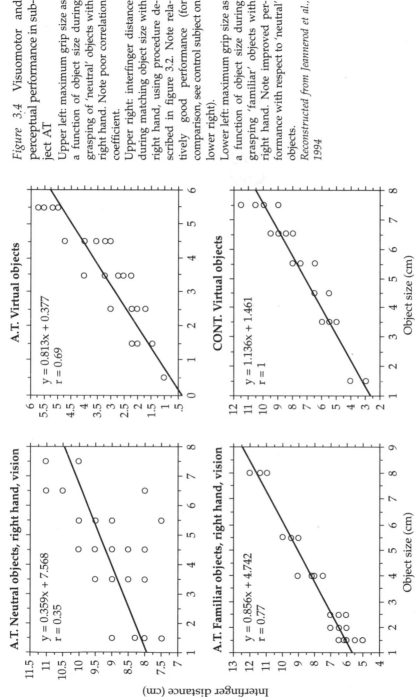

Figure 3.4 Visuomotor and perceptual performance in subject AT

Upper left: maximum grip size as a function of object size during grasping of 'neutral' objects with right hand. Note poor correlation coefficient.

Upper right: interfinger distance during matching object size with right hand, using procedure described in figure 3.2. Note relatively good performance (for comparison, see control subject on lower right).

Lower left: maximum grip size as a function of object size during grasping 'familiar' objects with right hand. Note improved performance with respect to 'neutral' objects.

Reconstructed from Jeannerod et al., 1994

parietal lesion, between impaired grasping and normal motor output based on perceptual judgement on the same objects or shapes, lends support to the notion that object-oriented responses are distributed in the two cortical visual systems: impaired grasping is a consequence of the damage of the dorsal system, whereas the intact ventral system still allows normal perceptual judgement for object size. This view, mostly advocated by M. Goodale, D. Milner and their colleagues (see Goodale et al., 1991; Goodale and Milner, 1992; Milner and Goodale, 1993), departs from that of Ungerleider and Mishkin (1982). Instead of contrasting an object and a space system and relegating form processing in the ventral system, it introduces a dual system for form processing. The anatomical and physiological data which have accumulated since the 1980s (see chapter 2) stress the fact that the dorsal system does more than simply analyze spatial relationships: its main function appears to be visuomotor transformation (and therefore goal-directed action). As action directed at objects necessarily implies processing of intrinsic object attributes, such as shape, it becomes difficult to keep holding the view that these attributes are processed entirely outside the dorsal system. This hypothesis, however, needs to be better qualified before it can be fully accepted. As it is formulated here, it relies on the premises that the mechanisms underlying responses to visual stimuli for 'action' and for 'perception', respectively, pertain to different anatomical systems. The problem is that object-oriented behaviour can hardly be conceived as composed either of pure 'action' tasks or pure 'perceptual' tasks. This point will be fully illustrated by experiments described in Section 3.5. For the present purpose, it can be documented by further observations in patient AT. Jeannerod et al. (1994) observed that AT's grasping performance was improved when familiar objects were used as targets, instead of neutral objects. In their experiment, these objects were of approximately the same size and shape as the neutral ones, but were clearly recognizable (a lipstick, a reel of thread, etc.). With these objects, the correlation between maximum grip size and object size increased up to normal values, as did the rate of aperture of the grip (0.86 cm in movements with

visual control of the hand, 0.70 cm without visual control) (figure 3.4, lower left). Note that the task of grasping familiar objects was a purely visuomotor one, as no perceptual judgement was required from the patient. Finally, AT was tested for her ability to match, with her fingers, the size of imagined familiar objects. The interfinger distance was strongly correlated with object size (r = 0.79).

These striking findings are good arguments in favour of an intact perceptual processing of visual form in AT. They also show that the two visual systems are not independent of each other. AT's behaviour in fact suggests that the functions of the impaired dorsal system were supplemented by information processed at the level of the intact ventral system. In the case of neutral objects, correct grasping could not be performed because the visual primitives related to object size could no longer be transferred to the parietal areas. No other cues could be used, as all objects looked alike. In the case of familiar objects, by contrast, cognitive cues were used, based on stored representations of their shape or size. The transfer of this information was made anatomically possible by the numerous anatomical connections existing between the two systems (Morel and Bullier, 1990).

3.2 Object-oriented behaviour in lesions of the ventral system

The above hypothesis of a dissociation between an 'action' and a 'perception' system implies that lesions in the ventral system should have an effect opposite to that of parietal lesions, namely, visual identification should be affected, whereas object-oriented action should remain intact.

Patients with object recognition problems following lesions of the ventral system (visual agnosia) have often been examined. These observations, however, are not always exploitable within the present framework, first because visual agnosia covers several different clinical entities (for a review, see Humphreys and

Riddoch, 1987), and second, because the issue of a dissociation between modes of processing has not been considered until recently. The important point is to know whether such patients would be able to make accurate gestures to objects that they would not recognize.

A clinical case corresponding to this criterion, that of patient DF, was studied by Goodale et al. (1991) and Milner et al. (1991). This patient suffered a large lesion of the occipital region, destroying areas 18 and 19 bilaterally and sparing most of area 17. Sensory testing revealed subnormal performance for visual acuity with high spatial frequencies (though detection of low spatial frequencies was severely impaired) and colour discrimination. Motion perception was poor. Perception of simple forms (for example, squares, rectangles) and shape detection were at chance and, as a consequence, DF was unable to recognize objects. Detection of line orientation was also impossible. By contrast, when line orientation was tested, not by perceptual judgement, but using reaching movements where the subject had to orient her hand through a slit, her responses were accurate. Similarly, whereas DF was unable to indicate with her fingers the size of visually inspected objects (the above size matching task), she performed accurate prehension movements, with the maximum size of her finger grip normally correlated with object size. These results (see figure 3.5) altogether demonstrate that the shape detection mechanisms in patient DF, who failed to perceive even the most elementary visual attributes, were impaired at a relatively low level of processing. Yet, the preserved capacities were sufficient for performing accurate grasps.

The early segregation between the two systems is confirmed by another interesting dissociation obtained in blindsight patients. As already mentioned in chapter 2, patients who have lost conscious vision in part of their visual field following lesion of the primary visual cortex (the banal lateral hemianopia, for example) may produce strikingly accurate responses when placed in a situation where no conscious experience of the visual stimulus is required, and where they are forced to respond. The early blindsight experiments (Weiskrantz et al., 1974; Perenin and

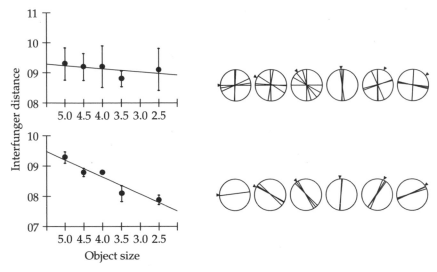

Figure 3.5 Dissociation of visuomotor performance from perceptual in one patient (DF) with a lesion in the ventral visual pathway
Upper row, left: inability to match interfinger distance with object size; right: inability to match hand orientation with orientation of a visual slit.
Lower row, left: correct maximum grip size as a function of object size during prehension movements; right: correct orientation of hand during reaching toward oriented slits. Arrows indicate orientation of slit; bars represent subject's responses.
From Goodale et al., 1991

Jeannerod, 1975) mostly tested the patients' ability to localize targets in their impaired visual field, by eye movements or by hand reaching. The possibility that object-oriented actions could be tested with the same method had been discarded (except for informal attempts, see Marcel, 1983), for the reason that blindsight patients are unable to discriminate visual forms. A new observation, however, clearly demonstrates that the responses in blindsight patients can extend to object attributes, such as orientation or size.

Perenin and Rossetti (1996) examined one patient (PJG) who sustained a lesion of the left occipital lobe severing the primary visual cortex and the optic radiations, following a vascular accident. A dense hemianopia of the right visual field was found. While the patient maintained visual fixation on a central visual target, objects were presented within his hemianopic field. These objects were a visual slit oriented at different angles, or a set of quadrangular blocks of different sizes. PJG was requested either to produce a movement toward these objects (for example, reach the slit with a hand held card as if for 'posting' the card through the slit; or reach and grasp the blocks, both movements relying on fast visuomotor transformation), or to match the angular orientation of the slit by rotating the hand and to match object size with the fingers (the above orientation and size matching tests based on perceptual analysis). The results were very clear-cut: the orientation of the hand during the reach was modified according to the orientation of the slit, and the maximum finger grip size during the reach-to-grasp movement correlated with object size. By contrast, no such correlation was found, neither for orientation nor for size, during the corresponding matching tests.

These results, which present some striking similarities with those obtained in patient DF, illustrate an extreme case of the dissociation between modes of processing of visual input in two different object-oriented situations. The first point to be discussed is their relevance to the hypothesis of an anatomical distribution of these modes of processing in different cortico-cortical pathways. In patient PJG, the lesion was not located in the ventral pathway, it was located at the origin of the cortico-cortical systems, in the striate cortex. The neurophysiological data presented in chapter 2, however, support the idea that a lesion located in V1 disconnects the ventral system from visual input, whereas the dorsal system is still visually afferented through subcortical visual relays. This pathway could thus account for PJG's preserved form detection in visuomotor performance. If this reasoning is true in PJG (and perhaps also in DF if we assume that her lesion in the prestriate areas damaged the cortico-cortical connections between V1 and the parietal cortex), then the pattern of connections for 'visuomotor' form detection departs from that postulated by Goodale and Milner (see also Ungerleider and Haxby, 1994). This point will arise again in the section 3.3 of this chapter.

It is interesting to contrast the effects of massive deafferentation of the ventral system from visual input, with those of more focal lesions. One such case, patient FB, was described by Sirigu et al. (1991). Patient FB presented a bilateral lesion of the temporal poles involving Brodman's areas 38, 20 and 21, as well as medial temporal structures (hippocampus and amygdala). He had severe difficulties recognizing visual objects, as well as colours, faces and places. FB's visual imagery was apparently correct, as he could draw objects from memory. He could also name objects when their function was verbally described to him. When shown a common object, FB described and performed actions that were congruent with the specific manipulation of that object, even if its function was not correctly identified. This is illustrated by the description of an iron: 'You hold it in one hand and move it back and forth horizontally (mimes the action). Maybe you can spread glue evenly with it' (Sirigu et al., 1991, p. 2566). In FB, the process of object recognition was thus likely to be impaired at the stage where the various perceptual attributes of an object come to be bound together. In other words, object recognition was not possible, although identification of the object attributes themselves was preserved, which shows that identifying the attributes of an object is not in itself a sufficient condition for accessing its semantic properties (function, use, name, etc.). Yet, as shown by the iron example, patient FB was able to make gestures that were plausibly related to the function of the object.

The dorsal function that remains in patients like DF and PJG as a residue after exclusion of the ventral system is a very impoverished one. It corresponds to the activity of subcortical projections to parietal areas which bypass V1, as part of a 'primitive' system for fast and crude reactions to visual stimuli (see Bullier et al., 1994). It might be that this system operates only in situations of emergency, automatic movements or decreased awareness. This point will be specifically addressed below in one experiment on normal subjects (see section 3.5.2). In fact, the type of function which is normally carried out by parietal structures is more than a simple, more or less direct, visuomotor transformation, and this function can only be underestimated when it is studied in patients like DF and PJG (see Carey et al., 1996). Parietal function does not operate in isolation, it is embedded in a broader system for producing action, which involves other areas, including those from the ventral system. Section 3.4 will aim to define the behavioural modes involved in producing object-oriented action, whether they rely on visuomotor transformation or are based on object perception and identification. Another type of deficit produced by parietal lesions, ideomotor apraxia, will provide further arguments for the existence of these mechanisms.

3.3   Brain activity mapping during object-oriented behaviour

Further arguments concerning a segregation of task-dependent pathways for visual processing can also be obtained using brain activity mapping in normal subjects. The hypothesis of two cortical visual systems in its simple version (that of Ungerleider and Mishkin, 1982) implied that a selective cortical activation should be obtained in tasks involving object recognition or spatial processing. If the task involved recognizing, memorizing or forming a visual image of an object, the ventral visual pathway should be primarily activated. If, on the other hand, the task involved spatial processing, the dorsal pathway should be activated.

In order to verify this point, Haxby et al. (1991) compared brain activation using the PET technique during a face matching task and during a dot-location matching task. As the experiment was limited to mechanisms for giving explicit perceptual responses, the tasks involved no directional movement and the responses were given by pressing a hand-held button. The results showed that the activated cortical areas partly overlapped in the two tasks. A large lateral occipital extrastriate area (corresponding to Brodmann area 19) was activated bilaterally in the two conditions. In addition, an occipitotemporal zone (Brodmann area 37) in continuity with the common occipital zone was found to be activated in the face matching task only, whereas a cortical zone located in the superior parietal lobule was activated during the spatial task (see also Ungerleider and Haxby, 1994).

Further developments of the hypothesis on the role of cortical systems, however, required that the dorsal function should be tested with a visuomotor task, rather than with a purely perceptual task. Indeed, posterior parietal areas have been found to be consistently activated during object-oriented actions. Grafton et al. (1992), also using PET, found an rCBF increase in the dorsal parietal region during tracking a visual spot with the index finger. The activation focus predominated in the superior parietal lobule (Brodmann area 7) and in the precuneate cortex. This location is in agreement with the localization of lesions that produce misreaching and impairment in hand shaping, as from Perenin and Vighetto (1988) (figure 3.1). The activation of posterior parietal areas in relation to visually-guided movements has been confirmed in several studies, with the difference, however, that the main focus of activation tends to be located more ventrally and more rostrally than initially described by Grafton et al. The main focus appears to correspond to areas 39 and 40, rather than to the superior parietal lobule (Decety et al., 1994; Stephan et al., 1995).

A new PET experiment by Faillenot et al. (in press) seems to provide an explanation for these differences. Subjects were instructed either to match complex shapes made of wooden blocks, or to grasp these shapes using a precision grip. A pure 'motor' task (pointing to the blocks) was used for subtracting the activation related to the arm movement itself. During the matching task, specific activations were found, not only (as expected) in the middle temporal gyrus (areas 21 and 37), but also at the occipitoparietal junction. During grasping, the main focus was located in the anterior and ventral part of parietal cortex (anterior part of area 40). In addition, another activation focus was found to be common for both matching and grasping: this focus was located in the dorsal and posterior parietal lobe (areas 19 and 7). Faillenot et al.'s interpretation of the data was that:

1   Object identification requires visual processing, not only in the ventral stream, but also in the dorsal stream.
2   Visual processing in the dorsal stream is, at least in part, common to object 'perception' and object-oriented 'action'.
3   The only activated area specific to grasping is located in the anterior part of area 40, in agreement with previous findings from several studies (figure 3.6).

One possible explanation for these results is that the area common to object matching and grasping in the parietal lobe is related to processing geometrical, three-dimensional, aspects of object shape, such as orientation, volume, etc., whereas the infero-temporal area is related to purely semantic aspects. One could argue against this hypothesis that object recognition is not affected following parietal lesions. This argument is not entirely correct, however: patients with parietal lesions often exhibit constructional apraxia. They are unable to assemble object parts for producing a coherent whole, specially when instructed to draw objects in perspective (see De Renzi, 1982). This suggests the existence of a specific mode of object perception for the purpose of generating action, that is, specialized for processing action-related properties of objects, particularly those properties which involve 3-D cues (see figure 3.7). Its destruction leaves unimpaired object recognition per se, which can be achieved in the absence of 3-D cues. At any rate, the Faillenot et al.'s results do not support the idea of identifying the parietal cortex with a pure 'action' system. They also question the notion of a double dissociation between the two cortical mechanisms for object-oriented behaviour, a notion drawn from pathological observations.

3.4   The representation of object-oriented actions

The point in this section will be to determine in which ways objects are represented as goals for action. The distinction we have previously used, between a dorsal 'action' system and a

Grasping

Left				Right	
Cortical Regions	BA			Cortical Regions	BA
Primary motor cx (hand area)	4			Intraparietal sulcus	7,40
Lateral premotor cx	6				
Mesial frontal cx	6				
Somatosensory cx	1,2,3				
Parietoinsular cx	2,40				
Ant. supramarginal gyrus	40				

Matching

Left				Right	
Cortical Regions	BA			Cortical Regions	BA
				Inferior temporal cx	37
				Prefrontal cx	10
				Intraparietal sulcus	7,40
				Posterior parietal cx	7,19

Figure 3.6 Complementarity of ventral and dorsal pathways in normal subjects
This diagram illustrates the Faillenot et al's results. During the grasping task, areas located in the left hemisphere, contralateral to the hand used for grasping the objects, were activated. In addition, one area was activated in the posterior parietal cortex of the right hemisphere. This area is common to that activated during the matching task.
During the matching task, areas located exclusively in the right hemisphere were activated. Several of those areas, in the parietal cortex, pertain to the dorsal visual pathway.

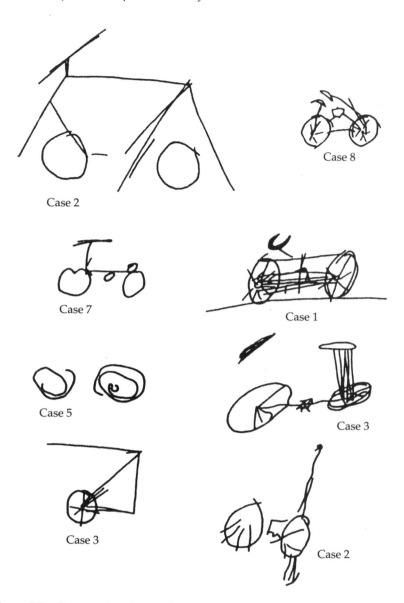

Case 2

Case 8

Case 7

Case 1

Case 5

Case 3

Case 3

Case 2

Figure 3.7 Constructional apraxia
Illustrative cases of drawing disabilities in patients with posterior parietal lesions.
From De Renzi, 1982

ventral 'perception' system, will now be replaced by a more general distinction, which is intended to remain independent of this strict anatomical dichotomy, between a 'pragmatic' and a 'semantic' representation for action (Jeannerod, 1994). A pragmatic representation will refer to rapid transformation of sensory input into motor commands (of which the visuomotor transformation is an example), whereas a semantic representation will refer to the use of cognitive cues for generating actions.

3.4.1 *Classifying object attributes*

Objects are perceived as phenomenal entities. This implies that the elementary visual features like local contour orientation, changes in contrast and spatial frequency, depth cues, area, colour, texture, motion etc., are integrated into higher order properties: volume has to be extracted from stereoscopic depth cues or coherent motion cues, form has to be extracted from contours and contrast cues, etc. The final percept thus arises from a supra-ordinate processing, whereby objects are attributed still higher order properties, largely semantic and contextual, which relate to their shape or function. These mechanisms are likely to be distributed over different brain areas. One of the essential steps for achieving overt identification of an object must be to 'bind' its many elementary attributes into a single identifiable and meaningful entity.

At variance with the above semantic processing, the representation involved in sensorimotor transformation has a predominantly 'pragmatic' function, in that it relates to the object as a goal for an action, not as a member of a perceptual category. The object attributes are represented therein to the extent that they trigger specific motor patterns for the hand to achieve the proper grasp. This function should, in principle, not imply binding of object attributes into a single entity, because each attribute contributes to the motor configuration of the hand by selecting the relevant degrees of freedom. This was the point of the Arbib's theory (see section 2.4) for explaining how motor schemas are assembled into an appropriate coordinated control program.

A consequence of this distinction between semantic and pragmatic processing is that object attributes should be classified, not with regard to putative anatomical channels, but rather with regard to their relevance to one or the other aspect of object-oriented behaviour. A large set of attributes are in fact relevant to both the semantic and the pragmatic processing: this is the case for those contributing to shape, size, volume, compliance, texture, etc. Others, by contrast, are probably irrelevant to the pragmatic representation (for example, colour) or are of little or no relevance to semantic processing (for example, weight). For this reason, a classification of attributes based on the classical distinction between a cortical channel for spatial vision and a channel for object vision may be incomplete or even misleading. Kosslyn et al. (1990), for example, consider that the mechanism of what they call 'spatiotopic mapping' should include, not only the processing of location and orientation of objects, but also parameters related to their size. Size, however, cannot be confounded with other purely spatial attributes: although phenomenal size depends on distance, this is not true for represented size which remains invariant with respect to distance. Represented size, not phenomenal size, is thus part of object identity and not of its spatial layout. The same could be said of shape which, although it changes as a function of the relative positions of the object and the perceiver, remains representationally invariant. To fully answer Kosslyn's argument, however, one would need to know whether preshaping of the hand is made after phenomenal or represented object size.

3.4.2 The frame of reference problem

These considerations raise the problem of the frames of reference used for describing objects in the different modes of representation. Marr (1982) suggested that some operations, like identifying, require an object-centred description, whereas others, like localizing, require a viewer-centred description. Accordingly, the central programme for reaching, because it deals with the object as a locus in space, not as a set of attributes, should be built in a viewer-centred (or egocentric) system of coordinates, that is, a system with the body as a reference. Shapes, however, should be recognizable from all vantage points. As stated by Marr (1982) and by Biederman and Cooper (1992), this can only be achieved by an object-centred coordinate system, independent of the position of the viewer with respect to the object. A viewer-centred description would impose a redescription of the shape each time the position of the viewer changes.

Does this imply that the program for preshaping, grasping and manipulating an object should be built in a system of coordinates related to the object and not to the body? It is difficult to follow this argument because of the tight coordination between the different arm segments involved in reaching and in grasping, respectively. Reaching, the function of which is to carry the hand to the appropriate location, is mostly achieved by the proximal joints of the arm. But this is not the exclusive function of proximal joints: they may also contribute to the formation of opposition space during prehension. To reach the same object at different orientations, for example, we may need to rotate the forearm (a proximal movement) to change the position of the fingers with respect to the object (e.g., Stelmach et al., 1994).

An essential aspect of object-oriented behaviour is therefore that the same object has to be simultaneously represented in multiple ways, simply because the environment asks different questions to the nervous system and because the answer to each of these questions requires accessing different types of representations. To illustrate this point, imagine, for example, the action of picking one apple from among many others. In order to make the appropriate choice, as Van der Heijden and Bridgeman (1994) put it, 'the pragmatic system that picks the real apple also has to pick the apple experienced in the semantic system'. Imagine that the apple to pick is red: we know that the pragmatic system alone does not have the capacity to choose the red apple among the green ones because the redness and the greenness are processed in the semantic system. Indeed, a patient with a colour agnosia will be unable to select the red apple and will pick one of the apples at random. One possibility (Van der Heijden, 1992) would be that the selection of the proper apple is made early in the processing of afferent information, at a level where visual areas are retinotopically coded. In other words, the motor representation would have the possibility of 'looking back' toward areas common to the ventral and the dorsal systems where both the visual primitives and some degree of spatial localization are present on the same map. This hypothesis refers to the classical Aristotelian notion that what arises from the same point in the external world pertains to the same object. This would explain why the red apple and the apple-to-pick coincide in space and appear as a single object in spite of being ultimately represented in two different systems. Small time differences in processing the data arising from this same apple but channelled in several different subsystems would remain unnoticed, so that the impression of the simultaneity (and sameness) of the red apple and the apple-to-pick would not be disrupted (see Jeannerod, 1992). According to this view, attentional mechanisms would play a role in binding different modes of representation into a single, higher order one (see figure 3.8 for a summary diagram).

It has been further proposed (for example, by Bridgeman, 1992) that the information used in 'motor' processes (those which are coded in egocentric coordinates) is unconscious, whereas the information used in 'cognitive' processes (independent of egocentric coordinates) is conscious. Frith (1995) takes this distinction as a cue for tracing a line between knowledge that can, or cannot, be shared with other individuals. 'Of all the representations held in the brain, that which is coded in non-egocentric coordinates will most closely resemble that held in the brain of another. It is these representations that will best enable prediction of the behavior of another creature . . .' (Frith, 1995, p. 683). Examples given below, however, will stress the difficulty of holding a strict distinction between modes of behavior, based on such dichotomies as 'space' versus 'object' systems, 'egocentric' versus 'allocentric' frames of reference, and 'conscious' versus 'unconscious' processing.

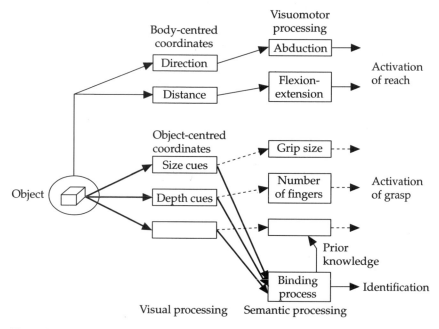

Figure 3.8   Diagrammatic representation of central processes involved in object-oriented behaviour

Extrinsic attributes of an object (related to its spatial position) are processed in body-centred coordinates, for activation of the reach. Its intrinsic attributes are processed in a different, parallel pathway for activation of the grasp, also pertaining to the dorsal visual pathway and to the posterior parietal areas. Shape analysis, using the same object primitives, is effected both in the dorsal pathway for visuomotor transformation and in the ventral pathway for perceptual identification. Only a few components of visual processing (for example, size cues, depth cues, etc.) are mentioned. Others are symbolized by the empty box. Semantic knowledge stored in the ventral pathway can improve visuomotor transformation using connections between the two pathways.

From Jeannerod, 1994

3.5   Task-dependent dissociations of visuomotor and perceptual responses

The arguments drawn from the effects of cortical lesions and, to a lesser extent, those drawn from brain activity mapping, had left us with the impression of two parallel systems for processing visual input, one for carrying out the transformation of elementary visual features into percepts, the other one for carrying out a different transformation for the purpose of generating visually oriented actions. However, in the foregoing descriptions of clinical cases, several observations indicated that this dichotomous thinking was an oversimplification. In addition, we already know that the anatomical and physiological organization of these systems does not fully support the conception of a separate functioning. In this section, we examine the problem of the generation of object-oriented responses in normal subjects, with the aim of determining their complementarity, rather than their differences. In doing so, we will try to show that there are several routes for action, rather than separate routes for action and perception.

3.5.1   Motor versus perceptual responses

Several experimenters have shown that perceptual illusions do not affect motor responses. A typical example is the so-called 'Roeloff effect', where a fixed visual target surrounded by a moving frame appears to drift in a direction opposite to the movement of the frame. In spite of this illusory displacement, subjects make no error when they are requested to rapidly point by hand to where they see the fixed target (Bridgeman et al., 1981). Wong and Mack (1981) reported similar results using saccadic eye movements instead of manual pointing. More recently, Gentilucci and Negrotti (1994) reported another dissociation between motor and perceptual responses. They showed that pointing by hand to the remembered location of a target, or reproducing its location by moving a laser beam, yielded different types of errors. Whereas target distance was underestimated when the subjects pointed, it was overestimated when they matched its location with the beam. Section 3.5.2 will show other examples, using experimental situations where the two modes of response to the same visual event have different time constants and are therefore clearly dissociated from each other.

3.5.2 Time-based dissociations

It has been argued that the processing leading to visuomotor responses would be largely automatic and unconscious, whereas the perceptual system would be consciously controlled (see below). This is indeed an old idea that can be tracked in the literature back to the origin of the theory of separate visual systems. Already at the end of the last century, subcortical visual systems were thought to mediate unconscious reflex motor responses, whereas only activities mediated by the cortex were supposed to be conscious. In fact, the experiments to be reported here do not fully support this distinction between 'conscious' and 'unconscious' systems. Instead, it will be shown that the awareness of our actions is related to the timing of motor events in our behavioural responses. This idea is illustrated by the fact that subjects can track the displacement of a target of which they are unaware. For example, if a target briskly changes its location during the ocular saccade that accompanies a pointing movement toward that target, the subjects remain unaware of the displacement (they see only one, stationary, target); yet, they can point correctly at the final target location (Bridgeman et al., 1975). Goodale et al. (1986) reported a similar pointing experiment where the target occasionally made jumps of several degrees, unnoticed by the subjects. They found that the subjects were nonetheless able to adjust the trajectory of their moving hand in order to reach the target. Interestingly, no additional time was needed for producing the correction, and no secondary movement was observed, suggesting that the visual signals related to the target shift were used without delay for adjusting the trajectory. Following these examples, the first experiment in this section will provide an illustration of a dissociation produced by perturbing visual input during visually-guided movements. The way the movement reorganizes, as well as the timing of motor and perceptual events during reorganization, will be discussed with regard to a possible dissociation between automatic and conscious processes.

There are situations in everyday life where actions in response to visual events are clearly dissociated from conscious experience of the same events. We respond first and become aware later. One example is, when driving a car, we have to make a change in trajectory because of a sudden obstacle on our way: we consciously see the obstacle after we have avoided it (and only then do we experience retrospective fear!). Castiello et al. (1991) designed a series of experiments where they measured this temporal dissociation. Subjects were instructed to reach by hand an object placed in front of them, as soon as it became illuminated. It took them approximately 330 ms on average to start moving. In a different set of trials, the instruction was simply that they signal (by a vocal utterance: Tah!) at what time they became aware of the illumination of the object. The vocal response took 380 ms to appear. Finally, on still another set of trials, the instruction was to perform the two tasks at the same time. Not unexpectedly, the values for both the motor and the vocal reaction times were found to be very close to those measured in the previous sets of trials, that is, the onset of hand movement aimed at the object preceded by a short delay (about 50 ms) the vocal response signalling the subject's awareness of its change in visual appearance. This difference was not noticed by the subjects, who felt their hand movement to coincide with their perception of the illumination of the object.

To answer the question of whether or not it takes the same time to generate a motor response to a visual event and a subjective experience of this same event, a situation was created where the motor reaction time was reduced. Subjects were facing three identical objects, separated from each other by about 10 cm. The instruction for the subjects was, as in the earlier version of the experiment, to reach for the object that got illuminated and to signal vocally the time at which they became aware of it. On most trials, the central object alone was illuminated. In 20 per cent of trials, however, the light was suddenly shifted to one of the other two objects: the shift occurred exactly at the time of onset of the hand movement (Paulignan et al., 1991a). In this event, according to the instruction, subjects had to correct the direction of their hand movement in order to track the second illuminated object, and to emit a second vocal signal to indicate the time at which they became aware of the shift in illumination. The first sign of correction of the hand trajectory appeared early (about 100 ms) following the shift in illumination. By contrast, the vocal utterance corresponding to this same event came much later, in the order of 300 ms after the beginning of the change in movement trajectory. The subject's reports were in accordance with this temporal dissociation between the two responses: they reported that they saw the light jumping from the first to the second object near the end of their movement, just at the time they were about to take the object (sometimes even after they took it!).

The clearest effect observed in this series of experiments is that the time to awareness of a visual event, as inferred from the vocal response, keeps a relatively constant value across different conditions (see Castiello et al., 1991 for details and control experiments). Under 'normal' circumstances (that is, where no time pressure is imposed on performing the task) this value is roughly compatible with the duration of motor reaction times. The consequence of this compatibility is that, when we make a movement toward an object, we become aware of this object near the time when the movement starts, or shortly after it has started. Hence, the apparent consistency between our actions and the flow of our subjective experience. This consistency does not seem to be affected by small differences in timing (up to 50 ms), but it breaks down when the difference increases, for instance when the motor reaction time shortens under conditions of time pressure, such as avoiding sudden obstacles or tracking unexpected object displacements.

It is tempting to speculate about the long duration of our motor reaction times in normal, unperturbed, conditions. Long reaction times might have the function of keeping our subjective experience in register with our actions. Imagine what our life would be if the above temporal dissociation were the usual case, and if our awareness of the external events were systematically delayed from our actions in response to these events!

More seriously, this dissociation between motor responses and subjective experience, when it happens, as well as the more usual synchrony between the two, reflects the constraints imposed by brain circuitry during the processing of neural information. Different aspects of the same event are processed at different rates. It happens that the global outcome is constrained by the slowness of the process that builds up awareness. The impression of simultaneity that we have is not an illusion or a *post hoc* reconstruction. The apparent synchrony of awareness with other events is in direct relation to the amount and the duration of neural processing needed to reach conscious experience. As confirmed by the above experiments, consciousness is not immediate, it takes time to appear (see Libet, 1985 for review). Adequate timing of neuronal activity in different brain areas is a critical condition for achieving subjective temporal consistency between external events.

The difference in processing time for the two types of responses suggests that the time needed to generate a motor response to a visual event may change as a function of the task in which the response is given, whereas, by contrast, the time to signal awareness would remain invariant. Castiello and Jeannerod (1991) tested this hypothesis in the situation where the size of the object, rather than its spatial location, was suddenly changed. In this experiment (a replication of Paulignan et al., 1991b), the object was made to suddenly increase its size at the initiation of a prehension movement. The first visible correction (a reincrease in grip aperture at the time where the grip began to close) took about 330 ms to appear. Total movement time was increased by 175 ms. When vocal responses signalling awareness were associated with the motor corrections, these responses consistently occurred more than 400 ms after the onset of the perturbation, a value very close from the 420 ms reported in the Castiello et al. (1991) experiment for conscious detection of changes in object position. The temporal difference between motor and vocal responses was thus reduced down to about 70 ms. The fact that the delay for subjective awareness of a visual stimulus remained invariant, whereas the time to the motor response was modulated as a function of the type of task (correcting for a spatial displacement or for a change in object size), reveals that awareness does not depend on a given particular neural system to appear. Instead, it is an attribute related to particular behavioural strategies.

These experiments raise the problem of where fast motor responses, like those produced in reaction to perturbations, are generated. Alstermark et al. (1990) concluded from a similar experiment in cats that these fast responses were of subcortical origin, as they disappeared after lesion of the tectospinal pathway. Keeping in mind the wide interspecies differences in neural organization between cat and man, it might be that the responses observed here are similar to responses obtained from blindsight patients (see above). Interestingly, an observation by Perenin and Rossetti (1996) in patient PJG shows that correct responses to object size or orientation in the blind hemifield can no longer be produced if the subject's movement is delayed. This result suggests that the delay implies the use of a different strategy (based on memory and, possibly, awareness) which, in turn, channelled the visual input to a different pathway. As this pathway was not available to the patient, the reponse could not be given.

New experiments are needed in normal subjects, using the same effector (for example, pointing) to assess the response, to determine whether a systematic change in the timing of the response results in qualitatively different movements, for example, with different patterns of errors, different kinematic structures, etc.

3.5.3 *Implicit functioning of pragmatic representations*

Grasping an object implies no explicit knowledge of the properties of that object. Even if the object is novel, the visual cues which are used for preshaping the hand are processed automatically. Finger grip sizes correctly, the appropriate number of fingers is selected, the hand orients . . . All these motor outputs are achieved effortlessly. By contrast, if questions are asked about the nature of the object, or about its physical properties (is it heavy? how big is it? etc.) the subject will immediately shift to another, explicit and effortful behavioural srategy. He/ she will produce overt responses bearing on estimates, comparisons, etc. In both cases, the same primitives of the object are processed. What changes is the task in which the subject is involved.

An experiment by Gentilucci et al. (1995) adds further to the differences and the similarities between the modes of processing used during the two tasks of grasping and matching. These authors used the same apparatus as shown in figure 3.2. The virtual image of a visual object (a plastic cylinder) was presented, which kept the same diameter (for example, 4 cm) throughout the block of trials. Another object, the size of which differed by +/− 0.5 cm was placed in optical coincidence with the visual one. The subjects were instructed to grasp this object, with their hand hidden below the mirror. After a few trials, the maximum grip size was adjusted to the size of the tactually experienced, invisible object. The subjects, in spite of adjusting their grip size, consistently failed to notice any discrepancy between the visual and the invisible object. However, when asked to consciously match the visual object size with their fingers (the size matching test), their interfinger distance matched the size of the invisible object. These results further demonstrate the implicit nature of the visual (or visuomotor) processing during grasping. They also tend to show that the two modes of functioning are not entirely isolated from each other, as size information gained in the 'implicit' task is transferred to the 'explicit' one. The fact that they do not ignore each other suggests that the form analysis performed in each system is accessible to the other one, and that the two tasks do not probe anatomically distinct systems. It could well be that the task (the question asked to the subject) selects a given mode of processing, characterized by a given repartition of activity within the same distributed structures.

3.5.4 *The semantic penetration of pragmatic representations*

Properties of behavioural strategies during object-oriented actions begin to emerge from these experimental results. These strategies involve processing of intrinsic object attributes in a way which seems similar to, and may use the same neural systems as, other behavioural strategies which do not involve action (form identification, for example). Yet, object-oriented actions are most often performed in an implicit mode, which does not involve conscious awareness.

It may be interesting in this respect to examine situations where subjects are involved in an explicit mode of processing during object-oriented actions. To what extent can subjects cognitively access parameters that they normally encode automatically? In order to approach this problem, Klatsky et al. (1987) classified hand shapes during functional interactions with objects, using criteria such as the size of the hand surface contacting the object and the type of hand posture (prehensile versus non-prehensile). They found that the pattern of hand movements objects elicit when they are to be grasped, used and manipulated could be classified into four broad categories: 'clench' (large and prehensile); 'pinch' (small and prehensile); 'palm' (large and non-prehensile); and 'poke' (small and non-prehensile). When subjects were asked which hand shape they would use in interacting with a given object and, conversely, when a hand shape is designated, to which type of object it corresponds, they made accurate responses. Conversely, when subjects were shown unfamiliar forms and asked to indicate which hand shape would be the most appropriate, they generated highly regular responses that could be predicted from the geometrical parameters of the forms (for example, the area of their projecting surface in the frontal plane). This differentiation of hand shapes according to the form of objects was retained in preshaping during actual reaching (see also Pellegrino et al., 1989). Finally, the same authors trained subjects to produce the various hand shapes in response to visual presentation of these forms. They showed that in the trained subjects, presenting a hand shape subsequently facilitated the judgements they made about the feasibility of interactions with objects. The same was not true if the cue was presented verbally (Klatzky et al., 1989).

These results, which demonstrate that the representation of a motor configuration of the hand influences knowledge about manual interactions with objects (and conversely), are reminiscent of the effects of motor imagery on motor performance, to be described in chapter 4. They suggest that knowledge of movements performed during interactions with objects can be accessed cognitively (which type of information is used to get such an access will be discussed in chapter 6). They point to the fact that, given the proper instructions, subjects can change their strategy and access the content of representations which were apparently inaccessible. If we assume that the prototypical hand shapes described by Klatzky and her colleagues (their 'exploratory procedures', see chapter 2) correspond to a variant of the motor schema concept, then the above results suggest that more or less elementary components of action can be consciously imaged. 'Thus, one might require that motor images have the content of actions, that they function to some extent like motor commands or motor output, and that they share processing avenues with the motor system' (Klatzky et al., 1993b, p. 301). The point that motor images might be 'windows' through which motor representations can be observed will be fully developed in chapter 4.

3.6 A note on apraxia

This chapter offers an interesting framework for discussing certain types of apraxic syndromes (the so-called 'ideomotor' apraxias, especially those following parietal lesions) as a specific disruption of the mechanisms of representing actions. The main problem met by these patients arises when they are requested to imitate actions, to reproduce actions from memory or to pantomime symbolic gestures. In a group of patients with left parietal lesions Heilman et al. (1982) also described difficulties recognizing gestures: the patients were unable to discriminate, among gestures performed by another person, those that were correct from those that were not (see also Rothi et al., 1985).

The impairment common to apraxic patients could be their inability to use stored motor representations, in other words, to activate 'from within' the set of schemas that correspond to those actions. To use Heilman's terminology, it could be that they have lost the 'visuokinesthetic engrams' needed for building up a representation of those gestures. Thus, the problem arises when the subject has to shift from a strategy where object-oriented actions are processed automatically, to a more cognitive mode. It is indeed a common observation that these patients can perform actions when they are embedded in a familiar course of action (use a glass to drink during the meal), but cannot do it when it is designated as a goal isolated from its normal context, like raise a glass as if to drink, or demonstrate the action of drinking without holding a glass in the hand. As the elementary motor schemas are preserved in such patients, their deficit should be in selecting and organizing schemas into a purposive action (or building up a coordinated control program, in Arbib's terms).

A patient (LL) with a bilateral posterior parietal lesion, described by Sirigu et al. (1995b), illustrates these points. LL complained of difficulties in using objects and performing everyday actions. She was tested for her ability to use simple objects (a spoon, a cigarette, etc.). Evaluation rested on adequacy of the grasp (shape of the hand, placement of the fingers on the object) and adequacy of the gesture when using the object. As a rule, hand and finger movements were inadequate when LL was instructed to use the object (for example, perform the gesture of eating soup with the spoon). The spoon was grabbed incorrectly, it was turned several times in the fingers, etc. By contrast, the transport of the spoon from the table to the mouth was better preserved. LL's problem was not a pure hand shaping deficit, as finger posture was correct and maximum grip size correlated with object size when she took the object, not for using it, but for handing it over to the examiner. The deficit also extended to recognition of correctness or incorrectness of hand postures during object use by the examiner. Finally, LL was equally poor at describing verbally hand postures in relation to unseen objects.

These findings support the notion of a specific alteration of stored gestures. The ability to store actions in, and to retrieve them from, the motor 'memory' is independent of the ability to recognize objects. It also seems different from merely recognizing visually a hand pattern, since the deficit in apraxic patients involves not only recognizing and describing these patterns or actions, but also performing them. In that sense, the deficit is more one of mentally evoking actions, or forming mental images of actions. As will be central in chapter 4, mental images of actions share many of the neural mechanisms for generating actions. A further logical step (which was explicitly considered by Roy and Hall, 1992) would be to examine apraxic patients for their ability to generate motor imagery, with the idea that their deficit in selecting and organizing motor schemas will also be revealed in evoking actions mentally.

The process of storing object-oriented actions (or actions in general) must be a complex one. It must first involve knowledge about the object itself and its function: these are explicit, verbalizable aspects of the process, which are likely to be laid down in a semantic store. It must also, and perhaps mainly, involve procedures for limb configuration, adequate handling and movement kinematics. These aspects are likely to remain implicit, to be poorly verbalizable and to be stored in procedural memories, properties which are those of a pragmatic representation. Different ways of using these stores may arise according to the task in which the subject is involved (see Rothi et al., 1991). Execution of the action in a purely procedural context will directly activate the procedural store; gesturing, pantomiming or generating a motor image will require a more explicit access to these procedures; finally, verbally describing the action will involve the most semantic mode. The basic elements of the representation remain the same, but the context in which they are used selects different subsets among the possible configurations and triggers different strategies. The effects of lesions reveal that these operations are not limited to a particular neural system, but involve a large network distributed across systems for semantic and pragmatic processing.

chapter four

The Contribution of Mental Imagery to Understanding Motor Representations

NO SUCH THING

The aim of this chapter is to investigate the concept of mental imagery in the context of motor actions. The process of motor representation, a largely non-conscious process, can be accessed consciously under certain conditions: it will be posited that a motor image is a conscious motor representation. According to this definition, motor images should be endowed with the same properties as those of the corresponding (covert) motor representation, that is, they should have the same functional relationship to the represented action and the same causal role in the generation of that action. In using this definition, we follow the general idea already illustrated in previous chapters, that actions are normally driven by internally represented goals rather than directly by the external world. Representations may be built from the environment, they may rely, at least partly, on knowledge acquired from the outside. Yet they require an additional processing whereby actions can be stored, retrieved, improved, or built anew. This representational step operates with fixed rules and relies on identifiable building blocks. A study of motor imagery can thus be considered a valid approach for describing the content and the structure of motor representations.

4.1   Motor imagery, a 'first person' process

NO SUCH THINGS [handwritten]

First, a brief description of the implications of motor imagery for a representational theory of action is in order. Motor imagery departs from other types of mental imagery. Visual images, for example, are experienced by the self in the same way as a spectator who watches a scene (the so called 'external' imagery of sport psychologists, see Mahoney and Avener, 1987). Motor images, by contrast, are experienced from within, as the result of a 'first person' process where the self feels like an actor rather than a spectator ('internal' imagery). During motor imagery the subject feels himself executing the action, whether it involves the whole body (as in running for example) or it is limited to a body part (as in writing, pointing to a target or holding pressure against an obstacle, for example). This process, therefore, requires a representation of the body as the generator of acting forces, and not only of the effects of these forces on the external world. A number of everyday situations correspond to this definition: watching somebody's action with the desire to imitate it, anticipating the effects of an action, preparing or intending to move, refraining from moving, remembering an action, etc., can be considered as putative motor images (see Annett, 1995).

NO SUCH THING AS A SELF [handwritten]

To illustrate, consider for example a pupil learning a motor skill such as playing a music instrument. The pupil watches the teacher demonstrating an action that he must later imitate and reproduce. Although the pupil remains immobile during the teacher's demonstration, he must image in his mind the teacher's action. Conversely, when the teacher watches the pupil's repetition, though not performing the action himself, he must be experiencing a strong feeling of what should be done and how. Similar feelings may be experienced by sport addicts watching a football game on television. They mentally perform the appropriate action to catch the ball (and indeed, they express their frustration when the ball has been missed by the player). The vividness of the imagined action in the watchers can be such as to induce changes in heart and respiration rates related to the degree of their mental effort (see section 4.3.2).

Using a cognitive psychology framework may also help understanding the specificity of motor imagery. Paivio, in his influential Dual Coding Theory (see Paivio, 1986) had proposed the existence of two different, non-exclusive, modes of generation for the mental content, the verbal and the non-verbal modes. Mental imagery would represent a typical example of the functioning of the second one, such that a visual image, for example, would be built by assembling modality-specific units (Paivio's 'imagens'), independent from language, and stored in visual memory. In the case of a motor image, the 'imagens' should pertain to several different modalities, including visual and kinesthetic. Although this theory implies that the verbal and the non-verbal (imagery) systems can be activated separately, they have to remain interconnected, in order to explain how it is possible to generate mental images through verbal instructions or to describe mental images verbally. The strength of the connection between the verbal and the non-verbal systems, however, should differ between types of imagery. Whereas common experience shows that visual images are easily described verbally, and that shape, colour, size of represented objects can be described in great detail, motor images, in contrast, are difficult to transfer into a verbal code. It is difficult, if not impossible, to describe the coordination of movements needed for swimming, for example: it is much easier to demonstrate the action directly by performing the movements. Annett (1986), in systematically studying the behaviour of subjects in tasks such as to explain 'how they take the two ends of a string and tie them together to make a bow', observed that they have great difficulties refraining to use their hands. They make incorrect and repetitious descriptions which take about three times more than it takes them to actually perform the action. Finally, they report to have to rely on motor imagery to support the explanation, and that their hesitations are due to temporary losses of the image (see also Annett, 1995). These observations point to the fact, already mentioned in the previous chapter, that motor representations are poorly coded verbally. Conversely, the use of language creates a context where motor procedures are poorly accessible. The 'lexicon' for actions should perhaps be sought for in the motor 'schemas', rather than in the verbal vocabulary.

4.2 What is represented in motor images

In spite of being poorly coded verbally, however, motor representations are accessible. Specific methods have to be used, such as measuring mental movement time, or matching the imaged movement with a real movement, for which the work of Klatzky and her colleagues has provided clear examples (Klatzky et al., 1987; see section 3.5.3). This section will thus address the problem of the content of motor images and, by extension, the content of motor representations. The main issues to be discussed will be: what are the parameters coded in motor representations?, how can these be accessed experimentally?, is it possible to identify in motor images, parameters that are encoded in the preparation of real actions? If preparation and imagery represent different degrees or aspects of the same phenomenon, and if they have the same objectives, they should contain the same information. In other words, parameters that are relevant to describing actual movements and are likely to be represented during motor preparation should also be represented in imagined movements. Conversely, the consciously accessible content of motor images should provide information as to which parameters are represented during motor preparation. There may be limits to this prediction, as some of the representational levels may not be consciously accessible, and therefore may not be 'imageable'.

Although any represented aspect of a movement ultimately has to be transformed into a set of neural command for muscle contractions, this is not to say that muscle contractions, for example, are represented. Let us assume that the detailed description of motor output is achieved by spinal interneurons acting as a closed-loop regulator under the control of cortical commands, as suggested by Loeb et al. (1990). If this were indeed the case, cortical commands would only specify the goal and the constraints of the action (in terms of speed and accuracy, for example), whereas execution problems (specification of dynamics and kinematics, linearization, changes from spatial to muscle coordinates, and so forth) would be worked out by the spinal regulator. One may conjecture that only the cortical commands would be easily accessible to the subject, and to the experimenter through the subject's report. It is thus critical to know at which level of complexity movements are actually represented, among the wide variety of possible representations: are they represented as the activation of a set of muscles, as an ensemble of functional synergies, or as a set of motor 'rules' (see Saltzman, 1979; Gottlieb et al., 1989)? In the following sections a number of possibilities will be reviewed, starting with the representation of relatively global movement parameters such as duration and force, as well as more specific kinematic rules. Duration and force have not been chosen arbitrarily: those are the parameters of motor preparation which are the most directly experienced by subjects during the motor imagery process and they have directly explorable introspective counterparts.

4.2.1   *The problem of the representation of time*

Experimental data point to the similarity between the time needed for performing an action mentally and overtly. Already in 1962, Landauer compared the time taken by a subject to say the alphabet or series of numbers aloud and to think them to himself. Finding that overt and implicit recitations took almost the same time, Landauer concluded that 'it seems that one does not think words and numbers appreciably faster than one can say them aloud, suggesting that the two behaviours may involve much the same central processes'. Decety and Michel (1989) reached the same conclusion in comparing actual and mental movement times in a writing task. The time taken by right-handed subjects to write their signature or a piece of text was found to be the same whether the task was executed overtly or mentally. The same temporal invariance was found (although movement duration was globally increased) when subjects used their left hand.

Further results suggest that the similarity of duration for overtly and mentally performed actions can be generalized beyond the category of learned skills. Decety et al. (1989) compared the duration of actually walking to targets placed at different distances with that of mental simulation of walking to the same targets. Blindfolded subjects were asked either to walk or to imagine themselves walking to previously inspected targets located at 5, 10 or 15 metres. Walking times were read from a stopwatch the subjects held in their right hand; they switched it on when they started to walk (overtly or mentally) and off when they stopped. In the overt walking condition, walking times were found to increase with the distance covered. The same effect was observed in the mental walking condition. Moreover, and most importantly, mental walking times were found to be very similar to those measured in the overt walking condition for the same subjects and for corresponding distances (figure 4.1A).

The fact that walking times were invariant across overt and mental conditions in such a basic task as walking to targets raises an interesting issue. Several authors (for example, Pylyshyn, 1973; see also Richman et al., 1979; Mitchell and Richman, 1980) would argue that the subjects had tacit knowledge of what should happen when they walk mentally for longer distances, namely, that duration of the action should increase. If this were actually the case, the observed temporal invariance would be simply due to a strategy of the subjects of replicating in the mental condition the temporal sequence registered in the actual condition (for a counter-argument, see section 4.2.2. below). It is not clear, however, whether and how the duration of movements is coded centrally. No simple answer can be given to the question of what are the cues used by subjects to determine the duration of a mental event. According to W. James (1890), we have no sense of empty time, we can only judge the duration of sensations or of mental states. Because a succession of feelings

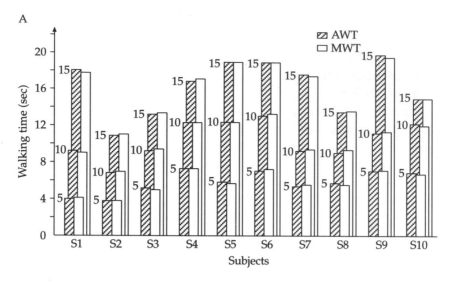

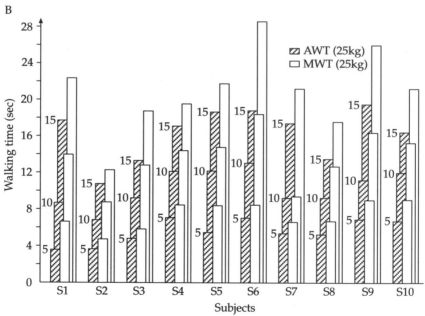

Figure 4.1 The timing of mentally simulated actions

A: subjects (S1–S10) actually walk to previously inspected targets located 5, 10, 15 metres away, or simulate the same action mentally. Actual walking time (AWT, dashed areas) and mental walking time (MWT empty areas) appear to be very similar.

B: same experiment in same subjects while carrying a 25 kg load. Note longer MWT.

From Decety et al., 1989

is not a feeling of sucession, we do not perceive time as such (see Debru, 1992).

The duration of a movement is a composite variable that arises from the unfolding of the movement itself: it depends on the force-mass relations involved in the action (for a complete treatment of this point, see Gottlieb et al., 1989). It is commonly observed that the duration of a simple movement (single joint, constant mass, no strong accuracy requirements) is a function of its extent, that is, of the distance to be covered. To produce movements of a greater extent in this condition, the command system has just to increase the amount of muscular force. Accordingly, maximum acceleration and maximum velocity tend to increase linearly (within limits) with the extent of the movement. However, the fact that greater force is associated with greater distance and with longer duration cannot be considered a general rule. For example, if the load of the moving limb increases, the same distance can still be covered within the same time, provided force is increased and additional energy is expended, which means that in this case greater force will no longer be associated either with greater extent or with longer duration of the movement. In addition, in actions involving small displacements and high accuracy requirements, the force, but not the duration, increases with the distance covered. The level of force programmed in the motor commands is thus associated with greater duration of the movement only in a restricted number of situations and therefore cannot be used as a cue for determining movement duration.

One possible way to further document this point is to compare the durations of actual and mental movements performed against an external load. If the duration required for performing the movement is encoded centrally within the motor representation, the external load should not affect the perceived duration of the imagined action. If, on the other hand, duration is represented as a function of other variables, such as muscular force, then the durations of the imagined and the overt movements should differ, because the load would exert its effect only in the overt condition and not in the mental condition. This possibility was tested in a further experiment by Decety et al. (1989) using the same subjects and the same setup as in the previous one. Blindfolded subjects were loaded with a 25 kg weight placed in a rucksack before being instructed to walk or to imagine themselves walking to previously inspected targets. Walking times in the overt walking condition with the load were in the same range as those measured in the same subjects in the first experiment without the load. By contrast, in the mental walking condition with the load, durations were significantly increased (by 30 per cent or more) in all subjects and for all target distances (figure 4.1B).

This second experiment revealed a clear dissociation between actual and mental walking times, demonstrating that subjects were not merely replicating in the mental condition the estimation of the durations they had experienced in the actual walking condition. It further suggests that force, rather than duration, is the encoded variable, and that estimated duration is merely derived from the level of centrally represented force. When the subjects carried the load, they centrally programmed a greater force to overcome the resistance. In the overt walking task, this increase in force resulted in maintaining the same speed as without load; in the mental walking task, where there was no resistance, the subjects 'read' the increase in felt force as an increase in felt movement duration, according to their common experience. Duration is thus not encoded in itself, and force must be one of the cues for evaluating movement duration.

4.2.2   *The representation of motor rules*

Is it possible to study mental kinematics? Though this may seem a bizarre question, it is an important one. The previous section 4.2.1, in showing a close similarity between neural processes for preparing, executing and imagining movements, implied that at least some of the kinematic rules that have been described for overt movements (that is, those which do not pertain to the interaction with the external force field) should already be found at the central level. This prediction can be verified using experimental data with several different categories of goal-directed actions.

Skilled movements like writing or drawing have well defined kinematic regularities. They have a temporal structure that cannot be ascribed to biomechanical factors alone and that pertains to central factors. First, because the tangential velocity of these movements is scaled to their amplitude, movements of different amplitudes tend to have the same duration. This so-called 'isochrony principle' (see Viviani and McCollum, 1983) seems to be maintained in mentally simulated movements: for example, subjects take the same amount of time to mentally write a small or a large signature (Decety and Michel, 1989).

A second principle is that the tangential velocity of the moving limb is a function of the radius of curvature of the movement, that is, it is minimum when the curvature is maximum (Lacquaniti et al., 1983). Subjects cannot depart from this relation between geometry and kinematics: when instructed to track a target moving with a different spatiotemporal pattern (for example, accelerating rather than decelerating in the curves), their performance deteriorates, in the sense that their movements during the attempts to track the target 'continue to bear the imprint of the general principle of organization for spontaneous movements, even though this is in contrast with the specifications of the target' (Viviani, 1990, p. 369). The main point of relevance here is that the same relation between velocity and curvature is also present in subjects' perceptual estimation of the regularity of the trajectory of a luminous target. A target moving at a uniform velocity is paradoxically seen as moving in a non-uniform way and, conversely, the condition for perceiving a uniform velocity is that the movement has a kinematic structure which retains the above velocity/curvature relation (Viviani and Stucchi, 1992a). According to the same authors, the explanation for this effect would be that perception is constrained by motor control, that is, by the implicit knowledge that 'the central nervous system has concerning the movements that it is capable of producing' (Viviani and Stucchi, 1992b). This experiment shows that there is a central representation of what a uniform movement should be and that this representation influences visual perception. If this interpretation is correct, then the kinematic structure of mentally produced movements should also follow the same rule. This remains to be tested.

The possibility of accessing the content of motor images has also been investigated by using the classical paradigm of mental chronometry. Besides the study of Georgopoulos and Massey (1987) showing the increase in reaction time – which they considered as a 'mental movement time' – for movements of increasing 'difficulty' (for a description of this experiment, see section 5.1.1), other attempts were made to measure the duration of a purely mentally performed action as a function of task difficulty. In the experiment of Decety (1991), subjects were instructed either to actually walk or imagine themselves walking on beams that had the same length but varied in width. The beam width was assumed to be a factor of difficulty, that is, the narrower the beams, the more difficult the task. A clear effect of task difficulty was found in both actual and mental movement times. A new experiment (Decety and Jeannerod, 1996) was undertaken to verify the validity of Fitts' law in purely mental actions. Normal subjects were instructed to walk mentally through gates of different widths positioned at different distances. The gates were presented to the subject with a 3-D visual display (a virtual reality helmet) which involved no calibration with external cues and no possibility for the subject to refer to a known environment. Subjects had to indicate the time they started walking and the time they 'passed through' the gate. Again, mental walking time was found to increase with increasing apparent gate distance and decreasing apparent gate width. Thus, it took the subjects longer to walk mentally through a narrow gate than to walk through a larger gate placed at the same distance (figure 4.2). (For another demonstration of Fitts law in mentally simulated actions, see Sirigu et al., 1995a.) Note that in the Decety and Jeannerod experiment, the subjects never experienced actually walking through the gates, neither did they ever see physical gates: their mental time estimates could not be derived from prior experience.

A

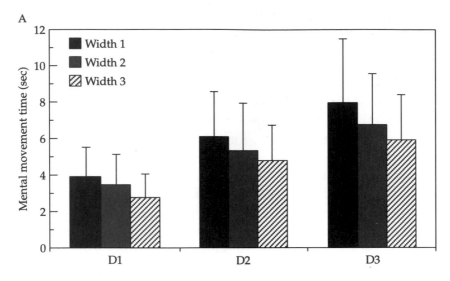

B

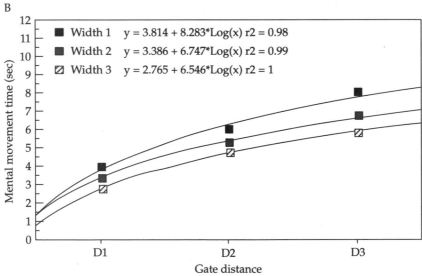

Figure 4.2 Speed-accuracy trade-off in mentally simulated action
A: mean mental movement time in 15 subjects walking through virtual gates of different widths (width 1, narrow) placed at different distances in virtual space (distance 3, D3, far). Note longer time for narrow gate at longest distance.
B: plot of same results showing log relationship between mental time and task 'difficulty'.
From Decety and Jeannerod, 1996

The point raised by these experiments is to determine at which level of action generation the description of the representation is made. One of the current interpretations given to Fitts' law holds that it governs not only the execution, but also the planning of actions, so that the movement, when executed, can be adjusted to the requirements of the task (see Meyer et al., 1982, 1990). Consider, for example, an everyday life situation where the same behaviour arises, for example, driving a car through gates of different widths. As the gates get narrower, the driver, even if he is aware that the car fits the gate width, will spontaneously slow down and nearly stop the car before getting through the gate. In other terms, the driver tends to adjust the velocity of his car to the accuracy requirement of the path: the greater the accuracy needed to drive the car safely through the obstacles, the slower the velocity. This example suggests that the driver's behaviour, as well as that of the subjects passing mentally through the gates, is determined by his representation of the action.

4.2.3   *Representation of motor constraints*

Other experiments reveal that the representation of an action takes into account the biomechanical constraints of the represented movement. In an interesting series of experiments, Parsons (1994) examined the time it takes to subjects to mentally rotate their hand from a starting position to a target position displayed on a photograph. The main result was that mental rotation times were very close to the corresponding real rotation times. For the less awkward postures, mental and real rotation times were equal, whereas for the most awkward ones, mental times were shorter than, but still correlated with, the real rotation times. Accordingly, when the picture of a hand at a given orientation was presented, the time it took the subject to determine its side (right or left) was close to the time for the real movement into its orientation (figure 4.3).

These results have interesting implications. First, they show that mentally rotating a hand into a target position follows the

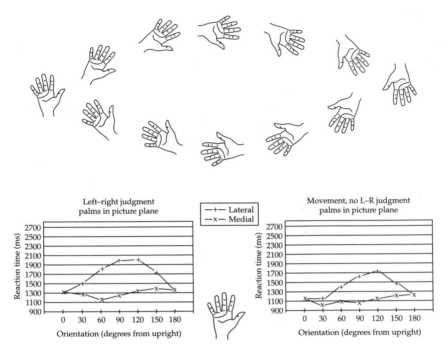

Figure 4.3 Reaction time for matching hands with different orientations
The drawing of a right hand in canonical orientation has to be matched with another drawing of a right or left hand presented at variable orientations (upper part). Reaction time to give the proper answer (lower left) is similar to the time to actually move the hand at the shown orientation (lower right).
From Parsons, 1994

same rules as mentally rotating other visual objects: mental rotation time is a function of the angle (Shepard and Metzler, 1971; Shepard and Cooper, 1982). Second, the fact that mental times were the same as real times suggests that mental rotation of a hand is constrained by the biomechanics of the hand as a body part. Indeed, in a previous sudy, Parsons (1987) had found that the times for mentally rotating a hand or foot into awkward target postures were consistent with the duration of movements along biomechanically plausible trajectories. These results lead to the prediction that, in certain conditions (for example, motor impairment), the duration of mental rotation of the hand should be dissociated from that of other visual shapes.

This prediction was recently verified in parkinsonian patients (see section 4.5).

One may wonder whether subjects would be able to image 'impossible' movements, that is, movements violating normal anatomical and biomechanical limitations. Although it has been reported that under conditions of perturbed proprioceptive input (for example, by tendon vibration, Roll et al., 1990) subjects may perceive their limbs in abnormal positions, there is no evidence that they would be able to simulate these positions during imagery in normal conditions. Experimental results of Shiffrar and Freyd (1990) showed that the perceived motion of human limbs (extrapolated by subjects from rapidly alternating pictures) tends to respect the biomechanical constraints and does not violate the laws of biological motion. A similar interpretation can be given to the results of Rosenbaum et al. (1990) and Rosenbaum and Jorgensen (1992). They found that the decision to form a given type of grip (for example, underhand versus overhand) for grasping an object is made according to the subsequent use of the object, so that awkward or uncomfortable hand postures are avoided and the time spent in extreme joint angles is minimized. They used a horizontally positioned bar and counted the number of times subjects (with their right hand) would make an overhand or underhand grip to take the bar and to position it vertically with its right or its left end on a surface. Subjects consistently made overhand grasps when they had to place the bar on its right end, and underhand grasps when they had to place it on its left end. Rosenbaum et al.'s hypothesis for explaining these results was that the representation does not specify which actions are allowed in which situations, but rather, which actions are *not* allowed.

4.3   Physiological correlates of mental simulation of movement

What is the situation of motor images among the other motor phenomena, such as motor intention, preparation, or execution?

Again, there are several possible ways of dealing with this question. A first hypothesis states that simulating a movement is the same thing as actually performing it, except that execution is blocked. An alternative hypothesis states that mental simulation is limited to rehearsing early stages of action, well ahead of execution. Whereas the first hypothesis generates specific predictions (for example, we should expect to find physiological correlates in motor imagery similar to those measured during real action), the second one is mostly a default hypothesis. It would only become plausible if sufficient convincing evidence for the first one could not be shown. In this and the following section, some of these arguments will be discussed under two main headings, the physiological changes occurring during mental simulation of movements, and the effects of mental training.

This approach of motor imagery seems justified by previous work on other types of mental imagery. Data drawn from the study of brain-lesioned patients or from brain-mapping experiments have revealed that visual imagery, for example, engages many of the mechanisms and neural structures that are also found to be involved in visual perception (Farah, 1989; Kosslyn et al., 1993). It seems therefore logical to look in the motor system for the same direct continuity between mechanisms for the representational stages of action and those for action performance.

4.3.1 Muscular activity

Physiological correlates have been recorded in many experiments involving mental motor imagery. Electromyographic activity (EMG) was frequently found to increase with respect to rest during motor simulation. Jacobson (1930, 1931) found micromovements and increased EMG in those limbs involved in imaginal movements, but not in the contralateral ones. These discharges were related to the requirements of the imagined task (for example, rhythm). Shaw (1940) found EMG increase to be proportional to the amount of imagined effort. Hence the common claim that the kinesthetic image of a motion pattern is accompanied by the same innervation pattern as during the motion itself (see also Hale, 1982; Harris and Robinson, 1986). Wehner et al. (1984) looked for a possible relationship between the amplitude course of EMG during mental motor training and processing task characteristics. They found frequency characteristics in the mental training EMGs similar to those in the active training EMGs, which shows that there are task-specific frequencies in the EMG of the relaxed arm during mental training. The fact that EMG was found to be quiescent in several experiments also involving motor imagery (for example, Yue and Cole, 1992) does not contradict the above idea. It may only reflect better inhibition of movement execution under certain conditions or in certain subjects. Conversely, the fact that muscular activity is sometimes only partially blocked during motor simulation (as shown by residual EMG) emphasizes the delicate equilibrium between excitatory and inhibitory influences at the motoneuron level and suggests that motoneurons are close to threshold during motor imagery.

There are only a few data concerning changes arising in the motor system during motor preparation. Experiments in the monkey by Mellah et al. (1990) showed that a small proportion of biceps motor units were active during the preparation period for a flexion of the arm preceding the instruction to move. These units, which had a low threshold and a low discharge rate, stopped firing shortly before the movement began. This preparatory muscular activity was suggested to influence a subsequent movement by increasing the stiffness of the muscle and reducing its time constant in responding to the phasic command. It could also be a source of information (via alpha-gamma coactivation) for facilitating the central neurons responsible for generating the phasic command. According to Mellah et al. (1990), the muscle fibres which fire during preparation belong to deep muscles and are likely to be of the slow tonic group, a type of fibres with a low metabolic rate. Experiments using surface EMG recordings or even NMR spectroscopy would thus fail to observe this activity. It is therefore possible that a similar muscular activity could be observed also during motor imagery if the appropriate recording technique was used. An incomplete inhibition of motor output (occurring as a consequence of instructions or of a subject's bias) would be a valid explanation for accounting for these muscular discharges.

The fact that mental simulation of movement activates motor output was confirmed by a recent study of spinal excitability during motor imagery. Bonnet, Decety, Requin and Jeannerod (unpublished) instructed subjects either to press isometrically on a pedal, or to simulate mentally the same action. Two levels of strength (weak and strong) were used. The main result of this experiment was that motoneuron excitability, as tested by the amplitude of spinal monosynaptic reflexes, was increased during mental simulation. This increase was only slightly less than the reflex facilitation associated with the current performance of the same movement. Tendinous reflex (T-reflex) amplitude was more increased than H-reflex amplitude. In addition, the change of reflexes in the leg imagined to be involved in the movement was larger for a strong than for a weak simulated pressure. In accordance with some of the foregoing results, a weak EMG activity was found during mental imagery.

The fact that the T-reflexes were more facilitated than H-reflexes deserves discussion. A first explanation for this phenomenon is that the H-reflex is a test for the excitability of all muscles of the stimulated leg, including those which are not involved in the simulated action. T-reflex, by contrast, specifically tests the excitability of the muscle involved in simulating the foot pressure. It is thus likely that the change in excitability should be more visible using T-reflex than using H-reflex. Another explanation is that, whereas both reflexes are conveyed via the same monosynaptic neuronal pathways, the effect of the stimulus is, by far, not equivalent: the H-reflex, which is triggered by the electrical stimulation of Ia fibers, short-cuts neuromuscular spindles, while the T-reflex, which is triggered by a tendon tap, is a response to stretching these spindles. In so far as the sensitivity of neuromuscular spindles to muscular stretch is under the control of gamma motoneurons, an increase in excitability of the T-reflex, but not of the H-reflex, would result from a selective increase in gamma motoneuron activity.

This possibility of a spindle activation during mental simulation of a movement is an interesting one. Spindle afferents are known to play a role not only during movement execution, but also for organizing the motor output during self-generated actions (Porter and Lemon, 1993). For example, passively executed movements or vibrations of the corresponding tendon strongly facilitate, via spindle activation, the initiation of voluntary movements when such an initiation has became difficult, or even impossible, for example after a lasting immobilization or a cerebral lesion.

4.3.2   Autonomic nervous system

Other effectors normally not submitted to voluntary control, such as the autonomic effectors, are also likely to be activated during motor imagery. This possibility was tested in two experiments by Decety et al. (1991, 1993). In the 1993 experiment, subjects were requested to either actually perform or mentally simulate a leg exercise at two levels of work. Heart rate, respiration rate and end-tidal PCO_2 were measured in both conditions. After only a few seconds of actual exercise, heart rate began to increase up to about 50 per cent over the resting value. In the mental condition, where no work was produced, this increase was about 32 per cent. Respiration rate also increased almost without delay during actual effort and during mental simulation. The average respiration rate was even higher during mental simulation than during actual effort (see also Wuyam et al., 1995) (figure 4.4). These results confirm earlier findings of Adams et al. (1987) who showed that heart rate and cardiac output already increased notably within about five beats after exercise was started and that respiration changed within one breathing cycle. A large fraction of this fast increase in heart and respiration rates at the onset of exercise (both real and mental) is thus likely to be due to the effect of motor preparation, not to metabolic changes. Vegetative activation during preparation to effort would be timed to begin when motor activity starts. This would represent an optimal mechanism for anticipating the forthcoming

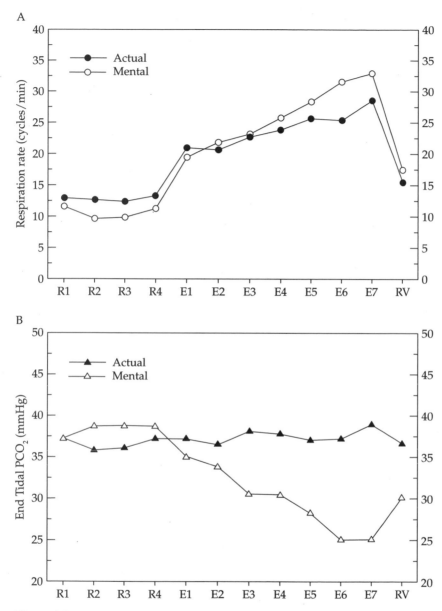

Figure 4.4 Autonomous response during mental effort

A: mean respiration rate in 10 subjects during actual (black symbols) or mental (open symbols) effort (pedaling against a 15 kg load with the right leg. Respiration rate is sampled each 17.5 seconds. R1–R4, sampling periods during rest. E1–E7, sampling periods during pedalling at increasing frequency. RV, beginning of recovery. Note faster rate during mental effort.

B: changes in end-tidal PCO_2 during the same experiment. Note drop in PCO_2 during mental effort, due to increased ventilation in absence of muscular catabolism.

From Decety et al., 1993

metabolic changes and shortening the intrinsic delay needed for heart and respiration to adapt to effort (for a review, see Requin et al., 1991). Autonomic activation during imagined action would pertain to the same phenomenon of preparation to action.

The possibility that these autonomic changes were a consequence of muscular activity can be ruled out. The spectroscopic analysis performed by Decety et al. (1993), showing no change in muscular metabolism during mental simulation, is against this possbility. In fact, the combination of increased respiration rate and unchanged muscular metabolism during mental simulation resulted in a progressive drop of PCO_2 in this condition: this never happens during physical effort where ventilation eliminates CO_2 at about the same rate as it is produced, and where PCO_2 remains constant. An additional argument in this direction is provided by an experiment of Gandevia et al. (1993b). They observed graded cardiovascular changes in paralyzed subjects attempting muscular contractions, a situation close to mental simulation. As paralysis was complete, these changes could not be due to residual muscular activity and had to be of a central origin.

4.3.3   Brain activity

The above physiological correlates of mental imagery ultimately reflect the activity of central neurons coding for simulated actions. To illustrate this point, let us consider again the example of the teacher and the pupil. While the pupil watches the teacher, neurons in the areas of his brain relevant to motor preparation and planning will fire as if he were actually performing the action he is viewing. Similarly, the teacher's feelings when he watches the pupil's performance must be based on the discharge of the same neurons, in his own brain, that were firing while he was executing the correct movements. Finally, when the pupil mentally rehearses what he observed from his teacher, the same neurons again should be activated. According to this description, the 'representation' neurons operating during observed and simulated actions should be the same as those activated during preparation for real action.

This is not an unrealistic hypothesis, particularly if we consider the activity of neurons recorded in an analogous situation in the monkey premotor cortical area (Di Pellegrino et al., 1992). As described in chapter 2, these neurons fire, not only during execution by the animal of a given hand movement, but also – and most strikingly – while the animal watches another animal or a person performing the *same* movement. Whether these neurons also exist in man is a matter of speculation. However, a recent experiment by Fadiga et al. (1995) strongly supports this notion. Subjects were requested to observe for 3 seconds grasping movements performed by an experimenter. At the end of the observation period a transcranial magnetic stimulus was applied to their motor cortex. The pattern of muscular response to this stimulus was found to be selectively increased with respect to control conditions. In addition, the set of muscles activated by the stimulus was the same as that recorded while the subject himself actually performed the movement. This result demonstrates an increased excitability of the motor system during the observation of actions. It is likely that the same effect would also be obtained during mental simulation, as indicated by the increased spinal excitability observed in this condition. These mechanisms might represent the neural basis for imitation, observational learning and motor imagery.

Brain activity during motor simulation has also been investigated using the mapping of brain metabolism. Following pioneering studies by Ingvar and Philipsson (1977), Roland et al. (1980) monitored rCBF with single photon tomography in normal subjects, during mental simulation of a rapid and skilled sequence of digit movements. They found a significant and localised rCBF change mainly in the supplementary motor area (SMA). Decety et al. (1988) studied normal subjects imagining a graphic movement (writing 'one, two, three', etc.). The subjects were instructed to imagine the movement at the 'first person perspective' and to try to 'feel their writing hand'. Regions corresponding to the prefrontal cortex, SMA, the cerebellum and the basal ganglia were significantly activated (see also Ryding et al., 1993).

A recent confirmation of these studies was provided by the PET data obtained by Decety et al. (1994) and Stephan et al. (1995). Stephan et al. compared the effects, on brain activation, of sequential joystick movements in three conditions: execution, mental simulation and preparation to move. During imagined movements a specific part of SMA (the rostral part of posterior SMA) was preferentially activated. This localization was different from that observed during executed movements, where activation was more caudal. This finding reinforces the notion of a parcellization of SMA into areas with different hierarchical status and different functional implications: the posterior zone would be purely executive (the SMA proper of Matelli et al., 1993), whereas the more anterior zone would be more related to cognitive activity, in this case, motor imagery. Stephan et al. (1995) also found a bilateral activation of the ventrolateral part of area 6 and of superior and caudal part of parietal lobes (areas 7 and 40). Stephan et al.'s data somewhat differ from those of Decety et al. (1994), also using PET. In the Decety et al. study, three-dimensional graspable objects (spheres and cylinders of different sizes, colours and orientations) were presented to subjects with the instruction to imagine themselves grasping the objects with their right hand. rCBF was found to be increased in several areas concerned with motor behaviour. At the cortical level, area 6 in the inferior part of the frontal gyrus was strongly activated on both sides as was area 40 in the contralateral inferior parietal lobule. Subcortically, the caudate nucleus was found to be activated on both sides and the cerebellum only on the left side. Another focus of activity was observed in left prefrontal areas, extending to the dorsolateral frontal cortex (areas 9 and 46; see also Fox et al., 1987). Finally, the anterior cingulate cortex (areas 24 and 32) was bilaterally activated.

The main difference between Decety et al. (1994) and Stephan et al. (1995) lies in the labelling of the SMA. The fact that this area was not activated in the Decety et al.'s experiment may be due to the fact that their subjects simulated visually guided reach and grasp movements directed at external objects. In studies where SMA was found to be activated (including that of Stephan et al., 1995), simulated movements were rapid sequential, internally generated movements, without external goal. This was also the case in the Parsons et al.'s (1995) PET study. These authors showed that discrimination of the side of a visually presented hand (which they suggested to be resolved by mentally moving your own hand until it matches the presented hand, see Parsons, 1994) also involved bilateral activation of SMA.

Consciously representing an action thus involves a pattern of cortical activation that resembles that of an intentionally executed action (for example, Frith et al., 1991). An important point remains to be determined, however: it is whether or not primary motor cortex is silent when no execution occurs. Activation of primary motor cortex during mental simulation of movement should in fact not be a surprising finding, as it was already suggested by the Georgopoulos et al.'s (1989) monkey experiments, where the directional activity of cortical cells was found to be modified during 'mental rotation' of the movement direction by the animal. In man, activation of primary motor cortex during mental simulation of movement or related processes is suggested by experiments measuring cortical responsiveness to transcranial magnetic stimulation. Pascual-Leone et al. (1995) reported that the size of the excitable area devoted to finger movements (as determined by transcranial stimulation) was increased as movements were repeated over training periods (a fact reported in animal experiments by Grunbaum and Sherrington as early as 1903). The important point is that a similar increase in the size of the excitable area was produced by imaginal training. Relevant observations were also made by Gandevia and Rothwell (1987), who showed that 'concentrating' on one hand muscle without activating it increased the effect of subthreshold magnetic stimulation of the cortical area corresponding to that muscle (and not of other muscles). Thus, there is a selective enhancement of responsiveness of motor cortical areas during motor imagery.

Experiments using metabolic brain-mapping provided more ambiguous results. Roland et al. (1980), Decety et al. (1994) and Stephan et al. (1995) in PET experiments and Sanes (1994) using fMRI found no activity in caudal area 4 during imagined movements. In contrast, Leonardo et al. (1995) and Kim et al. (1995), also using fMRI, reported sensorimotor cortex activation in this condition in two out of five subjects. This was confirmed by Roth et al. (1996) who found an unambiguous contralateral activation of area M1 in four out of six tested subjects during motor imagery of a repetitive finger/thumb opposition movement (figure 4.5). The activated zone overlapped that activated during execution of the same movement, although it was smaller. Premotor cortex also was activated, on both sides. Finally, SMA was activated bilaterally: in this structure, however, the area involved during motor imagery was located more rostral than that activated during execution (see also Tyszka et al., 1994).

Some of the results presented in this section raise the problem of the mechanism and the locus of motor inhibition during motor simulation. We know that, during preparation for a movement, inhibition occurs at the segmental spinal level: hence the decrease of spinal reflexes during the preparatory period and their reincrease shortly before the movement starts (Bonnet and Requin, 1982). The pattern of spinal excitability during motor simulation, with a marked increase in T-reflex, is thus closer to that of motor execution than that of motor preparation. The mechanisms by which the motor command is actively inhibited should thus differ for preparation and simulation. In the former case, the movement is blocked by a massive inhibition acting at the spinal level to protect motoneurons against a premature triggering of action (Requin et al., 1977). In the latter case, we could expect that the excitatory motor output generated for executing the action is counterbalanced by another, parallel, inhibitory output. This competition between two opposite outputs would account for the partial block of the motoneurons, as shown by residual EMG and increased reflex excitability. Where this inhibitory output originates is still an open question.

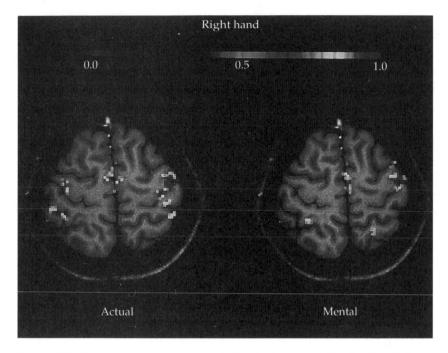

Figure 4.5 Primary motor cortex activity during mentally simulated finger movements

Functional magnetic resonance imaging of cortical blood-flow during actual execution (left) and mental simulation (right) of a sequential finger movement with the right hand in one normal subject. Note increase in blood flow in left hemisphere (appearing on right side of figures). Activated pixels concentrate in the M1 hand area and SMA. During actual execution, also note activation in premotor cortex on both sides.

From Roth et al., 1996

4.4   The effects of mental training

The strong relationships of motor imagery to the neural substrate, described in section 4.3, lead to the logical expectation that the central changes produced in the motor system during imagery will affect subsequent motor performance. Conversely, the observed changes might represent an explanation for those effects known to arise as a result of mental training.

The sport psychology literature in the early 1960s offers a large number of studies reporting measurable effects of mental imagery on subsequent motor performance. Comparison of the performances of subjects who had received 'mental practice' with those of control groups led to the conclusion that mental practice facilitates performance (for a review, see Feltz and Landers, 1983). Mental training has been shown to affect several aspects of motor performance normally thought to be specific outcomes of training, such as muscular strength (Yue and Cole, 1992), movement speed (Pascual-Leone et al., 1995), reduction of variability and increase in temporal consistency. The latter effect was demonstrated by Vogt (1995). He examined how subjects learned to replicate a periodic movement pattern displayed visually. Training was either physical (replicate the visual pattern by flexion-extension of the elbow), mental (form a mental image of the movement needed to replicate the pattern), or observational. Physical test blocks were performed (without visual feedback) after the training period in each modality. Physical and non-physical types of practice were found to exert closely similar effects on the replication of the movement, whichever parameter was considered (for example, movement form, spatial scaling, consistency of movement tempo, and consistency of relative timing).

The interpretation of the effects of mental training, however, differs widely among authors. According to Paivio (1986), the improvement in motor performance following mental practice might be due to motivational factors which increase the physiological arousal of the performer. According to others, mental imagery could have a beneficial influence on neural mechanisms involved in performing the subsequent action. Finke (1979) reported that subjects imagining pointing at visual targets during wearing laterally displacing prisms showed the same after-effects as if they had actually pointed with the prisms. This result, which involves a directional bias in executing the adapted movements, could hardly be explained by motivational factors. Similarly, Johnson (1982) studied the effects of imagined movements on the recall of a learned motor task. Prior experimental data had been reported (for example, by Stelmach and Walsh, 1973), showing that the recall of a learned movement was distorted if another movement was interpolated between acquisition and recall. The distortion was a bias of the to-be-recalled movement in the direction of the interpolated movement. Johnson conjectured that, if imagined and actual movements were functionally equivalent, then the same effect on recall should be obtained by interpolating an imagined movement instead of an actual one. This hypothesis proved correct in that the imagined and the actually produced movements led to the same direction error during recall.

The neural basis for these effects remains hypothetical. A first possible explanation is that efferent discharges generated during the imagining process represent the substrate for subsequent facilitation of motor performance through priming of the motor pathways by descending volleys. As already mentioned, mental imagery is accompanied by subthreshold motor activation and even small movements. Eye movements have been recorded during recall of visual scenes (for example, Jeannerod and Mouret, 1962). It could be argued that the centrally generated image 'leaks' into executive mechanisms which are held under (incomplete) inhibition and that the observed effects of training are due to purely central changes. This view is supported by recent work on mental muscular 'training'. Yue and Cole (1992) compared the increase in muscular strength produced by actual training (repeated maximal isometric contractions) and by mental training (imagining the same effortful contractions). In both conditions, the maximal force produced by the trained muscles increased significantly (by 30 per cent and 22 per cent, respectively). EMG recordings during the training sessions showed that, whereas high levels of contraction were produced during actual training, the muscle was quiescent during mental training. Yue and Cole (1992) came to the logical conclusion that the increase in muscle strength following mental training did not occur primarily as the result of changes at the execution level of the motor system. They suggested instead that neural changes occurred at higher (programming and planning) levels, and that the altered programs in turn achieved strength gains via actions on spinal circuitry.

This 'central' explanation, which is supported by the effects of magnetic transcranial stimulation of motor cortex described in an earlier section of this chapter, is an interesting one, as it has implications for the process of learning in general. Thus, there would be an inner regulation of external performance without recourse to actual movement and to the related sensory feedback and knowledge of results. This explanation is compatible with a hierarchical model of action generation where an internal representation of the action releases efferent signals in lower level mechanisms, and where a comparison of the efferent discharges with the internal stages of the action is performed (see Mackay, 1981). A similar model will be developed in chapter 6.

In the above hypothesis, the EMG activity observed during mental training has to be considered more as an effect than a cause of the processes taking place during learning. The recent findings on spinal reflexes during motor imagery reported in section 4.3.1, however, suggest an alternative – albeit complementary – interpretation. A tonic afferent discharge arising from the muscular spindles during imagery (possibly due to increased gamma motoneuron activity) could have implications for subsequent shaping of motor performance and improvement in learning. First note that this explanation differs from the classical interpretation postulating that the minimal muscular activity generated by mental motor imagery could generate sufficient kinesthetic feedback for supporting learning (Jacobson, 1931). Also note that it is compatible with the 'central' explanation above, as it also involves the activity of a central generator for triggering the spindle activity.

Determining unambiguously the type of the relationship of the EMG activity during motor preparation and motor imagery to the representational process would require a re-examination of these phenomena in de-afferented patients. This would involve testing the ability of generating an imagined movement with a de-afferented limb (in patients suffering peripheral neuropathy, for example). Persistence of vivid imagery in these patients, which is likely to be the case according to the observations mentioned earlier in this chapter, would rule out the peripheral origin of the image, even if EMG discharges were recorded.

4.5   Motor imagery in clinical disorders of movement and action

Finally, the close relationships observed between mental simulation of movement and changes in activity of the motor system suggest that motor imagery should be affected by pathological conditions affecting the central motor structures. The finding that, in normal subjects, mental movement times and real movement times are equal, or at least correlated, provides a means for verifying this prediction. Accordingly, a pathological condition producing a slowness of movements, for example, should also produce an increase in the time taken for simulating the same movements. A similar reasoning was used in chapter 3 for predicting disorganized motor imagery in apraxic patients.

Mental simulation was recently compared in normal subjects and in Parkinsonian patients by Dominey et al. (1995). Normal subjects were right-handed volunteers; patients were akinetic Parkinsonians selected at the early stage of their disease, with clinical signs predominating on the right side. Normal subjects and patients were instructed to perform, with either hand, a sequential finger movement (touching the pad of the thumb with the pad of the other four fingers) in conditions of motor execution and motor imagery. Parkinsonian patients were slower than normals in all conditions. During motor execution, their movements were slower than normals with both hands, although this effect was more marked with their right hand. The same slowness and the same asymmetry was observed for mental movements. Finally, the degree of asymmetry in both motor execution and mental imagery were significantly correlated with each other. This correlation was particularly clear in two of the patients who presented fluctuations of their motor performance as a function of their dopamine treatment: mental movement times increased or decreased to the same extent as motor execution times according to whether the patients were in their 'off' or in their 'on' periods, respectively (figure 4.6).

Impaired motor imagery in such patients could have been due to a general inability to generate mental images. In order to

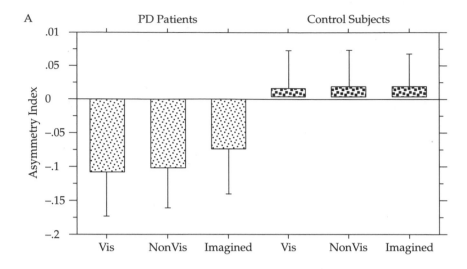

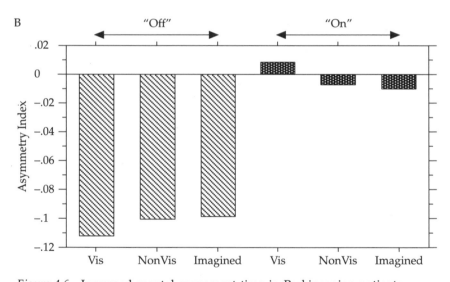

Figure 4.6 Increased mental movement time in Parkinsonian patients

A: asymmetry of movement times during both actual execution of a finger sequential movement with right and left hands (under visual control, Vis; without visual control, NonVis; during mental simulation, Imagined). PD patients were affected only on right side. Note negative values of asymmetry index, indicating slower movements with right hand. In normal controls, note small, non-significant, advantage of right hand.

B: the same experiment is shown in one Parkinsonian patient during an 'off' period, and immediately after treatment ('on'). Note sharp change in asymmetry index for both actual and mental performance.

From Dominey et al., 1995

control this point, Dominey et al. (1995) compared patients performance during two mental rotation tasks: a letter rotation task where the time to respond whether the letter was normally or mirror oriented was measured; a hand rotation task, where the response rested on whether the hand shown was right or left. Patients were slower for hand rotations than for letter rotations, and their performance in hand rotation correlated with their imagery performance in the sequential finger movement task. This result further supports the notion (Parsons, 1994) that hand rotation pertains to motor imagery, rather than to visual imagery (refer to figure 4.3).

Another example of the effects of central motor impairment on mental simulation of movement was reported by Sirigu et al. (1995a) in a patient with a left arm progressive hemiparesis due to a right rolandic lesion. The patient was tested for her ability to reproduce, physically and mentally, finger, wrist, elbow and shoulder movements displayed by the experimenter. The results showed that the left arm was slower executing motor tasks with the fingers and elbow, not with the shoulder. The same difference held for mentally simulated movements. It thus appears that motor cortical lesions, although they do not affect the ability to generate motor imagery, impair mentally performed actions to the same extent as they impair real movements.

chapter five

Action Planning

The description of the motor representation provided in the previous chapters dealt with relatively simple actions. Those are actions for which the goal is completely described by the stimuli arising from the external milieu. In the action of grasping an object, for example, it is sufficient to encode the attributes of this object for generating a perfectly appropriate movement. In this case, movement time is encoded in terms of movement kinematics and coordination between segments.

Yet, simple actions like grasping an object are rarely (except in laboratories) performed for themselves. They are usually embedded into more complex actions where achievement of the goal requires other steps to be performed prior to, and after them. Simple actions are thus under the dependence of higher order factors which represent the final goal of the overall action. An experiment reported by Marteniuk et al. (1987) can be used to illustrate this point. Subjects had to reach for a small disc, and then to either fit the disc into a tightly fitting well (fit condition), or to throw it into a larger container (throw condition). Marteniuk et al. found that the kinematics of the initial reach, which was common to the two conditions, differed according to whether the instruction was to fit or to throw. In the fit condition, the peak velocity of the reach was lower and a larger proportion of movement time was spent decelerating. These changes are not predicted by the kinematic requirements, nor by the coordination constraints of the movement itself; they pertain to the higher order mechanisms which modulate or 'penetrate' the lower levels. Motor representations expand in time far beyond the movement which is actually prepared or performed.

The ensemble of actions which concur to a single goal will be postulated to be represented within an 'action plan'. The main function of action planning is thus to select, from the stock of available motor schemas, those which will have to be performed, relate them to the proper internal and external cues, and organize them into an appropriate sequence. Selecting a given set of motor schemas implies inhibiting the non-desirable ones, specially those that may relate to intervening stimuli or distractors. This function may be essential for carrying out actions constrained by rules or by instructions. The specific part which has to be carried out by the plan is therefore a memory function: learn, memorize and retrieve the cues and the movements associated with them; store the subgoals during execution of the intermediate steps of the action; and check completion. Description of action plans thus adds to the motor representation a further dimension – time – which was not present as an independent parameter in the description of motor schemas.

There are two qualitatively different modes of adequately carrying out a task. One mode operates through the application of well-learned routines, whereas the other one requires a specific cognitive strategy for building up a new representation. Many complex actions (like getting dressed, preparing breakfast or going to work) may be so automatized that, once started, they unfold without wilful control: the association between cues and movements, the selection of the motor schemas and the organization of the temporal framework already exist and do not have to be done again. Other actions, by contrast, require going through a number of addtional steps for specifying the goal, drawing up a plan, and defining temporal contingencies.

This distinction between types of actions is important, because it implies that action planning depends on a number of separate, non-mandatory processes, some of which may, or may not, be activated according to circumstances. The processes that encode intentions, prior knowledge, instructions, etc. are likely to be bypassed in the case of routine actions. This view on organization of action, together with the previous descriptions of object-oriented action, progressively reveals the need for a hierarchical type of motor organization. This and the next chapter 6 will provide a more complete description of these levels of representation and will attempt transferring these descriptions into neural terms.

5.1   A cognitive approach to action planning

The notion that there are endogenous mechanisms which can account for the unfolding of complex actions is an ancient one. Triggered actions and actions released by electrical brain stimulation are examples of preorganized sets of motor commands, which are stored and ready to operate once started by the appropriate stimulus. Although this type of organization departs from the concept of action plans, it may give an idea of how actions are represented neurally. Lashley, in his famous paper on the problem of serial order in behaviour (Lashley, 1951) emphasized the role of a 'schema of order' in organizing rapid motor sequences, what he called the 'syntax of action'. Action sequences, he thought, were too fast to depend on reflex chaining, simply because there was not enough time for the sensory consequence of a given movement to trigger the next one in the series (for a recent reappraisal of Lashley's views, see Bruce, 1994). Although this timing argument is no longer considered as a crucial one (proprioceptive feedback can indeed be very short, see Jeannerod, 1991) Lashley's ideas on central organization of action (as opposed to peripheral chaining) are still widely accepted. Their influence can be tracked in Keele's definition of 'motor programs', still in use nowadays: 'a set of muscle commands that are structured before a movement sequence begins, and that allows the entire sequence to be carried out' (Keele, 1968, p. 387. For an overview, see Keele et al., 1990).

A major step in understanding the nature of action planning was the introduction in neurophysiology, of paradigms borrowed from cognitive psychology. Covert operations underlying motor preparation became accessible in experiments using trained monkeys, where the activity of single neurons could be correlated with behavioural events. In this chapter, two main approaches using this methodology will be described. One of these approaches refers to the well-known experimental paradigm of 'mental chronometry'.

5.1.1 Mental chronometry paradigms

The basic idea of mental chronometry is that the time taken to execute a motor task reflects the processes underlying the preparation of that task. These processes are thought to be time-consuming, and their durations to add to each other. Response time thus tends to increase when a greater number of informational elements must be taken into account before the response can be given. Sternberg, along with his former hypothesis of 'memory scanning' (Sternberg, 1966), proposed for actions involving repetition of rapid sequences, like speaking or typing, that 'motor programs' are built from relatively short sequences (1 second) and that these sequences are organized into larger action units. The main argument for this hypothesis was that the time needed to execute one sequence increases linearly with the number of sequences in the program. Thus the whole utterance influences the execution of each of its elements, which suggests the whole 'program' must exist before production of the utterance begins (for example, Sternberg et al., 1988). Sternberg's hypothesis thus favours the serial and hierarchical nature of motor representations (a bias which might relate to the type of actions – rapid sequential movements – studied by his group). Other experimenters, however, came to a similar conclusion concerning hierarchical organization, by studying discrete arm movements, and using motor reaction time (RT) as an index. By manipulating the advanced information provided to the subject, and by measuring the temporal costs or benefits of these manipulations, we can infer the structure of the preparation mechanism. Rosenbaum (1980) found that cueing certain aspects of the response to be given (for example, the direction in which the target will appear) produces a greater benefit than cueing other aspects (for example, the target distance). Hence the logical conclusion that direction should be represented at a 'higher' level than distance.

In the early 1970s, paradigms drawn from cognitive psychology began to be transposed into neurophysiological experiments in trained monkeys. Tasks involving a response specified by an instruction stimulus, which required that the animal held the instruction for a certain delay before the motor response could be given, were used. Neurons which were activated by presentation of the instruction stimulus and fired until the response was initiated ('set-related' activity) were recorded in several cortical areas, including prefrontal cortex, premotor cortex and even primary motor cortex. In motor cortex, Evarts and Tanji (1974) showed that corticospinal neurons responded differently to the same perturbation applied to the monkey's hand, whether the animal had been instructed to resist to the perturbation or to move with it. Thus the response was not related to the actually performed movement, but rather to a memorized instruction to move in a certain way.

This finding that task-related changes in motor cortical cell activity can occur during a relatively long waiting period in the absence of EMG activity, was followed by many experiments where the content of the instruction given to the animal was manipulated. S. Wise and his colleagues (for example, Weinrich and Wise, 1982; Kurata and Wise, 1988) found many neurons with set-related activity in prefrontal and premotor cortex (some of these neurons have already been examined in chapter 2; see figure 2.5). They clearly distinguished cells which were activated after an attentional cue had been presented, from those which were activated after presentation of a motor instruction cue (Boussaoud and Wise, 1993a). In the former case, the cue instructed the monkey where to wait for the motor instruction cue; in the latter case, it told her in which direction to move. As the same stimulus (for example, a green square), presented at the same location, could be used either as an attentional cue or as a motor cue, the neuron discharge only reflected the set-related activity. More neurons in the dorsal premotor cortex were influenced by the motor instruction cue than in the prefrontal cortex. Conversely, more prefrontal neurons were influenced by the attentional cue. The interpretation given to these results by Boussaoud and Wise (1993b) is that the dorsal premotor cortex encodes the motor significance of stimuli and that the activity of neurons therein is likely to reflect motor preparation. It should be stressed at this point, however, that action planning is more than simply preparing a movement in terms of which arm to use or in which direction to move. As will be emphasized below, planning involves encoding the many cues that define the long-term goal of an action and selecting the motor schemas for performing its intermediate steps.

Other experiments by J. Requin and his colleagues (Lecas et al., 1986; Riehle and Requin, 1989) also give some insight into action plans. They analyzed motor reaction times and changes in neuron activity in monkey premotor cortex, as a function of the nature and the amount of information provided by the preparatory signal about a forthcoming movement. The monkey could be cued on both direction and extent of the movement to perform, or on direction or extent only (Rosenbaum, 1980). When both informations were provided, RTs were short and neurons showed an intense activity during the preparatory period; providing information on direction only produced longer RTs with less preparatory neuronal discharge; finally, providing information about extent and not about direction resulted in still longer RTs with no preparatory activity. This result stresses the parallel between neuronal activity and processing of information during motor preparation.

Another exploitation of cognitive paradigms relevant to preparing motor actions, is the series of experiments by A. Georgopoulos and his colleagues on mental rotation and memorized movements. Imagine the following situation: you are requested to move a lever in a direction different from that indicated by a visual reference. The instruction is that you move it at a given angle (randomly selected by the experimenter on each trial) from the direction shown by the reference. The time you will need to give the motor response will be a linear function of the angle between the direction of the reference and that of the requested movement. Hence the conclusion that the reaction time is spent mentally rotating the movement vector until it matches the direction of the 'mental' target. Georgopoulos and Massey (1987) who performed this experiment first in normal human subjects interpreted their findings within the Fitts' law framework (Fitts, 1954, see section 4.2.2). The duration of reaction times, which they considered as a 'mental movement time', was correlated with mental movement 'difficulty' (calculated from the amplitude of the angles) as classically found for the duration of executed movements. Hence their conclusion that because Fitts' law was respected in this condition, 'both real and imagined movements might be governed by similar amplitude-accuracy relations' (Georgopoulos and Massey, 1987, p. 361).

Further support for this interpretation was obtained by Georgopoulos et al. (1989) by transposing the same paradigm in monkeys trained to move a handle at given angles with respect to the direction of a reference light. During the animal's performance, they recorded from neurons located in primary motor cortex, coding for movements in a given direction. Georgopoulos et al. computed the population vector (by summing the individual vectors encoded by many individual neurons; Georgopoulos, 1986) in relation to movements directed at visual targets, including the condition where the monkey had to make movements in a direction different from that of the target. In the latter condition they found that the direction of the population vector changed during the reaction time of the movement. The vector progressively rotated from the direction indicated by the reference to the direction of the intended movement. This finding explains the way parameters of movement execution (in this case, direction) are coded centrally during motor preparation and provides a physiological rationale for the expression of such an universal motor rule as Fitts' law. Although only motor cortex, so far, was explored with this type of task, it is likely that the mental transformation that leads to the correct response is generated upstream with respect to motor cortex.

In another series of experiments, Georgopoulos and Lurito (1991) directly applied the memory scanning paradigm of Sternberg (1966). Subjects made a series of movements from a central position to successively presented peripheral lights. After a warning signal, one of the lights (except the last in the sequence) was presented again and subjects were instructed to move in the direction of the light which was next in the previously shown sequence. The RT duration for this movement was found to be a linear function of the number of lights, hence suggesting a mental scanning of the whole set of lights before generating the motor response. A variant of this experiment was performed in trained monkeys. Motor cortex cells were recorded and their population vectors computed. It was found that the vector abruptly shifted during the reaction time from the direction of the test-stimulus to that of the motor response (Pellizzer et al., 1995). The fact that the shift was abrupt seems to indicate that memory scanning is composed of discrete jumps, as opposed to the progressive adjustment of direction observed during mental rotation.

These experiments provide a validation of the RT paradigm for studying motor preparation. They demonstrate (perhaps unsurprisingly) that the time taken to assemble the components of motor preparation reflects underlying neuronal activities which, in turn, predict the behavioural responses and their delays. They do not provide information, however, on the real neural mechanisms at play for organizing the motor response as a function of a long-term goal. These mechanisms are located in the frontal cortex. To answer this question, the next sections will provide a review of the relevant anatomical and functional aspects of frontal cortex and will present clinical data drawn from patients with frontal lesions.

5.2 A neuropsychological approach to action planning

Planning has traditionally been assigned as one of the functions of prefrontal cortex. Planning, however, is a broad process which can be analyzed and decomposed into more elementary operations. As prefrontal cortex (the so-called granular frontal cortex) is known to be a mosaic of subareas, there is a possibility that these subdivisions could match the elementary operations that compose planning. In addition, prefrontal cortex is part of several circuits involving, not only other cortical areas such as the cingulate cortex, but also the basal ganglia. Anatomical and neurophysiological data from animal experiments, as well as clinical and neuroimaging data in man will be explored below for answering some of these questions.

5.2.1 *Anatomical connections of the frontal granular cortex*

The pattern of connections to and from the frontal granular cortex has been extensively studied. A summary of these connections will be given, with emphasis on those which are most likely to be related to motor control (figure 5.1).

At the subcortical level, afferent connections first arise from the thalamic mediodorsal nucleus. The magnocellular (medial) portion of this nucleus projects preferentially to the orbital and medial portions of prefrontal cortex, and the parvocellular (lateral) portion, to its dorsolateral part. In addition, the part of cortex in the convexity of the arcuate sulcus (area 8) receives a predominant input from an intermediate mediodorsal zone, located between the parvo and the magnocellular portions, as well as an input from the pulvinar. These thalamocortical projections relay to prefrontal cortex inputs from the mesencephalic reticular formation, the amygdala and inferotemporal cortex. It is also important to mention dense direct interconnections with the limbic system, which are not to be detailed here (see Goldman-Rakic, 1987 for review). Most of these subcortical connections are reciprocal. The basal ganglia apparently make no exception. Prefrontal neurons massively project to the caudate nucleus and putamen, where the sites of termination of the dorsolateral and orbital projections remain segregated. In turn, the striatum, via the reticular part of substantia nigra and the internal part of the pallidum, finds its way back to prefrontal neurons (Ilinsky et al., 1985; Hoover and Strick, 1993). These pathways also indirectly connect prefrontal cortex to premotor cortex and to primary motor cortex.

At the cortical level, reciprocal connections arise from nonprimary areas, mainly the posterior parietal area 7, temporal area 22 and inferotemporal area 21. Because these areas are them-

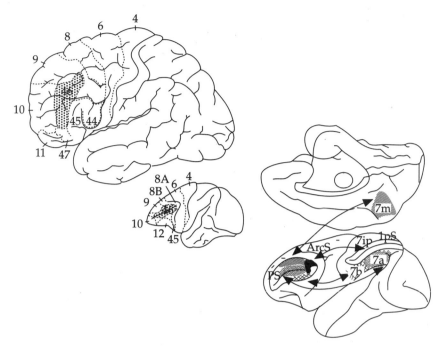

Figure 5.1　Parieto-frontal cortical connections in monkey

Upper left: layout of the corresponding areas of the convexity of the frontal lobe in man and monkey. Numbers refer to Brodmann areas.

Lower right: parieto-frontal connections in monkey. PS, Principal sulcus; ArcS, Arcuate sulcus; IpS, Intraparietal sulcus. Note unfolding of PS to show embedded area 46.
From Goldman-Rakic, 1987

selves connected with modality-specific sensory areas, the re-sulting pattern is that of a convergence on prefrontal cortex of transcortical pathways related to visual, auditory and somesthetic modalities (Jones and Powell, 1970). These 'sensory' inputs do not converge on the same cortical zones but rather tend to remain segregated: they tend to be grouped in modality specific columns interdigitated with other columns which receive transcallosal input from the controlateral prefrontal cortex (Goldman-Rakic and Schwartz, 1982). Area 21 is connected with the cortex ven-tral to the sulcus principalis, area 22 with the cortex dorsal to the sulcus and parietal areas 5 and 7 with both banks of the sulcus. The connections with area 7 are topographically organized: area 7a (a predominantly visual associative area) is connected with the fundus of the sulcus principalis, whereas area 7b (predominantly somatosensory) is connected with the ventral rim of the sulcus (Goldman-Rakic, 1987; see also Petrides and Pandya, 1984) (figure 5.1).

Prefrontal cortex is also reciprocally connected with anterior cingulate cortex (areas 24 and 32, Pandya et al., 1981). It is of particular interest that prefrontal cortex is tightly connected with motor cortical areas, specially the premotor areas. Not only are there direct reciprocal connections between the ventral part of the sulcus principalis in and around area 46 and inferior area 6 (Matelli et al., 1986), or the anterior SMA (Muakkassa and Strick, 1979); but there are also other routes by which the prefrontal cortex is only a few synapses away to and from primary motor cortex, via cingular cortex or the basal ganglia complex. Direct corticospinal projections have been found to arise from this part of mesial cortex: it is more likely, however, that they originate from SMA rather than from the anterior cingulate cortex proper (Luppino et al., 1993)

There is a striking similarity between areas surrounding the principal sulcus, particularly area 46, and the frontal eye field (area 8), which are both concerned with motor control. They both receive inputs from parietal areas 7a and 7b and they both send projections to the caudate nucleus. By contrast, however, their projections to premotor areas are different, as area 8 projects to a very limited area of premotor cortex, whereas area 46 has connections with large portions of area 6.

5.2.2   Frontal lobe lesions in monkeys

The remarkable development of frontal lobes in primates and specially in man has long been a source of speculation for physiologists. The most common claim was based on analogical reasoning: the parallel development of frontal lobe volume and intellectual abilities in man called for an implication of the frontal lobes in higher nervous activities, those which are related to

intellectual faculties. This claim, however, could hardly be transferred into an acceptable experimental paradigm. The only available experimental approach to frontal lobe function consisted
in studying the effects of ablation. Using the newly discovered
electrical stimulation as a method to delineate the excitable zone
of the precentral cortex, the first experimenters, like Ferrier,
removed the non-excitable part of the frontal lobes and observed
the effects on spontaneous behaviour of the animal. Following
large ablations of the cortex rostral to the arcuate sulcus, Ferrier
(1876) reported the lack of any motor or sensory disturbance.
He noticed that the monkeys were less interested by their sur-
roundings, they appeared to be somnolent, apathetic and unable
to sustain attention. From this observation, Ferrier conjectured
that the main frontal lobe function was maintenance of attention, a function achieved by inhibiting movement and preventing sensations from being immediately transformed into motor
acts (as it occurs in children, for example). Motor inhibition,
which developed with education, was a condition for fixating
attention and 'concentrating consciousness'. Even though Ferrier
was basically correct (it is true that frontal ablation produces
behavioural disinhibition, hyperactivity and distractedness), his
results were considered as premature: if we waited long enough,
Bianchi (1895) said, attention recovered. Bianchi was struck by
the fact that his frontal monkeys had lost their social abilities.
This was because, he thought, they were no longer able to syn-
thetize sensations arising from various sensory and motor areas
and to build coherent representations. Hence his conclusion that
the frontal lobes were the organs for fusion and coordination of
impressions necessary for triggering a goal-oriented motor
sequence. These early intuitions concerning frontal lobe functions
still remain valid.

Another important step in the description of the effects of
frontal lobe ablation (and in the parcellation of its function into
more sizeable units) was the introduction, by C. F. Jacobsen, of
quantifiable testing. The test Jacobsen used (the classical delayed
reaction task), consisted in presenting the animal with a piece
of food at one of two possible locations, hiding it for a variable

delay and testing its retrieval by the animal. Many improvements of this basic task (delayed alternation task, delayed matching to sample, etc.) were subsequently developed by Jacobsen himself or by his followers. Experimental animals were chimpanzees and monkeys (baboons), which had been operated on by J. Fulton. The most consistent finding was a failure of these animals to perform the delayed reaction task, hence the conclusion that they had lost their 'immediate memory' (Jacobsen et al., 1935). Further experiments, however, where the effects of hyperactivity and distractedness on delayed response task were better controlled, led to some hesitation about this interpretation.

There is a clear topographical specialization for delay tasks: a lesion limited to the middle part of the sulcus principalis is sufficient for producing most of the effect (Butters and Pandya, 1969). The nature of the deficit is less clear. On the one hand, it cannot be characterized as a pure memory deficit, simply because monkeys with a lesion of the sulcus area still normally can learn discriminations, for example. On the other hand, because both time and space intervene as factors in the classical delay tasks, the failure could be determined by difficulties in manipulating spatial as well as temporal information. Both the cue that the animal has to memorize and the action it has to generate to indicate its choice are coded in spatial coordinates. A predominant deficit in processing the spatial localization of the cue was emphasized by Mishkin (for example, Mishkin et al., 1969).

The deficit, in fact, would be better characterized as a difficulty in mastering the temporal aspects of a spatial discrimination task and, for this reason, would be maximal in the performance of spatial tasks with a delay. Indeed, in an experiment by Passingham (1985), monkeys with arcuate lesions (area 8) were found to be unable to learn a sequential task where they had successively to press a button, pull a handle and depress a lever. Passingham interpreted this effect as due to the fact that the three manipulanda were in different places, and that the animals could not learn their spatial arrangement. When monkeys with similar lesion (in a previous experiment, Halsband and Passingham, 1982) were tested for performing a sequence of movements with the same manipulandum, they succeeded. Disentangling the respective influence of temporal and spatial aspects of the tasks used to test deficits following frontal lesions thus would be important for understanding the precise mechanism of the memory impairment associated with these lesions. Experiments comparing animal performance in delay tasks following inactivation of prefrontal or parietal areas should be a good way towards answering this question, since parietal lesions are known to affect primarily spatial processing. The difference in the effects of the two lesions could thus be attributed to the function of prefrontal cortex. Fuster and his colleagues (for example, Quintana and Fuster, 1993) produced temporary inactivation (by cooling) of the sulcus principalis area and the intraparietal sulcus area. They used delay tasks which involved, or did not involve, spatial contingencies. During prefrontal inactivation, the monkeys failed in the two types of tasks and the number of errors increased with the delay. During parietal inactivation, by contrast, the same animals were impaired only during the task with spatial contingencies, and the duration of the delay was without influence on the pattern of response.

Lesions of the ventral part of prefrontal cortex (below the sulcus) affect the animal's ability to perform tasks based on discrimination between different stimuli, such as delayed object or colour matching tasks, or delayed object alternation tasks (Mishkin and Manning, 1978). The problem is with the discrimination of object properties, not with the delay, as demonstrated by the fact that ventrally-lesioned animals fail even at the shortest delay (Passingham, 1975). Another test where these animals fail is discrimination reversal. Once a habit has been learned (which the animal can do if the two objects are presented simultaneously, not in succession), the discrimination is reversed and the animal has to produce the response that was previously incorrect. Animals with ventral lesions tend to perseverate in the ancient behavioural set. These perseverative errors are one of the major aspects of the deficit due to ventral prefrontal lesions. It is hard to determine whether they reflect the loss of the ability to suppress or inhibit interfering tendencies (Fuster, 1989), or, more simply, the loss of ability to discriminate object properties, as suggested by Bachevalier and Mishkin (1986) for example. Both deficits, however, are likely to severely affect the ability of frontal animals to plan actions ahead in time.

A general conclusion on the effects of prefrontal lesions in monkeys could be that this region is primarily involved in tasks that require the integration of 'temporally discontiguous' elements of cognition (Fuster, 1989). Within this unitary framework, however, each part has its own specialization: the dorsolateral part is more specialized in processing the temporal contingencies of tasks involving spatial aspects, whereas the ventral part controls responses based on intrinsic objects properties. This functional duality may reflect the pattern of the afferent connections, which originate in posterior parietal cortex for the dorsal part and in inferotemporal cortex for the ventral part.

5.2.3   *Paradigms for studying neuronal activity in prefrontal areas*

The advent of the trained monkey preparation in neurophysiology has radically changed the approach to prefrontal functions. Using experimental paradigms issued from lesion studies, it has became possible to correlate neuronal activity with behavioural reponses in trained normal animals. Firmer conlusions can be drawn from the pattern of these correlations on the role of prefrontal cortex in organizing and planning actions.

Most of the unit studies of prefrontal cortex have used motor tasks involving delays. Neuronal firing rate has been correlated with the various events that compose the sequence, namely, presentation of the cue; delay between presentation of the cue and presentation of the test; motor response reflecting the choice of the animal. Units were found which responded specifically to a given type of cue, or to a given aspect of the response. The most interesting ones, however, are those which change their firing rate during the delay, that is, in the absence of the stimulus itself, and prior to the response. These neurons are more likely to encode contingencies of the planned action (for example, to perform the action or not according to the type or to the localization of the cue; to select the type of motor response to be prepared; to determine the order of the response in a sequence, etc.), than simple stimulus or response characteristics, as 'sensory' or 'motor' neurons would do.

Fuster (1973), in an experiment using the classical delayed response task, found prefrontal neurons firing during the delay period. These neurons were concentrated on both banks of the sulcus principalis and at the bottom of the cingulate sulcus. Most of them presented a sustained activation throughout the delay (up to 25 seconds) between presentation and test, and were uninfluenced by the fact that the animal had to give the correct response either with the left or the right arm. When distracting stimuli were presented during the delay, which eventually led the animal to produce an incorrect response, the sustained neuronal discharge often decreased during the presentation of the distractor. Fuster (1973) also tested a group of neurons from the posterior parietal region (area 5) in the same conditions: no such increase of firing during the delay was observed. Instead, the discharge of these neurons was strictly related to the motor response and was contingent on the side of the arm used to produce the response. Fuster's conclusion was that sustained activation of prefrontal neurons during the delay period is important for establishing a temporal bridge between the cue and the response and rehearsing this information for prospective use. Niki and Watanabe (1979), also using a simple delay task found that, among the neurons related in one way or another to the task, about 45 per cent in the dorsal prefrontal cortex and 43 per cent in the anterior part of the cingulate gyrus had a sustained firing during the delay. Such neurons seem to be equally affected by the fact that the monkey has to give a motor response to the cue (the 'go' condition) or to inhibit the motor response (the 'no go' condition) (Watanabe, 1986).

More refined delay tasks were used after the lesion data had challenged pure attentional or mnemonic explanations of prefrontal functions. Funahashi et al. (1989) designed a delay task where the cue was spatial location and where the response was an eye movement, the direction of which, when the response was correct, corresponded to the localization of the cue. In this task, the cue was a visual target presented at one of eight different possible locations. During presentation of the cue (for 0.5 sec), the animal fixated a central fixation point, and kept fixation during the delay period (up to 6 sec). When the central fixation point was turned off, the animal had to produce a saccade at the point in space where the cue had been previously presented. Animals learned this task quite well and reproduced the cue position with reasonable accuracy (though accuracy tended to decrease with increasing delays). A large proportion of neurons from the principal sulcus area were found to be related to the task and showed a significant sustained excitation or inhibition during the delay period. A highly relevant finding was that in most cases, the delay period activity was directional, that is the neuron fired in anticipation to the response for a preferred direction, while presentation of the cue in other directions was without effect on firing rate (figure 5.2; Funahashi et al., 1989; see also Funahashi et al., 1990, 1991). Similar characteristics were found for a smaller sample of neurons located in the arcuate area.

These neurons, which fire in the absence of an overt stimulus and in anticipation to a movement (response ceases as soon as movement starts), fulfill the typical criteria for the representation of an action plan, as will be stressed in chapter 6. Indeed, during error trials (those which ended with a saccade in an erroneous direction), the delay period activity was unchanged with respect to background activity. The discharge of each of these neurons seems to represent an elementary 'spatial memory', and the whole set of neurons seems to represent a memory map of visual space, by which movements can be guided in the direction of the relevant cues. The anatomical connections of the recorded area with the parietal cortex may be responsible for determining the direction of the response, so that a cue in a given spatial location activates the neurons with the corresponding memory fields. It is also possible that posterior parietal neurons themselves have memory fields. Some parietal neurons are known to present typical set-related activity in delay experiments. In addition, prefrontal cortex and inferior parietal cortex are coacti-vated in working memory tasks, as revealed by a deoxyglucose functional mapping study (Goldman-Rakic et al., 1993).

Prefrontal neurons (and, possibly also parietal neurons) are thus reflective of central mnemonic processes that guide the correct choice at the end of the delay: they provide a mnemonic code (their 'memory field', Goldman-Rakic, 1987; Funahashi et al., 1989) for directing the action. The notion of domain-specific working memories which could play the role of action plans has been further elaborated in experiments combining the spatial and the temporal aspects of the cue. Barone and Joseph (1989) trained monkeys to watch a panel where three lamps were dis-played. For each given trial, while the monkey was fixating a central fixation point, the lamps were briefly turned on in a given sequence (for example, 132, 231, etc.; figure 5.3). After all the lamps were turned off, and after waiting for a variable delay, the monkey had to replicate the sequence by fixating the lamps by eye and pressing them by hand in the correct order. Neurons related to this task were recorded in the superior arcuate area and in the caudal part of the sulcus principalis. A first cat-egory of cells were influenced by the visual aspect of the task. As a rule, these cells were spatially selective, that is, they dis-charged while the monkey fixated the central fixation point after one of the three lamps had been presented. Some of them (the 'visual-tonic' cells) were in addition temporally selective, as their activation depended on the sequential order of illumination of the specific target. Activation was present only if the specific target appeared, say, first in the sequence, not if it was second or third. Visual-tonic cells kept discharging until the eye posi-tion was shifted toward that target. The tonic discharge thus encoded a spatially and temporally defined visual goal for an action. This striking property is displayed in figure 5.3.

Other cells ('context' cells) were activated in relation to the execution of the task. They discharged later in the sequence, dur-ing fixation of one of the targets, but depending on which other targets had been, or were going to be, pressed. This sustained discharge thus also presented spatial and temporal selectivity.

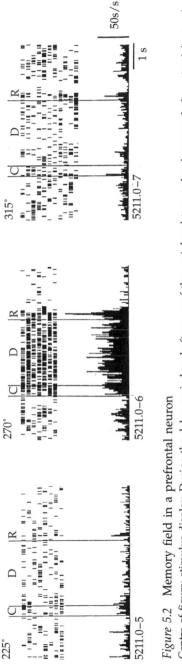

Figure 5.2 Memory field in a prefrontal neuron

Centre of figure: stimulus display. During the delay period and after one of the peripheral targets has been cued, the animal fixates the central point FP. The rasters and histograms of discharge of one single neuron are shown at locations corresponding to each target. Note preferential discharge during the delay period, only for target located at 270°. On each histogram, C, presentation of cue; D, delay period; R, onset of oculomotor response.
From Funahashi et al., 1989

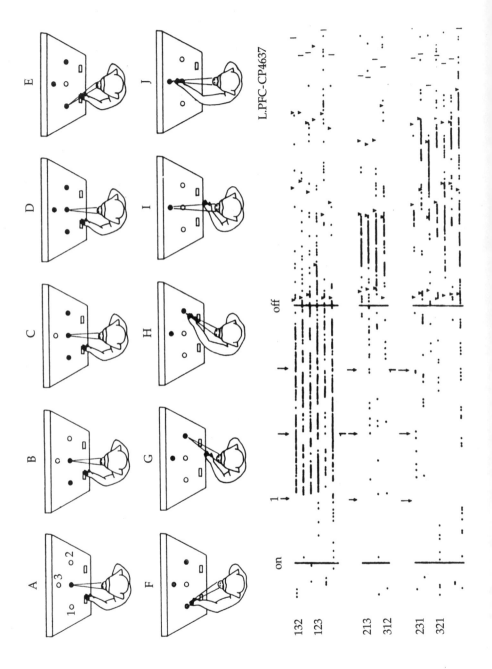

L.PFC-CP4637

Barone and Joseph considered that the context cells were down-stream with respect to the visual-tonic cells: they would receive from visual-tonic cells information about the location and the rank of the targets, and determine the sequence of the corre-sponding movements. This mechanism would ensure that a movement is terminated before the next one is started, even in the absence of cue indicating the state of execution. Indeed, Barone and Joseph report that the animals were able to perform the task even if the three targets remained illuminated during the whole sequence of movements, that is, exclusively on the basis of the memorized information.

Whereas neurons in the immediate vicinity of the sulcus prin-cipalis, which are likely to be connected with parietal areas, are good candidates for spatial working memory, neurons in the ven-tral areas, connected to the inferotemporal cortex, are candidates for processing object related informations (intrinsic object prop-erties). Rosenkilde et al. (1981) showed that change in activity of ventral neurons during the delay was predominantly related to the visual cue. Wilson et al. (1993) used both a spatial delayed response (as in the Funahashi et al. experiment shown in figure 5.2) and a pattern delayed response. In the latter case, the mon-key had to direct her eyes right or left according to the pattern that was presented as a cue: in other words, she had to memo-rize the pattern cue. A large proportion of ventral neurons were found to present a delay period activity in the pattern delayed

---

Figure 5.3   Temporally selective prefrontal neuron

Upper part: experimental protocol. While the animal fixates the central fixation light and presses the key with her left hand, stimuli appear in a definite order (panels A–D). After the central light is turned off, the animal replicates the sequence with both eye and arm movements (panels E–J).

Lower part: neuron discharge during experimental trials where targets were illuminated in different sequences (for example, 132, 123, etc.). Neuronal discharge is synchronized with onset of target 1 which occurred first (upper rows), second (middle rows) or third in the sequence (lower rows). Note preferential discharge when target 1 is presented first. Large vertical bars refer to onset and offset of central fixation light at the end of the delay period. Small black triangles indicate monkey's movements to the targets; small vertical bars indicate the time of reward at the end of the sequence.

From Barone and Joseph, 1989

response, not in the spatial delayed response. These neurons might be the basis for stimulus-selective actions, and might represent still another type of specialized (domain-specific) working memory, to be used when performance of a given task is conditional to the presence of a particular object (a face, for example). Together with the results of lesion experiments, these single unit data can be interpreted within the general framework of the two cortco-cortical pathways described in chapter 2. Indeed, the dorsal part of the principal sulcus area, which receives predominant posterior parietal projections, would represent the termination of the dorsal pathway for processing spatial relationships. The ventral zone, connected with the inferotemporal cortex, by contrast, would be the termination of the ventral pathway for processing object identity (see Ungerleider and Mishkin, 1982).

The unifying concept for prefrontal cortex function, therefore, is that of 'specialized working memories' (Goldman-Rakic, 1987). Depending on the connections and inputs of each individual neuron, the sustained discharge encodes, not only the spatial characteristics of the target, but also its semantic value and the emotional context of the task. These parameters are retained by the specific neurons until the corresponding action had been executed. Execution, in turn, provides these neurons with signals for 'zeroing' the memory and returning their discharge to the resting level. The mechanism of sustained discharge is thus a key mechanism for action planning. This point will be further elaborated in chapter 6.

5.2.4   *Planning deficits following frontal lesion in man*

The observers of deficits following frontal lesions in humans have insisted on the deleterious effects of these lesions on several aspects of action planning and decision making. Under this respect, the famous case of Ph. Gage provides a prototypical example of the human frontal syndrome which results in abnormal social conduct with its negative personal consequences (for a recent assessment of the extent of Gage's lesion, see Damasio et al., 1994). Clinically, distractedness, hyperactivity or, alternatively, loss of initiative and apathy are the most frequently observed symptoms of such lesions.

Exaggerated dependence with respect to external events, which can account for hyperactivity and distractedness, has been documented by Lhermitte (1983) under the name of 'utilization behavior'. Frontal patients, when shown usual objects, tend to use these objects in a compulsive way: given a pack of cigarettes and a lighter, they smoke; given a glass and a bottle of water, they drink, etc. This behaviour fits the concepts of 'lack of inhibition' and of 'release of automatic behaviour' which have been used in the past to characterize frontal behaviour. Denny-Brown and Chambers (1958), for example, considered that normal behaviour resulted from the combination of two opposite tendencies, a positive and a negative tropism to the environment. The parietal cortex was the site for initiating actions whereas frontal cortex was the site of action inhibition. Lhermitte's interpretation of utilization behaviour was that frontal damage suppressed modulating and inhibiting influences normally exerted by the frontal lobes on parietal cortex, with the result that the activity of the parietal cortex created dependence of the subject with respect to external stimuli. This explanation would account for the striking Lhermitte's observation that the patients performed these actions without any apparent 'internal motivation': they drank several glasses of water in a row, they kept eating after lunch, etc. Utilization behaviour is highly relevant to the role of frontal lobes in organizing action by demonstrating its role in inhibiting incorrect actions.

The lack of planning and anticipation of the consequences of action is demonstrated by the social behaviour of frontal patients. This was the case of patient EVR described by Eslinger and Damasio (1985). Damasio et al. (1990) conjectured that the patient, in spite of being able to recognize the *manifest* meaning of situations, failed to represent to himself the *implied* meaning of these situations (their future implications). In addition, they thought, the patient would be 'unable to mark those implications with a signal that would automatically distinguish advantageous from pernicious actions . . .' (1990, p. 82). The authors proposed that the signal marking the correct actions could be an emotional (positive or negative) label acquired from previous success or failure. Since implied meaning is based on activation of many component records for defining the possible consequences of a given situation, and requires that the activated records can be held across long delays, its access is likely to be deficient after a massive frontal lesion. In addition, failure to reactivate the emotional signal would deprive the subject from cues about the good decision to make. In order to validate this theory, Damasio et al. (1990) tested autonomic responses to socially meaningful stimuli in patient EVR (as well as in other frontal patients): they all showed highly defective responses. This theory, although it refers heavily and rather uncritically to behaviourist psychology, has the merit of introducing emotional and motivational processing within the mechanisms of action planning and anticipation of the consequences of actions.

Modern research has operationalized these broad deficits in terms of testable performance. Simple motor tests similar to those used in monkeys were applied to humans with prefrontal lesions. Guitton et al. (1985) used an 'anti-saccade' test where the subject was instructed to look opposite to a visual cue. If, for example, the cue briefly appeared right of the fixation point, the task of the subject consisted, after a variable delay, to look at an equal distance to the left where another target appeared for a brief period of time. The task therefore involved:

1   memorizing the instruction.
2   memorizing the position of the cue (right or left).
3   preparing a saccade to the opposite side.
4   performing the saccade immediately at the end of the delay, that is, fast enough to report the visual content of the target.

Frontal subjects were consistently unable to suppress unwanted (reflex-like) saccades in the direction of the cue and to generate the appropriate movement in the direction of a forthcoming target. There are at least two interpretations to this effect of frontal lesion. One is that prefrontal areas (in this case, the frontal eye fields, area 8) exert an inhibitory control on subcortical structures, such as the superior colliculus, in order to prevent the oculomotor system to react undifferentially to any target appearing in the visual field. The cortical lesion would thus release a 'primitive' reflex tendency (the visual grasp reflex, see Hess et al., 1946), normally prevented by a 'cancellation signal' for the unwanted saccade. A second possible explanation is that the specialized working memory for directing the saccade in the proper direction was destroyed by the lesion. It remains that Guitton et al.'s observations clearly illustrate the typical symptoms of distractedness and excessive reactivity of frontal patients to external stimuli.

Inhibition, however, is not the only way by which behaviour is organized. Inhibition would only allow to decide not to execute an action depending on a stimulus or triggered by a situation, it would not allow independent initiation of a new action. Prefrontal areas are also essential for positively organizing behaviour and planning new actions. Other 'frontal' tests similar to those used in monkeys were designed, such as delayed response tasks, delayed alternation and non-alternation tasks (Dubois et al., 1994), as well as tests involving elaboration of response criteria, storage of these criteria over trials and adaptation to changing criteria between blocks of trials (the Wisconsin card sorting test, see Milner, 1964). Frontal patients fail in these tests, due to their tendency to use previously acquired behavioural sets and to rely on more 'primitive' or automatic patterns of behaviour.

Planning abilities were also tested using tasks that required orderly successive steps to find the solution of a problem (the 'Tower of London', Shallice, 1982; see Owen et al., 1990). According to Shallice and Burgess (1991), however, many of the tests used in neuropsychology are unable to reveal the core of the frontal deficit, because they tackle isolated aspects of performance, they do not involve manipulable delays and they imply unambiguous answers. For these reasons, Shallice and Burgess designed tests with open-ended multiple subgoal situations, where frontal patients would theoretically have problems. These tests involved performing a series of subgoals within a fixed amount of time and using a prescribed set of rules. Subgoals were open-ended tasks (carrying arithmetic problems, dictating a route on a tape-recorder, writing names of pictures or collecting information which required going out in the street, reading the newspaper, etc.), the grouping of which required the application of a global strategy. Frontal patients produced many errors in these tasks, by performing inefficiently, breaking rules, etc. These errors can be described and predicted using a specific model of action planning (see section 5.5 of this chapter for details).

5.3   Study of human brain activity during motor preparation and action planning

Complementary information concerning neural mechanisms involved in action planning can be obtained in normal subjects by using brain-imaging techniques. Unfortunately, the tasks used so far by most of the authors of these studies are not always adequate for an approach of action plans.

The pattern of brain activity was compared during 'voluntary' movements (usually self-paced repetitive movements) and externally-triggered movements. Roland et al. (1980; see also Roland and Friberg, 1985) have shown that performing repetitively a finger movement sequence activates not only M1, but also the SMA (on both sides) and, to a lesser extent, the superior prefrontal area. Deiber et al. (1991) examined rCBF in several conditions: repeating a learned sequence; making movements randomly in any desired direction; moving in the direction specified by the intensity of a tone; moving in the direction opposite to that specified by the intensity of a tone. The random condition was the most effective in activating bilaterally prefrontal areas (9, 10, 46), as well as the cingular cortex, the premotor area 6 and the SMA. Posterior parietal cortex was activated in nearly all conditions. Performing the learned sequence also affected (although to a lesser extent) the premotor cortex but not the SMA. The latter finding, which is somewhat in contradiction with earlier studies, can be explained by the fact that Deiber et al.'s subjects had been trained prior to the experimental session. It could have been that SMA activation decreased when the performed movement becomes more automatic. Seitz and Roland (1992) showed that the activation of SMA in sequential motor tasks is maximal at the beginning of the learning phase and decreases throughout acquisition (see also Jenkins et al., 1994). The involvement of SMA in higher motor control will be discussed further below.

Activation of prefrontal cortex has been claimed to be specific of willed action. Frith et al. (1991) used a task where the subject, upon a tactile signal, chose to lift either one of two fingers. Control conditions were: lifting the finger that has been touched, or lifting the finger that has not been touched. Bilateral activation of area 46 was found, only in the choice condition (figure 5.4). Activation of area 46 in this condition thus clearly relates to internal response generation, a point recently confirmed by Jahanshahi et al. (1995). A similar involvement of dorsolateral frontal cortex, however, was also observed, both by Frith et al. and by others (Petersen et al., 1988; Wise et al., 1991), during word generation tasks. Although this observation is consistent with the general function of prefrontal cortex in willed action, it raises the question of a more specific role of this area in semantic processing. To test this possibility, Kapur et al. (1994) instructed subjects to produce manual responses (pressing buttons) upon seing words on a screen, in three different tasks. In the 'lexical' task, they had to respond if the word contained, or not, the letter 'a'. In the 'semantic' task, if the word concerned a living or a nonliving thing. In the 'baseline' task, the word was replaced by an arrow, and the response had to be given according to the direction in which the arrowhead pointed. They found that the left dorsolateral prefrontal cortex was specifically activated by the semantic task, not by the other two. Hence their conclusion that activity of this area does not reflect willed action, but rather 'working with meaning' of a stimulus to reach a goal in an instructional context. This interesting observation raises the

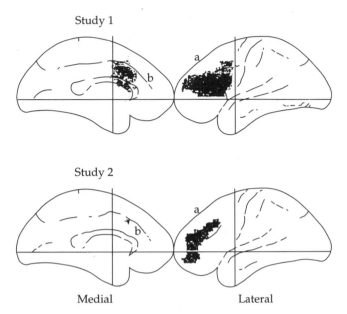

Figure 5.4   Increased prefrontal activity in two studies involving willed responses

Study 1: word generation task. Subjects had to respond to a signal by producing any word beginning with an S or with an F.

Study 2: sensorimotor task. Subjects had to respond to a signal by raising a finger of his right hand.

In both tasks, note increased blood flow (using a PET technique) in prefrontal areas in the left hemisphere.

From Frith et al., 1991

question of a possible functional asymmetry of prefrontal cortex in man. It could well be the case that the left area would be specialized for generating responses in relation to semantic cues, whereas the two sides would equally contribute to the more general function of internal response generation in all sorts of situations. This would explain the bilateral involvement of prefrontal cortex in the Frith et al.'s motor task and in motor imagery tasks (Fox et al., 1987, Decety et al., 1994) as it was reported in chapter 4.

In addition, what was true for SMA is also true for prefrontal cortex. Its involvement (on the left side for verbal tasks, on both sides for motor tasks) seems to be specific of effortful, nonautomatic response selection and/or inhibition. Prefrontal activation during a verb generation task disappears in trained subjects (Raichle et al., 1994). This finding is consistent with the general idea that this area of cortex is concerned with internalized knowledge necessary to guide behaviour in the absence of external cues. By contrast, automatic response selection would not require prefrontal activity and would rather involve other neural pathways, such as the basal ganglia (see section 5.4).

Another cortical area, the anterior cingulate cortex, is also consistently found to be activated during complex motor tasks (for example, Frith et al., 1991). Paus et al. (1993) compared cingulate cortex activation during tasks involving a motor response to a cue: in one version of the task, the response to the cue was overpractised. In another version, the response had to be reversed, hence requiring a new cue-response combination. The same tasks were repeated with three types of motor responses (manual, oculomotor, speech). A typical overpractised task was responding 'them', 'her' and 'him' to hearing the words 'take', 'join', 'find', respectively; in the reversal task, new combinations were assigned. Paus et al. found activation in an area in the dorsal bank of the cingular sulcus (corresponding to the dorsal part of area 24 and part of area 32) at the transition between frontal cortex (areas 6 and 8) and limbic cortex. Close but distinct activation foci were found for the three tasks. The 'manual' focus was the most dorsal and caudal one. In addition, in the manual and speech tasks, activation foci were also found in the lateral prefrontal cortex. The cingulate cortex activation occurred mostly when the subject was forced to choose from a set of competing responses (reversal task), rather than to rely on well established associations (overpractised task). Paus et al.'s interpretation of these results is that information on motor plans processed in the dorsal prefrontal areas is sent to cingulate cortex, where it can be modulated by other incoming inputs (for example, from dopaminergic systems) before being transferred to motor cortex. This interpretation is consistent with Posner et al.'s (1988) suggestion that the anterior cingulate area is part of an attention system that selects information for action.

The activation of areas 24 and 32 in complex motor tasks may be difficult to disentangle from activation of close-by areas, also related to movement, such as SMA. A recent PET study by Matelli et al. (1993) clearly demonstrated the inhomogeneity of human frontal mesial cortex. In their study, aimless proximal and distal arm movements activated an area caudal to the vertical line through the anterior commissure (VCA). This area (which, according to Matelli et al., represents the 'SMA proper'), differs from the cortical zone located immediately anterior to it, which they found to be unaffected by the simple movements, and which is more likely to pertain to a 'cognitive' area with a function similar to that of area 32. The finding of a bilateral SMA activation during 'internally generated' repetitive movements, as was reported in several studies using different brain-mapping techniques (for example, Orgogozo et al., 1979; Roland et al., 1980), probably involves both SMA proper and the more anterior zone.

This heterogeneity of mesial cortex explains the effects of mesial cortex lesions in humans, which include SMA but also often encroach on the neighbouring cingulate cortex. These lesions are known to produce severe reduction of spontaneous motor activity, including speech (Laplane et al., 1977). Extensive midline lesions involving the anterior cingulate cortex on both sides produce akinetic mutism. These explanations, however, leave open the question of the participation of SMA 'proper' in motor planning. Halsband et al. (1993) reported that two patients with lesions limited to the left SMA had difficulties in reproducing rhythmic movements from memory, although they were able to produce the same sequences under auditory pacing. This observation fits recent experiments in monkey which clearly demonstrate the existence within SMA of cells with typical memory fields (Tanji and Shima, 1994), which suggests that this area should also play a role in higher levels of motor control, specially in the generation of sequences that fit into a precise motor plan.

5.4 The role of basal ganglia in action planning

The participation of the basal ganglia in the processes underlying action planning is demonstrated by a large amount of data.
Comparison of neuronal activities in prefrontal cortex and in
the caudate nucleus, however, indicates that the two structures
basically encode the same events, but in different ways. Prefrontal
cortex builds the motor representation for each new action
according to the prescribed rules, to the available cues and to
the goal to be achieved, whereas caudate neurons encode a copy
of the plan and use it to determine when to start and when to
stop a given step of the action.

Neurons from the basal ganglia complex, which are massively
connected with the prefrontal cortex, have properties which indeed resemble those of prefrontal neurons. Hikosaka and Wurtz
(1983) found in the reticular part of substantia nigra many
neurons which altered their discharge in delay tasks, such as performing an ocular saccade to a previously cued target (memory-
contingent responses, see also Hikosaka and Wurtz, 1989). More
recently, Kermadi and Joseph (1995), using the same task as
Barone and Joseph (1989, see above), also found anticipatory
discharges related to various aspects of the task. A category of
neurons anticipated the sensory cues that signalled the unfolding of the task, such as the offset of the central fixation point, or
the onset of the first target, etc. Other neurons fired in advance
with respect to the movements performed by the animal. For
example, a neuron fired when the animal made a saccade toward
a given target, but its activity was sequence-specific: it was
contingent upon the rank of the target in the sequence. Both
Hikosaka and Wurtz and Kermadi and Joseph reported that the
duration of these anticipatory discharges was shorter than those
recorded in the same conditions in the prefrontal cortex. These
characteristics are suggestive of a role of caudate neurons in
signalling the next step to be performed in a given action (for
example, Marsden, 1987), and also signalling that the previous
step has been terminated. By contrast, caudate neurons would

not be suited, neither for assembling the spatial plan, nor for holding it for a sufficiently long time to guide the action to its goal. These operations are more likely to be under the control of the prefrontal cortex.

Data from human PET experiments are consistent with this view. Basal ganglia appear to be clearly involved during action planning (Decety et al., 1990) or during motor imagery (Decety et al., 1994). The differential involvement of frontal cortex and basal ganglia in motor representations is demonstrated by an experiment by Seitz and Roland (1992). They mapped the brain activity of normal subjects at different stages of learning a sequential hand movement. They showed that while cortical activity tended to disappear as learning progressed, the reverse was observed in the basal ganglia (putamen and globus pallidus) on the side opposite to the trained hand. This finding suggests that, whereas frontal cortex is critically involved in establishing the motor routines, the basal ganglia have the function of handling these routines for carrying out the action.

Deficits in action planning can also be observed following lesions or functional impairments of the basal ganglia. It is thus interesting to compare the pattern of errors produced by patients with basal ganglia lesions and by frontal patients. Harrington and Haaland (1991) have tested Parkinsonian patients during the execution of sequences of hand postures. A pictorial display of the sequence was presented on a screen and the patient had to reproduce it at an imperative stimulus which occurred after a variable delay. Sequences were 'repetitive' (repeating the same movement several times) or 'heterogenous' (making several different movements in a row). Parkinsonian patients were more impaired in complex sequences (long and heterogenous) than in simple ones, including when they performed the first movement of the sequence. This suggests that they were unable to use the program displayed on the screen as a whole: rather, they progressed step by step and had difficulties switching from one movement to the next. The deficits of this type of patients in performing a predictive saccade task (Ventre et al., 1992) can also be attributed to their poor ability to use advance information about forthcoming movements (for a similar result in monkeys following dopamine depletion of the caudate nucleus, see Kori et al., 1995). A similar explanation accounts for the results obtained by Dominey et al. (1995), already reported in chapter 4. Using a mental motor imagery paradigm, they showed that Parkinsonian patients were impaired, not only in producing a sequence of repetitive finger movements, but also in simulating the same sequence mentally. The patients' difficulty was thus to internally shift from one movement to the next, not to execute these movements. This deficit is illustrated by the experiment of Cooper et al. (1994), who showed that impairment in response speed increased with choice complexity, even if the motor response remained constant in all cases. Consistent with the above findings is the fact that some of the areas normally activated during volitional tasks (such as putamen, SMA and cingulate cortex), fail to be activated in Parkinsonian patients when they are off treatment (Playford et al., 1992). The impaired SMA activation can be reversed in these patients when their akinesia is treated with apomorphine (Jenkins et al., 1992).

Patients with Parkinson's disease also show increased performance times for frontal tests, such as the Tower of London. Unlike frontal patients, however, they are not impaired in planning the steps of the action of reconstructing the tower: instead, they are globally slower in initiating solutions, correct or not (Owen et al., 1992; note that the cognitive deficit observed here could not be explained by motor factors, as the version of the test used in this study excluded movements). Similarly, whereas both frontal and Parkinsonian patients fail in a version of the Wisconsin card sorting test requiring a shift in response mode (for example, responding to a previously irrelevant dimension), the reason of the failure is different in the two cases: frontal patients cannot respond to a novel dimension because they perseverate in the previous response mode; Parkinsonian patients are unable to refocus attention on a previously irrelevant dimension (see Robbins et al., 1994).

5.5   A synthetic conclusion on action planning

Action planning is one of the highest levels of the motor representation. It can be activated, either directly (for example, by external cues) in the case of automatized actions, or by endogenous processes which will determine the generation of a more 'voluntary' type of action. The neural elements which function during action planning are likely to be distributed over a large network of neural structures, both cortical and subcortical (see Requin, 1992).

A synthetic approach of the planning mechanisms themselves first requires to build a model which would be compatible with the experimental data. In addition, this model should take into account the ideas which have revealed useful in describing motor representations. One of those is that planning operates by selecting and activating a number of stored elements of action (or schemas), and by organizing their modality and time of expression. T. Shallice (see Norman and Shallice, 1980; see also Shallice, 1982, 1988; Shallice and Burgess, 1991) has proposed such a mechanism (which he called 'contention scheduling'), based on interactions between the activated schemas, such that the level of activation of the cooperative schemas is reinforced and that of competing ones is decreased. The notion of schema used here is broader than that of motor schemas already described in previous sections. It includes, not only the motor schemas themselves, but also less elementary representational units, which Shallice calls 'source-schemas': those are structures which control complex actions, not simple movements. Using an everyday life example, a schema like 'prepare breakfast' would be a typical source-schema. It would itself be composed of smaller component schemas (for example, 'make coffee') and so on until the level of the motor schemas would be reached. (figure 5.5).

Although routine actions can be controlled directly by the contention scheduling mechanism, newly performed actions require an additional instance for establishing a new schedule. Schemas have to be reassembled and new activation values carrying the

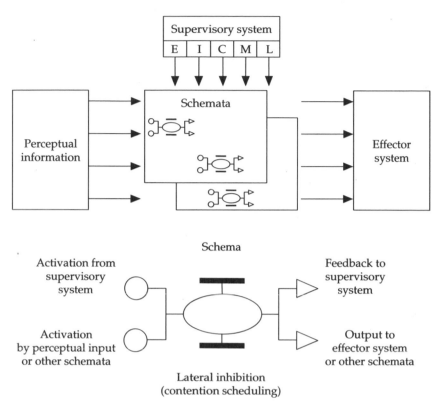

Figure 5.5   A model for planning mechanisms
Upper part: schemas needed for transferring information between perceptual and effector
systems are selected under the influence of the supervisory system.
Lower part: detail of one schema with its input and output connections. The contention
scheduling system is reponsible for the coordination between schemas.
From Stuss et al., 1995

intention have to be introduced. Shallice's assumption is that
these values are based on redirection of attention, hence the
term of 'supervisory attentional system' for this additional control mechanism. A similar view is held by Duncan (1986), who
postulates the existence of a 'goal-based search process' for scanning the store of schemas and selecting the action structure which
will best satisfy the goal. Following Shallice, planning of the
action by the supervisory system does not necessarily require a
complete representation of its whole course: part of the process

may be carried out on-line by the contention scheduling system, as opportunities and difficulties arise during execution. The intention would operate through the activation of 'markers' which could be triggered at a later time to modulate the on-going behaviour. 'A marker is basically a message that some future behavior or event should not be treated as routine and instead, some particular aspect of the situation should be viewed as specially relevant for action' (Shallice and Burgess, 1991, p. 737). The role of the marker, once triggered, would thus be to inhibit the ongoing behaviour and to switch in or out the particular course of action linked to the marker. Goal selection, marker creation and triggering would make possible on-line evaluation and modification of the action plan.

It is tempting to transfer these theoretical notions into neuro-physiological terms. The fact that patients with prefrontal lesions are impaired in decision making, anticipation of action conse-quences, adaptation to changing rules, resistance to distracting stimuli, strongly suggests that the frontal lobes play a major 'executive' role in generating intentions and supervising action (Luria, 1966; Shallice, 1988; Frith, 1992). In Duncan's (1986) terms, we should expect that, if an action is under the control of a goal list, it should continue until the goal is satisfied; and that a failure of this process should trigger the search for another, more appropriate, action structure. This is exactly what frontal patients cannot do: their performance may be interrupted although the goal remains unsatisfied, or, conversely, may continue in spite of violation of goal satisfaction. This deficit is illustrated by frontal patients impairment in reconstructing verbally or pictorially the sequence of movements needed to achieve an action. Grafman has used the term of 'scripts' to designate neu-rally represented mental entities that have to be assembled to organize an action sequence (Grafman, 1989). Frontal patients would be impaired in managing the syntax of scripts, that is, in ordering the actions that compose a given script according to the context or to priority rules (see Sirigu et al., 1995c). This inability to consciously access the content of representations of action is also typical in certain types of apraxia (Lehmkuhl and

Poeck, 1981). By contrast, these same patients may be able to automatically perform relatively complex well-learned routines or stimulus-driven actions, those which are controlled by the contention scheduling mechanism. They may even remain 'stuck' in the well-learned set and perseverate into it, or they may compulsively imitate actions performed in front of them. This ability to carry on 'preplanned' actions might correspond, in the frontal patients, to the residual function of the basal ganglia and would be consistent with the role of these structures in timing and checking the sequence of actions. This hypothesis is consistent with the notion that the basal ganglia may contribute to the process of habit formation.

Identifying the supervisory system with the frontal lobes, however, requires some revision of the initial theory, which considered this system in terms of a unitary process. The above experimental data in monkeys suggest that frontal lobes should be fractionated in several modules for domain specific working memories (Goldman-Rakic, 1995). In a recent paper, Stuss and his colleagues together with Shallice suggested that the frontal syndrome should be divided into several clinical entities, corresponding to an equal number of functional systems within the frontal lobes (Stuss et al., 1995; see also Shallice and Burgess, 1991).

chapter six

Design for a Motor Representation

This concluding chapter will emphasize some general principles for the design of the motor representation, which should apply to all the levels which have been described in the previous chapters. The main problem to be discussed is the way motor representations (whether they are considered at the level of elementary schemas or at the level of larger ensembles) are implemented neurally. This point is critical for understanding how a representation is built, how it is activated or disactivated, and ultimately, how it can have a causal effect on behaviour.

6.1   Requirements for representation neurons

The basic postulate will be that representations are built on sustained neuronal discharge arising in structures relevant to the various stages of the preparation of motor acts. The neural layout of the representation can be figured out as a network where the goal information (the information about the action to be performed) appears as an array of enhanced activity (see Jeannerod, 1990). This activated state will persist until completion of the action. For each individual unit of the network, however, the duration of the sustained activation will be determined by the hierarchical position of that unit in the network. A unit located upstream in the sequence of events that lead to the final goal will remain activated as long as the full action has not been completed. By contrast, a more local unit will remain activated only for a short time, that is, the time to complete the intermediate step of the action encoded by that unit. In other words, the last unit to return to its resting state will be that with the highest hierarchical position. This description implies that return to rest does not occur until a signal is given that the goal encoded by each unit has been attained. The nature of this 'completion' signal will be discussed in the section 6.2, where the internal architecture of the network will be detailed.

In order to be considered for the substrate of a representation these neuronal activities will have to fulfill a number of criteria:

1 They must be related to the preparation of an action, but not necessarily to its execution.
2 They must present a sustained discharge for as long as the action is not completed.
3 They must not be influenced by the presence or absence of an actual target.

In other words, the neuronal discharge corresponding to a motor representation in the sense used here should encode an internal goal, not a target and should relate to an intention, not to a movement. Modern cognitive neuroscience is now used to deal with such 'private' events, where task-related neural activity in specific brain areas can be monitored and studied in the absence of overt behavioural changes. These criteria can thus be used to select, among the neuronal populations which have been described in relation to action in the previous chapters, those which fulfill the definition of 'representation' neurons.

The term of representation as it has been considered in this book is rather broad: it can apply to global aspects of an action (or even to an action in its entirety), as well as to more local aspects of that action. The concept of schema has been used throughout as a way to connect these different levels of description. According to this definition, a given neuronal population fulfilling the above criteria can 'represent' the complete action (for example, press targets 1, 2 and 3 in a given order to get a reward), whereas other populations can 'represent' more limited aspects (for example, move the right arm to target 1, or move the eyes to target 2, etc.). Neurons from the monkey prefrontal and cingulate cortices, for example, have properties which are relevant to relatively global aspects of the organization of an action. Such neurons may fire during the delay between presentation of a cue and selection of a given target, but only if that target appears, say, second in the sequence, as if they 'knew' the order in which the movements have to be performed (the so-called 'context neurons', see Barone and Joseph, 1989). Other neurons, by contrast, encode more elementary aspects of the action, and are little or not influenced by what happened before, or what is going to happen next. They may code a single movement, like reach or grasp, whatever the context in which this movement appears: the 'motor dominant' neurons of Taira et al. (1990), for example, are good candidates for these 'motor schema' neurons. The cortical areas where they are located (for example, the inferior parietal lobule, the premotor cortex) are reciprocally connected with the prefrontal areas. It is thus tempting to speculate that the action plan generated or selected by the prefrontal cortex can 'gate' the elements required for implementing that action.

The coexistence of neurons coding for global and for local aspects of an action raises the problem of the temporal order in which they are activated. Although we would *a priori* think of a serial 'downward' activation (from global to local), several arguments suggest that activation is more likely to be simultaneous than serial. A first argument in support to this statement is anatomical: because most cortico-cortical connections are reciprocal, information can circulate in both directions and be simultaneously available in many areas. Also, the sequential aspect of many actions does not reflect the way the planning stage operates: the study of human skilled activities such as speech or typing for example, shows that individual movements are planned several steps ahead, in such a way that forthcoming steps influence those which are under execution (Sternberg et al., 1990). Note, however, that a conception involving parallel processing, simultaneous activation and distributiveness of information is *not* incompatible with that of a hierarchical organization. The concept of hierarchy implies dependence between levels of processing: it deals with the nature of the information that flows between levels, not with the timing or the direction of information flow. In addition, although the information that propagates within the network under consideration here goes in both directions, this does not imply that it is the same information that goes 'downward' and 'upward'. The downward flow could carry signals to control lower levels, whereas upward flow would simply carry completion signals indicating the current state of the lower levels to the upper ones (see section 6.3.2).

6.2 The internal structure of motor representations

Neurons with set-related activity are the core features of the different levels of the motor representation. In order to understand in which way they can efficiently influence motor behaviour, it appeared useful to propose a functional model which would, not only be compatible with the neurophysiological data, but also could provide a framework for studying the cognitive phenomena – normal and pathological – associated with motor representations. As this model has antecedents in the literature, a brief historical survey is in order.

6.2.1   The corollary discharge concept

Some of the classical theories concerning motor control and sensorimotor coordination will be reviewed first, as they carry interesting concepts for understanding the internal structure of motor representations. A highly influential conception, which appeared in the modern literature some fifty years ago, was that of R. Sperry. In 1943, Sperry observed that fish with inverted vision caused by surgical 180° eye rotation tended to turn continuously in circles, when placed in a visual environment. In a later paper, Sperry (1950) interpreted this circling behaviour due to inverted vision as the result of a disharmony between the retinal input generated by movement of the animal and a compensatory mechanism for maintaining the stability of the visual field. The mechanism postulated by Sperry for this stability was a centrally arising discharge that reached the visual centres as a corollary of any excitation generated by the motor centres and normally resulting in movement (hence the term 'corollary discharge', used by Sperry to designate this mechanism). In this way, the visual centres could distinguish the retinal displacement related to a movement of the animal, from the displacement produced by moving objects. Visual changes produced by a movement of the animal were normally 'cancelled' by a corollary discharge of a corresponding size and direction, and had no effect on behaviour. If, however, the corollary discharge did not correspond to the visual changes (for example, after inversion of vision), these changes were not cancelled and were read by the motor system as having their origin in the external world. The animal thus moved in the direction of this apparent visual displacement. Based on similar observations in insects, von Holst and Mittelsteadt (1950) independently came to the same conclusion. They postulated that each time the motor centres sent a command signal to the effector for producing a movement, they also sent a 'copy' of this command (the 'efference copy') to some other centre. The effector activated by the command signal produced a reafference which returned to the same centre. Von Holst and Mittelstaedt further postulated that the efference copy and the reafference were of opposite sign. When they exactly compensated one another, nothing further happened; when the reafference was too small or too large, a difference remained, which had definite effects according to the particular organization of the system (for example, they could influence the movement itself or ascend to higher centres to produce a perception, etc.; see von Holst, 1950). Corollary discharge and efference copy thus represent two nearly identical formulations of the fact that the nervous system can inform itself about its current state and use this information to monitor and regulate its own activity. A clear account on how such a mechanism could regulate ongoing movements is outlined by Bernstein's famous diagram, first published in 1957 (see Bernstein, 1967) (figure 6.1). Imagine the act of seizing a visible object from a table top: 'this may be regarded as a constant process of estimation of the rate of diminution of that section of the path over which the hand must still travel to meet the object' (1967, p. 129). The position of the object (Sw in figure 6.1) represents the required value to achieve. This value is compared to the the current value of the position of the hand (Iw). When the difference Dw between Sw and Iw equals zero, the system self stabilizes and the movement stops.

The corollary discharge was thus part of a mechanism for comparing outflow signals generated by the command apparatus and reafferent signals generated by the effects of the outflow on the environment. This definition, which recalls that of homeostatic regulation, can be extended to any mechanism which implies a comparison between two causally related signals. The revival of the outflow theory prompted some authors to use the comparator concept for a variety of regulations (see Teuber, 1960). Held (1961) extended the simple corollary discharge model to explain the effects of situations where visuomotor coordination was modified as a result of a systematic conflict between a desired and an observed motor output. Such situations can be created by exposure to laterally displacing prisms, for example. To explain adaptation to this type of conflict, Held included in the model a correlation storage mechanism where traces of previous combinations of concurrent efferent and reafferent signals were stored. When a goal-directed movement was performed, the currently monitored outflow signal selected the trace combination containing an identical efferent trace and the reafferent trace combined with it. This reafferent trace was compared with the current reafferent signal. If the two coincided, the trace combination was reinforced; if they did not coincide, the mismatch between the selected trace and the current reafferent signal was stored and eventually became the basis for a new combination which built up until adaptation was complete. In the meantime, error signals corresponding to the degree of mismatch were generated by the comparator and sent to the motor system for immediate correction. This hypothesis accounts for the emphasis

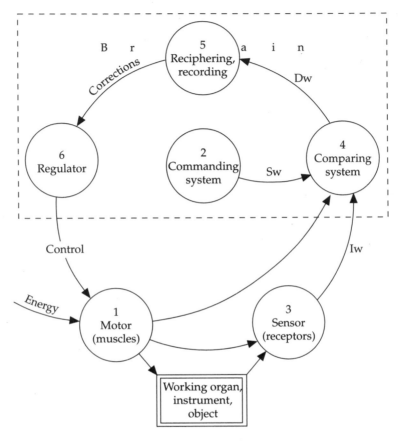

Figure 6.1   Bernstein's comparator model
The information (Iw) generated by the commanding system (Sw) is compared with reafferent input resulting from movement execution. The output of the comparator (Dw) determines the global output of the system.
From Bernstein, 1967

that Held and his colleagues put on the role of self-generated movements, not only in producing adaptation, but also in developing and maintaining normal coordination (see Held and Hein, 1963). Schmidt (1975) proposed a similar hypothesis for motor learning, where the final response resulted from a comparison between central and peripheral events, until the actual outcome of the movement would correspond to the desired (represented) outcome. Finally, more detailed models using the same principle, such as the Robinson model for the control of eye and head movements (Robinson, 1975), will be further mentioned below.

6.2.2 Comparator models

The above concepts of internal model, comparator and reafferent signals all refer to the theme of the control of action by its desired results. It is quite remarkable that many authors from such different areas as cognitive psychology, psychopathology or neuroscience have proposed this mechanism for explaining the control of cognitive functions. An early example is that of S. Freud's 'Project' where the desired goal was compared with the result of the action generated to obtain it: the degree of match between the two was a factor of satisfaction or dissatisfaction of the desire (for a reappraisal, see Pribram and Gill, 1976). A more recent example is provided by the Gray's model of the septo-hippocampal system for explaining anxiety which, by several of its features, is relevant to the problem of the control of actions (Gray, 1982). Gray's model includes several subunits. One is a 'generator of predictions', which operates on the basis of current sensory events and stored (previously experienced) environmental regularities. The generated predictions issued by this subunit trigger exploratory action programs, the function of which is to test the predictions. The resulting information is sent back to another subunit, the 'comparator', which also receives a copy of the prediction. If the comparator detects a coincidence between the prediction and the reafferent information, the system goes on by generating new predictions, and so on. If, by contrast, a mismatch is detected, the comparator shifts to a 'control' mode of functioning and sends outputs back to the generator of predictions. On the basis of known connectivity of the septo-hippocampal system and of experimental results, Gray identified the comparator with the subicular area, and the generator of predictions with the cingular cortex. In case of normal functioning (that is, when no mismatch is detected), the cingular cortex triggers exploratory programs by its action on the motor system. In case of mismatch, the action of the comparator on the cingular cortex results in behavioural inhibition. This effect, together with an increase in arousal and attention, would represent the neural substrate of anxiety. This mechanism is not very different from that postulated for the higher level of the motor representation. Indeed an intentional system is nothing but a generator of predictions. It uses stored knowledge and a number of internal cues as building blocks for anticipating actions. When these actions fulfill the prediction and the comparator is disactivated, the whole representation is strenghtened and stored. If a mismatch occurs and the comparator remains activated, the activity of the module is modified accordingly (for an application of the same model to consciousness, see Gray, 1995).

The diagram outlined in figure 6.2 will now be used to specify some of the characteristics of comparator models (see Jeannerod, 1995). The first point to be discussed is hierarchical organization. Although the diagram apparently assumes that the functional (and possibly, anatomical) steps of the action are organized serially, this impression must be corrected by available experimental evidence. First, as was mentioned earlier, it is difficult, if not impossible, to isolate processing steps (like intention, planning, etc.) from each other on the basis of anatomical localization: the system involved in the representation of action is a highly distributed one, types of neuronal activity overlap borders between areas, and the information processed at each given location simultaneously flows, not only in the direction indicated by the arrows on the diagram, but also in the opposite direction. The result is that, soon after the upper stages have been activated, it should become impossible to recognize a serial organization. In addition, to account for the fact that subactions pertaining to the same action plan are processed simultaneously, the diagram, at least for what concerns its distal steps, should be considered as one of many parallel lines with a similar structure. In other words, the proposed model departs from the classical concept of Miller et al. (1960), who conceived the motor representation as a computer program with a fixed sequence of steps. Before moving from one step to the next, the program had to check for

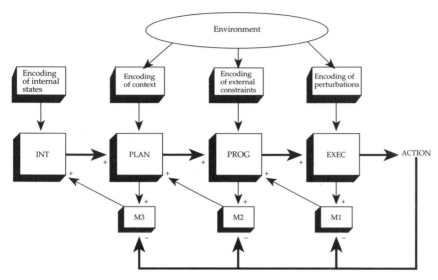

Figure 6.2 A flow chart model for explaining ongoing regulation of action
For details, see text.
From Jeannerod, 1995

completion of the operation (the Test Operate Test Exit (TOTE) system). What is left from a hierarchical organization in the diagram of figure 6.2 is that the complete internal model of the action to be performed must be stored at the highest level, and that during the initial activation the information has to flow in a precise direction. Indeed, it would be counterproductive that global specifications concerning the action plan directly reach the execution level, without being previously implemented into more detailed commands by the other intermediate steps. The action schemas embedded in each of the levels do not all have the same degree of specificity. As was argued in the chapter 5, source-schemas, component schemas and motor schemas represent different degrees of integration of the same action.

The other important point is the comparison mechanism for testing the degree of match between the desired and the current state of the system. Goal-directed behaviour implies that the action should continue until the goal has been satisfied. The description of the motor representation must account for this property, that is, it must involve, not only mechanisms for steering and directing the action, but also mechanisms for monitoring and eventually correcting its course, and for checking its completion. In the diagram of figure 6.2, this testing mechanism is effected in parallel at all levels of processing: the outflow information (or a copy of it) is sent into devices where the degree of match between operations arising at each level and the actual effect of these operations on the environment is determined. This mechanism implies a short-term storage of information processed at each level in as many memories as there are levels. The memories thus represent a distributed comparator for controlling the unfolding of the action. Reafferent input picked up at the periphery and documenting the current state of the action are fed into the memories and are used to signal its degree of completion. If the desired action has been completed, the reafferences and the content of the memories will coincide, and the latter will be erased. If the action is incomplete, residual activity will persist in the memories, which will reactivate the corresponding module and generate corrections (an advantage of the distributed nature of the comparator is that errors detected at a given level can generate appropriate corrections without interfering with the whole system). Finally, if the desired action does not take place, memories will not be erased, which in turn will maintain the whole system activated.

The storage process involved in the distributed comparator must be distinguished from the more stable memories where motor procedures (schemas) are stored and wait until they are selected and used. The motor representation includes only the activated schemas, those which have been selected for the purpose of the intended action. Because the motor representations are dynamic structures they must be reassembled *de novo* for each action: external constraints differ and the context in which the action takes place changes, so that the same action is never repeated several times in exactly the same way.

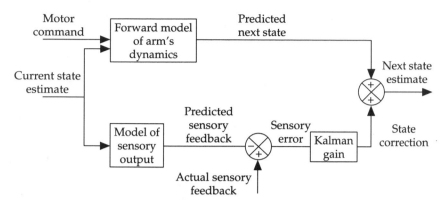

Figure 6.3 An internal forward model for predicting limb position during target oriented movements
For details, see text.
From Wolpert et al., 1995

6.3 Testing the validity of comparator models

Motor representations as they are outlined here resemble the internal 'forward' models, as they are used in engineering. Those are models which mimic the causal flow of a process by predicting its next state. In other words, they can estimate the outcome of the action without waiting for the sensory reafference, or even without performing it. This is exactly what one would expect from a mechanism accounting for planning and controlling execution of an action, as well as for (mentally) simulating the same action. Wolpert et al. (1995) have used such a model for analyzing the errors made by subjects in estimating the position of their hands at the end of movements made under externally imposed forces (figure 6.3). They describe their model as a combination of two processes: 'The first process uses the current state estimate and motor command to predict the next state by simulating the movement dynamics with a forward model. The second process uses a model of the sensory output process to predict the sensory feedback from the current state estimate. The sensory error – the difference between actual and predicted sensory feedback – is used to correct the state estimate resulting from the forward model' (Wolpert et al., p. 1881). Thus, the comparison process as it is shown here is twofold: a first comparison occurs between efferent commands and their predicted effect (a purely internal mechanism which has sometimes been termed 'internal feedback' – see Evarts, 1971), and a second comparison using actual feedback from the periphery.

6.3.1   Perturbation experiments

Having set the stage for a comparator model, it is now interesting to test its explanatory power in a particular type of behavioural experiments, those where perturbations are applied at the onset, or during the execution, of a movement. The perturbation produces a mismatch between the desired and the current trajectory or, to be more concrete, between the command sent by the program level to the execution level and the pattern of reafferent input (for example, visual, proprioceptive). The consequence is that this pattern does not correspond to the representation of the desired state stored in the working memory, which will not be cancelled. An error signal will be transferred to the program level which will have to change its specifications until execution is finally correct.

This comparison mechanism has to be very fast for preventing the error signal from propagating to higher levels. This fact is illustrated by an experiment made by Abbs and Gracco (1984). They described rapid corrections during perturbations applied to articulators during speech. The lower lip was unexpectedly pulled down during production of the phoneme /ba/. Yet, the lip closure was nevertheless achieved and the phoneme was correctly pronounced in spite of the perturbation. Such a compensation, which implied that lip closure was performed by a larger lowering of the upper lip, was thus effected within a delay compatible with the correct production of the phoneme. Indeed, EMG activity of the relevant oro-facial muscles was found to be modified very shortly after the onset of the perturbation. Activation of the orbicularis oris superior, responsible for upper lip depression, occurred within 22–55 ms, which accounted for the close-to-normal lip closure. By contrast, activation of the orbicularis oris inferior (the lower lip elevator), occurred several tens of milliseconds later. Abbs and Gracco concluded that activation of these two independent muscles reflected two different compensatory mechanisms. They suggested that late activation of the lower lip elevator reflected reprogramming triggered by proprioceptive feedback, whereas early activation of the upper lip depressor reflected an open-loop adjustment, 'a strategy, in Arbib's terms, whereby a controller directly monitors disturbances to a system and immediately applies compensatory signals to the controlled system, rather than waiting for feedback on how the disturbances have affected the system' (Arbib, 1981, p. 1466).

Another example of motor reorganization following a perturbation was already described in chapter 2. In this example (Paulignan et al., 1991a), the subjects had to reach and grasp a vertical dowel which occasionally jumped (at movement onset) by 10° to the right or to the left. The correction began to appear some 100 ms after the jump and drove the hand to the target with an excellent accuracy. A complex rearrangement of movement kinematics took place during the movement (sudden deceleration followed by reacceleration of the reach, recalibration of the finger grip), for preserving the coordination between the reach and the grasp. In spite of these kinematic changes, the movement duration was unchanged, except for the additional 100 ms visuomotor delay. The forward model designed by Hoff and Arbib (1993) accounts for these corrections. In this model, the command signal sent to the motor apparatus is compared with reafferent velocity signals picked up at the execution level. Since reafferent signals are normally delayed with respect to the command signal, the comparator looks ahead in time and produces an estimate of the movement velocity corresponding to the command. The image of this estimated velocity is used for computing the actual position of the limb with respect to the target. Simulation experiments showed that accurate corrections compatible with the behavioural data were generated when target position was perturbed, without notable increase in movement duration. This computer experiment thus confirms that the comparison between the outflow signal and the incoming signal must be a dynamic one. It is only because the current state of the action is monitored on line (rather than after the movement terminates), that corrections can be applied without delay as soon as the deviation of the current trajectory from the desired trajectory is detected.

6.3.2   *The role of the reafference*

In order to be useful for the comparison process, the reafferent signals must be compatible with the efferent ones. In other words, the two must be coded in the same 'language' for being mutually understandable and for the matching process to be possible. The ideal situation would be that where the reafference is a mirror image of the representation (what von Holst suggested by using the analogy of a negative and a positive of the same photograph that cancel each other). This is not physiologically absurd: the discharge of muscle spindles in the agonist muscle during a movement (due to the coactivation of the gamma motoneurons) exactly fulfills the criterion for an efference copy that propagates 'upwards' and copies the motor input to the alpha motoneurons. This signal, which is a direct image of the contraction of the muscle, could well be used for comparison with incoming signals resulting from the limb movement (Miles and Evarts, 1979).

This ideal, however, can hardly be reached in practical terms, for the reason that transformations occur between command signals and actual movements. As Bernstein (1967) conjectured, the two do not map entirely onto each other, for the reason that execution involves biomechanical constraints related to implementation by the musculoskeletal apparatus, and distortion by external forces which are not necessarily represented centrally. Describing the overt action thus does not give full access to the central process; and conversely, fully describing the representation (if this were at all possible) would not tell exactly what the corresponding action would be. In addition, representations are likely to be endowed with properties (partly built on experience from previous actions) which may not be apparent in their eventual motor counterpart. They seem to be structured with several levels of organization; they use cognitive rules for establishing the serial order of action parts, for assembling programs, etc. To be provocative, the overt movement is not a reliable source of information on its own representation.

An alternative mechanism for the comparison between efferent and reafferent signals is that the representation encodes, not joint rotations or kinematic parameters, but final configurations (of the body, of the moving segments, etc.) as they should arise at the end of the action. In other words, the goal of the action, rather than the action itself, would be represented. This idea of the representation of a final state of the system (a representation of the state of the organism when the goal has been reached) is appealing, because the difference between the present state (before the action) and the final state (after the action has been completed) *is* the action. In the familiar example of grasping an object, the representation would encode the final posture of the hand with respect to the object. It would remain active as long as the requested configuration (appropriate grip size and orientation of the hand) has not been obtained, which, in this particular example would be signalled by tactile cues arising from contact with the object. This mechanism imposes a strong constraint on the comparison process, which in fact fits some of the properties of a distributed comparator, namely, comparison must occur at several levels simultaneously for signalling completion of all the elements which contribute to the final configuration.

Although this mechanism is still highly speculative, it is supported by experimental arguments. Desmurget et al. (1995) recorded reach and grasp movements directed at an elongated object (a handle that had to be grasped with a power grip). When the orientation of the handle was suddenly changed at the onset of a movement, the arm smoothly shifted from the optimal configuration initially planned to reach the object to another optimal configuration corresponding to the object in its new orientation. The shift was achieved by simultaneous changes at several joints, (shoulder abduction, wrist rotation), so that the final grasp was effected in the correct position. In this case the comparison between the desired and the actual arm position could be effected dynamically through a process similar to that which has been proposed to solve the problem of coordinate transformation during goal-directed movements. The position of an object in space is initially coded in extrinsic (for example, visual) coordinates. In order to be matched by the moving limb, however, this position must be transferred into an intrinsic co-ordinate frame. If the position of the object in extrinsic coordinates and the position of the extremity of the limb in intrinsic coordinates coincide (that is, if these positions correspond to the same point in the two systems of coordinates), the action should logically be considered as terminated (see Carrozzo and Lacquaniti, 1994). This explanation which is valid for unrestrained movements, does not apply to movements constrained by an external contact (for example, moving a lever, tracing on a table, etc., see Desmurget et al., in press).

This hypothesis of a representation of actions based on final configurations has a direct relevance to clinical disorders like apraxia. Apraxic patients have difficulties in performing, but also imitating, gesturing or describing actions, precisely because they lack the procedures for building the appropriate configurations corresponding to object-oriented actions. A direct observation of this deficit was reported by Poizner et al. (1995). They showed that patients who were instructed to gesture actions like cutting bread, for example, failed because they could not produce the correct arm configurations.

A final point to be discussed is the relevance of this model to motor images. It is noteworthy that, in conditions of normal execution (that is, when the executed and the represented actions coincide), there is usually no awareness of the content of the representation at any level, and that no image is experienced. This is explained by the fact that motor imagery and execution have different time constants. Because imagery, unlike execution, implies subjective awareness, it takes longer to appear. If imagery actually occurred in conditions of normal execution, it would be delayed with respect to the corresponding action. This effect would be even more pronounced in cases of fast movements or during the occurrence of corrections (see chapter 3 for a discussion of this point). By contrast, awareness is common experience in conditions where the action is delayed, incompletely executed or blocked. According to the above model (figure 6.2), those are conditions where the motor memories are not or incompletely erased, and where the representational levels are kept activated: this persisting activation would thus be the substrate for (conscious) motor images. In addition, because activation persists at all levels of the system when action is not performed, there is a possibility that the content of the motor image reflects the activity of any of these levels. The actually experienced image would depend on the level which would be probed by the experimenter, with the proviso that this level would be consciously accessible.

6.4   Monitoring intentions

The extension of the notion of a comparison process to the most cognitive levels of the motor representation, and to cognitive functions in general raises several questions. How do we know that we are the authors of our own movements? How do we distinguish a self-produced movement from a movement imposed from the outside? Is it because we feel self-generated movements as 'endogenous'? And, if this is the case, on the basis of which signal? This section will analyze data concerning the monitoring of intentions and the nature of the cues which signal the intentional character of an event.

6.4.1   *Sensations of innervation*

There are interesting discussions in the literature about the origin of the sensations generated by these 'internal' signals (see Scheerer, 1987). Two opposite conceptions (that is, whether they are of an endogenous origin, or whether they arise from peripheral receptors) have been held. The conception of a central origin of position sense and muscular feelings was mainly heralded by J. Müller's school in Germany, where the notion of 'sensations of innervation' was developed (see Jeannerod, 1983). These were sensations from a central origin, no longer of a peripheral origin, transmitted by motor nerves, not by sensory nerves, by which subjects could feel the motor impulses emitted by their brain toward their muscles. Wundt argued that, because sensations originating from the act of will are normally fused with those arising from muscles during the movement, they would only be observed separately when a paralysis abolishes the movement and preserves the will to make it (see Ross and Bischof, 1981). Self-observations reported by people experiencing pathological paralysis fulfill this requirement. The physicist Ernst Mach, for example, provided a description of his own impressions after he experienced hemiplegia due to a stroke (Mach, 1906). At first, when paralysis of his arm was complete, Mach noted that the efforts of will he made to move it, although clearly perceptible, were not accompanied by any real sensation of effort. Later, after recovery had begun and the paralysis was less dense, each effort of will was accompanied by the sensation of having the hand or foot held down by enormous weights. The sensation of effort was perceived as a sensation of heaviness or resistance which opposed movement (see also Brodal, 1973).

Sensations of innervation have been studied both in patients with complete or partially recovered paralysis, and in normal subjects during transient neuromuscular block or during fatigue. In studying patients with paralysis of central or peripheral origin, Gandevia (1982) replicated some of the self-observations of Mach (1906). In conformity with these earlier findings, hemiplegic patients reported that attempts to move completely paralysed limbs produced no feeling of heaviness. When ability to move began to return, their attempts were accompanied by a feeling of intense heaviness. Finally, the sensations of heaviness decreased as movements became easier and regained strength. By contrast, in patients with paralysis of peripheral origin, attempts to move the paralysed limbs were always associated with sensations of heaviness. A recent longitudinal observation by Rode et al. (1996) on a patient with a pure motor hemiplegia fully confirms these findings. A weight matching task was used for measuring the degree of effort produced to move the paralyzed arm during the four month post-stroke recovery: the subject had to determine, by moving his unaffected arm against a weight, the amount that corresponded to the effort needed to produce a test movement (shoulder forward flexion or elbow flexion to the horizontal, full hand grip) with the affected arm. The change in the degree of effort exactly mirrored the regain in muscular strength. At the beginning of the study, when no muscular force could be produced, the subject reported no sensation of effort. By contrast, when the slightest muscular contraction became possible, he complained of an intense sensation of effort, which was paralleled by respiratory changes and increase in heart rate. Later on, as muscular force reappeared, the sensation of force dissipated.

Experiments involving transient paralysis in volunteer subjects have led to more ambiguous results. Several authors using ischemic block or local injection of curarizing agents to produce paralysis of one hand, failed to observe sensations of effort during their attempts to move (Laszlo, 1966; McCloskey and Torda, 1975). However, another less direct, but more objective, way to test the perception of efferent activity is to ask subjects to indicate the quantity of effort that they have to put for achieving a given task. Gandevia and McCloskey (1977) asked subjects to press a lever with one thumb (the reference thumb) in order to produce a reference tension, displayed visually on an oscilloscope screen. With the other thumb, they had to press another lever so as to match, without visual control, the muscular contraction or effort produced by the 'reference' thumb. During partial curarization on the side of the reference thumb, the subjects could still produce the reference tension by pressing the lever, by putting more effort into the action in order to overcome the partial neuromuscular block. Accordingly, with their other thumb, they indicated a much larger muscular effort than normally required to produce the same tension. The same authors (Gandevia and McCloskey, 1977) also used the perceived heaviness of weights as a measure of muscular effort. The same matching technique as above was used, that is, subjects chose weights with one arm until the heaviness perceived with that arm matched the reference weight lifted by the other arm. During partial paralysis, the subjects chose exaggerated weights, hence indicating an increase of the heaviness perceived with the weakened arm. The same result was obtained with muscular fatigue instead of partial paralysis. McCloskey et al. (1974) showed that after the reference arm supported the weight for some minutes and became fatigued, weights heavier than the reference weight were chosen to match it.

Other aspects of sensations of innervation (their temporal organization) can also be measured using purely introspective methods. These aspects can be inferred from judgements subjects make about when they release the command to move a limb. In the McCloskey et al. (1983) experiment, subjects were instructed to perform a test movement at will. The instructions also implied that they should disregard the movement, and concentrate on their issuing of the command to the limb ('think about when you tell it to move'). Finally, they were given a reference stimulus which occurred at a variable delay with respect to the onset of their movement (as judged from EMG onset). It was found that the reference stimulus had to be given about 100 ms prior to EMG onset in order to be judged by the subject coincident with onset of the motor command. In order to avoid possible cues arising from contracting muscles, the same experiment was repeated under ischemic block of the arm: in that case, where no muscle contraction occurred, the efferent volleys were recorded from the nerve upstream with respect to the block. Again, the reference stimulus had to precede significantly the nerve volleys to be felt coincident with the subjective central command. This experiment therefore demonstrates that subjects can identify the neural signals related to their central commands, and that they can distinguish these signals from those arising from muscles at the time of the movement itself. Several arguments demonstrate that the command related sensations are unlikely to have arisen from the muscle. The sensations are in advance with respect to EMG; they persist under ischemic block; in addition, muscle spindles, which might represent a possible source of signals for these sensations, do not seem to discharge during isometric muscle contraction prior to the movement (Vallbo, 1973).

The problem that remains to be solved is the precise nature of these 'sensations'. Are they real sensations? Or, alternatively, are they based on cognitive judgements? Gandevia (1982) proposed an interpretation for the sensations of effort reported by subjects with weakened muscles (by neuromuscular blockade, fatigue, or other ways) on their attempts to move, as well as for their perception of increased heaviness as measured psychophysically. He suggested that neural traffic in motor corticofugal paths might be read off and used as the relevant signal for the observed illusions. Indeed, complete paralysis following pyramidal lesions at the cortical level is not accompanied by sensations of increased effort or heaviness, precisely because no traffic occurs in the motor pathways after such lesions. Sensations reappear during partial recovery of movements, when neural traffic re-establishes. The same hypothesis would account for permanence of sensations of effort in all cases of distal paralysis, where corticofugal pathways are not altered. In a more recent paper, the same author (Gandevia, 1987) proposed that the discharge responsible for these sensations does not arise directly from the corticofugal pathway, because transcranial electrical stimulation of this pathway does not produce a sensation of effort. Instead, the subject experiences a passive movement. This observation conforms with Penfield's observations during direct electrical stimulation of the cerebral hemispheres in conscious patients: when such stimulations produced a movement, the patient invariably experienced having been moved passively by the experimenter, and had no sensation of having been the author of his/her movement (Penfield and Boldrey, 1937). It can therefore be suggested that the relevant discharges for the sensations of innervation arise from structures such as premotor cortex or basal ganglia, which subsequently impinge upon primary motor cortex and on the descending pathway.

6.4.2   *The problem of awareness of intentions*

There are limitations, however, to this monitoring of efferent activity. Several experimental results suggest that intentions for carrying out voluntary action are generated without explicit awareness. Libet et al. (1983, see also Libet, 1985) instructed subjects to perform *ad libitum* simple hand movements and to report the instant (W) at which they became aware of 'wanting to move' (by reporting the clock position of a revolving spot). In addition, readiness potentials were recorded from the subjects skull. EMG was also recorded for measuring the precise onset of the movement. W was found to lag the onset of readiness potentials by about 345 ms. In Libet's terms 'This leads to the conclusion that cerebral initiation . . . of a spontaneous voluntary act . . . can and usually does begin *unconsciously*'. '. . . The brain "decides" to initiate or, at least, to prepare to initiate the act before there is any reportable subjective awareness that such a decision has taken place' (1985, p. 536). This interesting result is hardly compatible with the notion of monitorable 'sensations' in relation to voluntary acts, unless one considers that intentions can only be consciously perceived after a certain intensity threshold has been crossed.

An experiment by Nielsen (1963) deals with the same question. Nielsen used a paradigm where subjects were unknowingly shown an alien hand in exact concordance with their own hand (figure 6.4). Subjects were asked to follow with their (invisible) hand a straight line shown in a mirror: while they were doing so the (visible) alien hand gently deviated to the right. Subjects were consistently found to deviate their own movement to the left, as if they tried to compensate the visually perceived rightward deviation. In addition, almost all subjects (18 out of 20) experienced that the hand they saw was their own hand, and tried to interpret the rightward deviation by 'inattention' or 'tiredness' or by the action of external forces. In other

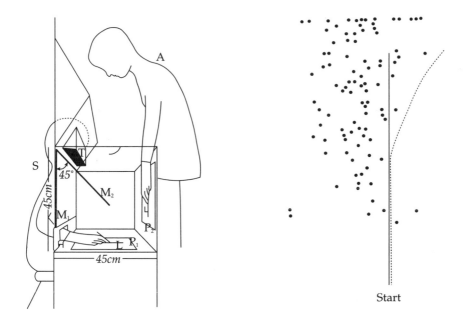

Figure 6.4   An experiment designed for studying attribution of intentions
Left: subject (S) sees his own hand or an alien hand (that of experimenter A) according to the position of mirror M2. Optical arrangement is such that the images of the two hands superimpose.
Right: endpoints of subjects tracings when the alien hand produced tracings (dashed line) that departed from straight line. Note concentration of endpoints on left side, opposite to alien hand trajectory.
From Nielsen, 1963

words, the subjects 'preferred' to rely on visual information rather than on their own motor outflow.

It is interesting to compare conditions where efforts of will are consciously perceived with conditions where they are not (like in the Nielsen experiment). Comparison reveals that efforts of will may not be consciously perceived unless action is blocked or grossly impaired. This happens in abnormal situations like paralysis; it may also be the case in conditions of motor imagery where action is purposively inhibited (this condition was described in chapter 4). It remains that, in spite of not being consciously perceived, efferent signals are nonetheless monitored at some point of the system in order to produce corrections, as in the experiment by Higgins and Angel (1970), for example. The distinction made by Searle (1983) between 'intention in action' (the implicit step that precedes an overtly executed action) and 'prior intention' (a conscious desire to do something) is quite relevant here. This is because this distinction provides a phenomenological description of two different situations, however, and not because it corresponds to a radical difference between those situations. Consider, for example, the case where the movement of raising my arm is impossible because of paralysis. If I must raise my arm to catch an object (an intention in action), the movement will not be performed. But I will shortly realize that I in fact intended to raise my arm (a prior intention). Why should we introduce formal analytical distinctions between conditions that experimental situations reveal to be continuous with one another?

The notion of a central monitoring (conscious or not) of efferent signals related to motor intentions provides a tentative conceptual framework for describing the pathological functioning of motor representations. A defect in this monitoring process has been proposed as a possible basis for a neuropsychological theory of schizophrenia (Feinberg, 1978). In the domain of motor actions, this theory predicts that schizophrenic patients should no longer be able to monitor efferent signals resulting from their intentions and should therefore have defective functioning of their motor representations, namely the process of comparison between the efferent and the reafferent signals should no longer be possible (Frith, 1992). Accordingly, it has been shown that schizophrenic patients have difficulties in generating motor corrections. Malenka et al. (1982) found that these subjects, in the absence of visual feedback from their movement, were unable to correct the direction of a tracking movement when the target displacement was reversed. Similarly, Frith and Done (1989), also using a motor task with error correction, noticed that psychotic patients with experiences of alien control of their thoughts were less likely to make corrections than other types of psychotic patients. The failure of the 'intention monitor' (Frith and Done, 1989) thus explains why schizophrenics may not be able to keep track of whether an action was produced as the result of a prior intention, or whether it was triggered by an external stimulus. If we follow Feinberg (1978) in considering thinking as a motor process, then delusional experiences commonly reported by schizophrenics, such as mind control by external agents 'might simply represent culturally determined interpretations of an experience in which thoughts seem to arise independently', as a result of 'failure or derangement of corollary discharge mechanisms' (1978, p. 638).

The failure of still another mechanism, the 'intention editor', would explain why certain patients (with Gilles de la Tourette syndrome) cannot select among competing intentions when they are instructed to perform two tasks in alternation, for example (Baron-Cohen et al., 1994). It is likely that new 'operators' will soon be added to this list for completing the cognitive structure of the motor representation.

6.4.3 *Understanding intentions of others*

As most intentions are generated implicitly and not consciously, it is critical that they are automatically referred to their origin. The monitoring of intention-related signals is thus a key mechanism for correctly attributing intentions to their authors. This is in fact true for the detection of mental states in general: the attribution of mental states to other people would be based on our ability to monitor our own mental states. Note that this is exactly what the classical corollary discharge theory, described earlier in this chapter, was about. It dealt with the neural mechanism for differentiating a self-produced movement from a movement arising from the external world. The difference was in the presence or absence, respectively, of centrally generated signals corollary to the motor output. A movement not accompanied by such signals would be automatically referred to a source (an intention) distinct from the self. In other words, the intention would be monitored as a reference against which the motor output and the related perceptual changes would be matched. In the absence of this differentiating mechanism a subject would not experience his own actions as originating from himself and might feel that he is being influenced or driven by the actions of other people. The same subject would also be deprived from the ability to detect others' intentions or even to attribute intentions to other people, hence again the possibility of misinterpretations and delusions.

There are still very few experimental studies of the ability to detect intentions. Dasser et al. (1989), for example, showed that pre-school children can correctly detect whether a movement pattern (two balls moving on a TV screen) was produced intentionally or not. It would be interesting to extend these experiments to the determination of the cues used by subjects to decide whether a movement was intentional or not, or to decide what was intended. Among the relevant cues are those that characterize 'biological motion': complex motion patterns produced by subjects (for example, dancing) can be recognized visually without difficulty, even if they are described in a very succint way (for example, by a few luminous dots placed at the level of the moving joints, on a dark background, see Johansson, 1977). This very striking ability suggests a coupling between motor and perceptual processes, whereby certain properties of the motor system influence perceptual interpretation of a visual stimulus (for example, Viviani and Stucchi, 1992a). It is tempting to generalize this statement, by saying that the properties of the motor representational system can determine the perceptual interpretation of motion patterns produced by other individuals. This interpretation would be the basis for understanding intentions.

6.4.4   *Imitation and observational learning*

Understanding the intentions and actions of others is the basis for imitation behaviour. Observation thus plays a prominent role, not only in initiating communication between individuals, but also as a basis for motor skill learning. The problem is to know 'what' is actually imitated. Can we conceive of a direct mapping of the perceptual scene into motor commands? Imitation studies in six-week-old infants suggest that this is not the case: these children are able to produce imitative mouth movements after a relatively long delay. In other words, they can produce a movement of a part of their body that they cannot see to match a target-action which is no longer visible (Meltzoff, 1995). This result stresses the existence of a storage mechanism between the perceptual and the motor processes.

Earlier in this book a description was made of a category of neurons in the monkey ventral premotor cortex. These neurons, which encode discrete hand actions (like picking food) also fire when the recorded animal observes a person (or another monkey as well) performing the same discrete action ('mirror neurons', see Rizzolatti et al., 1996). These neurons are thus activated both during observation of an action and during the performance of that action. This means that the action (and perhaps also the intention) to be imitated is stored in terms of an action code, not a perceptual code: the observed action is transformed into a potential action. This transformation would represent a possible explanation for perceptual phenomena like those reported by Viviani and others (for example, Viviani and Stucchi, 1992b), showing that the way an action is perceived is influenced by the motor capacities of the perceiver. This confirms the idea that has often been put forward throughout this book, that such processes as intending, imagining, observing/imitating and performing an action share common structural and functional mechanisms. The programme for the future will be to disentangle the specific signals that make us and the others know what, among all these possibilities, is happening in our motor brain.

Bibliography

Abbs, J. H. and Gracco, V. L. (1984): Control of complex motor gestures: Orofacial muscle responses to load perturbations of lip during speech. *Journal of Neurophysiology*, 51: 705–723.

Adams, L., Guz, A., Innes, J. A. and Murphy, K. (1987): The early circulatory and ventilatory response to voluntary and electrically induced exercise in man. *Journal of Physiology*, 383: 19–30.

Alstermark, B., Gorska, T., Lundberg, A. and Petterson, L. C. (1990): Integration in descending motor pathways controlling the forelimb in the cat. 16. Visually guided switching of target-reaching. *Experimental Brain Research*, 80: 1–11.

Andersen, R. A. and Gnadt, J. W. (1989): Posterior parietal cortex. In: *The neurobiology of saccadic eye movements*, R. Wurtz and M. E. Goldberg (Eds) Elsevier, Amsterdam, pp. 315–335.

Andersen, R. A., Essik, G. K. and Siegel, R. M. (1985): Encoding of spatial location by posterior parietal neurons. *Science*, 230: 456–458.

Annett, J. (1986): On knowing how to do things, In: *Generation and modulation of action patterns*, H. Heuer and C. Fromm (Eds), Springer, Berlin, pp. 187–200.

Annett, J. (1995): Motor imagery. Perception or action? *Neuropsychologia*, 33: 1395–1417.

Apter, J. T. (1946): Eye movements following strychnization of the superior colliculus of cats. *Journal of Neurophysiology*, 9: 73–86.

Arbib, M. A. (1981): Perceptual structures and distributed motor control. In V. B. Brooks (Ed.). *Handbook of Physiology, Section I: The nervous system, Vol. 2: Motor control*, Baltimore: Williams et Wilkins, pp. 1449–1480.

Arbib, M. A. (1985): Schemas for the temporal organization of behaviour. *Human Neurobiology*, 4: 63–72.

Arbib, M. A. and Hesse, M. B. (1986): *The construction of reality*. Cambridge University Press, Cambridge.

Arbib, M. A., Iberall, T. and Lyons, D. (1985): Coordinated control programs for movements of the hand. *Experimental Brain Research*, Supplement, 10: 111–129.

Arshavsky, Y. I., Deliagina, T. G., Gelfand, I. M., Orlovsky, G. N., Panchin, Y. V., Pavlova, G. A. and Popova, L. B. (1990): Neural control of heart beat in the pteropod mollusc *clione limacina*. Coordination of circulatory and locomotor systems. *Journal of Experimental Biology*, 148: 461–475.

Bachevalier, J. and Mishkin, M. (1986): Visual recognition impairment follows ventromedial but not dorsolateral prefrontal lesions in monkeys. *Behavioral Brain Research*, 20: 249–261.

Baleydier, C. and Morel, A. (1992): Segregated thalamo-cortical pathways to infeior parietal and inferotemporal cortex in macque monkey. *Visual Neuroscience*, 8: 391–405.

Balint, R. (1909): Seelenhammung des 'Schauens', optische Ataxie, raümliche Störungen des Aufmersamkeit. *Monastchrift für Psychiatrie und Neurologie*, 25: 51–81.

Bandler, R. (1988): Brain mechanisms of aggression as revealed by electrical and chemical stimulation: suggestion of a central role for the midbrain periaqueductal grey region. *Progress in Psychobiology and Physiological Psychology*, 13: 67–154.

Baron-Cohen, S., Cross, P., Crowson, M. and Robertson, M. (1994): Can children with Gilles de la Tourette syndrome edit their intentions? *Psychological Medicine*, 24: 29–40.

Barone, P. and Joseph, J. P. (1989): Prefrontal cortex and spatial sequencing in macaque monkey. *Experimental Brain Research*, 78: 447–464.

Berkeley, G. (1734): *A new theory of vision and other writings*. New Edition, Dent, London (1972).

Bernstein, N. (1967): *The coordination and regulation of movements*. Pergamon Press, Oxford.

Bianchi, L. (1895): The functions of the frontal lobes. *Brain*, 18: 497–522.

Biederman, I. and Cooper, E. R. (1992): Size invariance in visual object priming. *Journal of Experimental Psychology. Human Perception and Performance*, 18: 121–133.

Bisiach, E. and Luzzatti, C. (1978): Unilateral neglect of representational space. *Cortex*, 14: 129–133.

Bonnet, M. and Requin, J. (1982): Long loop and spinal reflexes in man during preparation for intended directional hand movements. *Journal of Neuroscience*, 2: 90–96.

Bonnet, M., Decety, J., Requin, J. and Jeannerod, M. Mental simulation of action modulates the excitability of spinal reflex pathways in man. Unpublished.

Bortoff, G. A. and Strick, P. L. (1993): Corticospinal terminations in two new-world primates. Further evidence that cortico-motoneuronal connections provide part of the manual substrate for manual dexterity. *Journal of Neuroscience*, 13: 5105–5118.

Boussaoud, D. (1995): Primate premotor cortex. Modulation of preparatory neural activity by gaze angle. *Journal of Neurophysiology*, 73: 886–890.

Boussaoud, D. and Wise, S. P. (1993a): Primate frontal cortex: neuronal activity following attentional versus intentional cues. *Experimental Brain Research*, 95: 15–27.

Boussaoud, D. and Wise, S. P. (1993b): Primate frontal cortex: effects of stimulus and movement. *Experimental Brain Research*, 95: 28–40.

Boussaoud, D., Ungerleider, L. and Desimone, R. (1990): Pathways for motion analysis. Cortical connections of the medial superior temporal and fundus of the superior temporal visual areas in the macaque. *Journal of Comparative Neurology*, 296: 462–495.

Boussaoud, D., Di Pellegrino, G. and Wise, S. P. (1996): Frontal lobe mechanisms subserving vision-for-action versus vision-for-perception. *Behavioural Brain Research*, 72: 1–15.

Bridgeman, B., Hendry, D. and Stark, L. (1975): Failure to detect displacement of the visual world during saccadic eye movements. *Vision Research*, 15: 719–722.

Bridgeman, B. (1989): Modeling separate visual pathways for spatial and object vision. *Behavioral and Brain Sciences*, 12: 398.

Bridgeman, B. (1992): Conscious vs unconscious processes. The case of vision. *Theory and Psychology*, 2: 73–88.

Bridgeman, B., Lewis, S., Heir, G. and Nagle, M. (1979): Relation between cognitive and motor-oriented systems of visual position perception. *Journal of Experimental Psychology: Human Perception and Performance*, 5: 692–700.

Bridgeman, B., Kirsch, M. and Sperling, A. (1981): Segregation of cognitive and motor aspects of visual function using induced motion. *Perception and Psychophysics*, 29: 336–342.

Brinkman, J. and Kuypers, H. G. J. M. (1972): Splitbrain monkeys: cerebral control of ipsilateral and contralateral arm, hand, and finger movements. *Science*, 176: 536–539.

Brinkman, J. and Kuypers, H. G. J. M. (1973): Cerebral control of contralateral and ipsilateral arm, hand and finger movements in the split-brain rhesus monkey. *Brain*, 96: 653–674.

Brodal A. (1973): Self-observations and neuroanatomical considerations after a stroke. *Brain*, 96: 675–694.

Bruce, D. (1994): Lashley and the problem of serial order. *American Psychologist*, 49: 93–103.

Bullier, J., Girard, P. and Salin, P. A. (1994): The role of area 17 in the transfer of information to extrastriate visual cortex. *Cerebral cortex*, 10: 301–330.

Bullock, D. and Grossberg, S. (1988): Neural dynamics of planned arm movements. Emergent invariants and speed-accuracy properties during trajectory formation. *Psychological Review*, 95: 49–90.

Butter, C. M. (1987): Varieties of attention and disturbances of attention. A neuropsychological analysis. In: *Neurophysiological and neuropsychological aspects of spatial neglect*, M. Jeannerod (Ed.), Advances in psychology n. 45, North Holland, Amsterdam, pp. 1–23.

Butters, N. and Pandya, D. (1969): Retention of delayed alternation. Effects of selective lesions of sulcus principalis. *Science*, 165: 1271–1273.

Buys, E. J., Lemon, R. N., Mantel, G. W. H. and Muir, R. B. (1986): Selective facilitation of different hand muscles by single corticospinal neurons in the conscious monkey. *Journal of Physiology*, 381: 529–549.

Cajal, S. R. (1909): *Histologie du système nerveux de l'homme et des vertébrés*. Paris: Maloine.

Caminiti, R., Johnson, P. B. and Urbano, A. (1990a): Making arm movements within different parts of space: dynamic aspects in the primate motor cortex. *The Journal of Neuroscience*, 10: 2039–2058.

Caminiti, R., Johnson, P. B., Burnod, Y., Galli, C. and Ferraina, S. (1990b): Shift of preferred directions of premotor cortical cells with arm movements performed across the workspace. *Experimental Brain Research*, 83: 228–232.

Caminiti, R., Johnson, P. B., Galli, C., Ferraina, S. and Burnod, Y. (1991): Making arm movements within different parts of space: the premotor and motor cortical representation of a coordinate system for reaching to visual targets. *Journal of Neuroscience*, 11: 1182–1197.

Caminiti, R., Ferraina, S. and Johnson, P. B. (1996): The sources of visual information to the primate frontal lobe. A novel role for the superior parietal lobule. *Cerebral Cortex*, 6: 319–328.

Cannon, W. S. (1932): *The wisdom of the body*. New York.

Carey, D. P., Harvey, M. and Milner, A. D. (1996): Visuomotor sensitivity for shape and orientation in a patient with visual form agnosia. *Neuropsychologia*, 34: 329–337.

Carrozzo, M. and Lacquaniti, F. (1994): A hybrid frame of reference for visuomanual coordination. *Neuroreport*, 5: 453–456.

Casagrande, V. A., Harting, J. K., Hall, W. C., Diamond, I. T. and Martin, G. F. (1972): Superior colliculus of the Tree Shrew: a structural and functional subdivision into superficial and deep layers. *Science*, 177: 444–447.

Castiello, U. and Jeannerod, M. (1991): Measuring time to awareness. *Neuroreport*, 2: 797–800.

Castiello, U., Paulignan, Y. and Jeannerod, M. (1991): Temporal dissociation of motor responses and subjective awareness. A study in normal subjects. *Brain*, 114: 2639–2655.

Chapman, E. and Wiesendanger, M. (1982): Recovery of function following unilateral lesions of the bulbar pyramid in the monkey. *Electroencephalography and Clinical Neurophysiology*, 53: 374–387.

Chen, D. F., Hyland, B., Maier, V. Palmeri, A. and Wiesendanger, M. (1991): Comparison of neural activity in the supplementary motor area and in the primary motor cortex in the monkey. *Somatosensory and Motor Research*, 8: 27–44.

Chieffi, S. and Gentilucci, M. (1993): Coordination between the transport and the grasp component during prehension movements. *Experimental Brain Research*, 94: 471–477.

Chieffi, S., Fogassi, L., Gallese, V., and Gentilucci, M. (1992): Prehension movements directed to approaching objects: influence of stimulus velocity on the transport and the grasp components. *Neuropsychologia*, 30: 877–897.

Christel, M. (1993): Grasping techniques and hand preferences in Hominoidea pp. 91–108. In Preuschoft, H. and Chivers, D. J. (Eds), *Hands of primates*, New-York, Springer-Verlag .

Cole, K. J. and Abbs, J. H. (1987): Kinematic and electromyographic responses to perturbation of a rapid grasp. *Journal of Neurophysiology*, 57: 1498–1510.

Colebatch, J. G. and Gandevia, S. C. (1989): The distribution of muscular weakness in upper motor neuron lesions affecting the arm. *Brain*, 112: 749–763.

Cooper, J. A., Sagar, H. J., Tidswell, P. and Jordan, N. (1994): Slowed central processing in simple and go/no-go reaction time tasks in Parkinson's disease. *Brain*, 117: 517–529.

Cowey, A. and Stoerig, P. (1995): Blindsight in monkeys. *Nature*, 373: 247–249.

Craik, K. J. W. (1943): *The nature of explanation*. Cambridge University Press, Cambridge.

Crammond, D. J. and Kalaska, J. F. (1990): Cortical neuronal activity recorded in a delay task that dissociates location of cue stimulus and movement endpoint. *Society for Neuroscience Abstracts*, 16: 423.

Damasio, A. R., Tranel, D. and Damasio, H. (1990): Individuals with sociopathic behavior caused by frontal damage fail to respond autonomically to social stimuli. *Behavioral Brain Research*, 41: 81–94.

Damasio, H., Grabowski, T., Frank, R., Galaburda, A. M. and Damasio, A. R. (1994): The return of Phineas Gage. Clues about the brain from the skull of a famous patient. *Science*, 264: 1102–1105.

Dasser, V., Ulbaek, I. and Premack, D. (1989): The perception of intention. *Science*, 243: 365–367.

Debru, C. (1992): La conscience du temps. De la phénoménologie à la cognition. *Revue de Métaphysique et de Morale*, 2: 273–293.

Decety, J. and Michel, F. (1989): Comparative analysis of actual and mental movement times in two graphic tasks. *Brain and Cognition*, 11: 87–97.

Decety, J. and Boisson, D. (1990): Effect of brain and spinal cord injuries on motor imagery. *European Archives of Psychiatry and Clinical Neuroscience*, 240: 39–43.

Decety, J. (1991): Motor information may be important for updating the cognitive processes involved in mental imagery of movement. *European Bulletin of Cognitive Psychology*, 4: 415–426.

Decety, J. and Jeannerod, M. (1996): Fitts' law in mentally simulated movements. *Behavioral Brain Research*, 72: 127–134.

Decety, J., Philippon, B. and Ingvar, D. H. (1988): rCBF landscapes during motor performance and motor ideation of a graphic gesture. *European Archives of Psychiatry and Neurological Sciences*, 238: 33–38.

Decety, J., Jeannerod, M. and Prablanc, C. (1989): The timing of mentally represented actions. *Behavioural Brain Research*, 34: 35–42 .

Decety, J., Sjoholm, H., Ryding, E., Stenberg, G., and Ingvar, D. (1990): The cerebellum participates in cognitive activity: Tomographic measurements of regional cerebral blood flow. *Brain Research*, 535: 313–317.

Decety, J., Jeannerod, M., Germain, M. and Pastene, J. (1991): Vegetative response during imagined movement is proportional to mental effort. *Behavioural Brain Research*, 42: 1–5.

Decety, J., Jeannerod, M., Durozard, D. and Baverel, G. (1993): Central activation of autonomic effectors during mental simulation of motor actions. *Journal of Physiology*, 461: 549–563.

Decety, J., Perani, D., Jeannerod, M., Bettinardi, V., Tadary, B., Woods, R., Mazziotta, J. C. and Fazio, F. (1994): Mapping motor representations with PET. *Nature*, 371: 600–602.

Deiber, M. P., Passingham, R. E., Colebatch, J. G., Friston, K. J., Nixon, P. D. and Frackowiak, R. S. J. (1991): Cortical areas and the selection of movement. A study with positron emission tomography. *Experimental Brain Research*, 84: 393–402.

Denny-Brown, D. and Chambers, R. A. (1958): The parietal lobe and behaviour. *Research Publications of the Association for Nervous and Mental Diseases*, 36: 35–117.

De Renzi, E. (1982): *Disorders of space exploration and cognition*. Wiley, New York.

Desmurget, M., Prablanc, C., Rossetti, Y., Arzi, M., Paulignan, Y., Urquizar, C. and Mignot, J. C. (1995): Postural and synergic control for three-dimensional movements of reaching and grasping. *Journal of Neurophysiology*, 74: 905–910.

Di Pellegrino, J. W., Klatzky, R. L. and McCloskey, B. P. (1992): Time course of preshaping for functional responses to objects. *Journal of Motor Behaviour*, 21: 307–316.

Dineen, J. J. and Hendrickson, A. E. (1981): Age-correlated differences in the amount of retinal degeneration after striate cortex lesions in monkeys. *Investigative Ophthalmology and Visual Science*, 21: 749–752.

Di Pellegrino, G., Fadiga, L., Fogassi, L., Gallese, V. and Rizzolatti, G. (1992): Understanding motor events: A neurophysiological study. *Experimental Brain Research*, 91: 176–180.

Dominey, P., Decety, J., Broussolle, E., Chazot, G. and Jeannerod, M. (1995): Motor imagery of a lateralized sequential task is assymetrically slowed in hemi-Parkinson patients. *Neuropsychologia*, 33: 727–741.

Dubois, B., Verin, M., Teixeira-Ferreira, C., Sirigu, A. and Pillon, B. (1994): How to study frontal lobe functions in Humans. In: *Motor and cognitive functions of the prefrontal cortex. Research and Perspectives in Neurosciences*, A. M. Thierry, J. Glowinski, P. S. Goldman-Rakic and Y. Christen (Eds), Springer-Verlag, Berlin Heidelberg, pp. 1–16.

Duchenne de Boulogne (1862): *L'éléctrisation localisée; son application à la pathologie et à la thérapeutique*. Baillère, Paris.

Duncan, J. (1986): Disorganisation of behaviour after frontal lobe damage. *Cognitive Neuropsychology*, 3: 271–290.

Ekman, G. and Junge, K. (1961): Psychophysical relations in visual perception of length, area and volume. *Scandinavian Journal of Psychology*, 2: 1–10.

Elliott, J. M. and Connolly, K. J. (1984): A classification of manipulative hand movements. *Developmental Medicine and Child Neurology*, 26: 283–296.

Eslinger, P. J. and Damasio, A. R. (1985): Severe disturbance of higher cognition after bilateral frontal lobe ablation. Patient EVR. *Neurology*, 35: 1731–1741.

Evarts, E. V. (1968): Relation of pyramidal tract activity to force exerted during voluntary movement. *Journal of Neurophysiology*, 31: 14–27.

Evarts, E. V. (1971): Feedback and corollary discharge. A merging of the concepts. *Neuroscience Research Program Bulletin*, 9: 86–112.

Evarts, E. V. and Tanji, J. (1974): Gating of motor cortex reflexes by prior instruction. *Brain Research*, 71: 479–494.

Fadiga, L., Fogassi, L., Pavesi, G. and Rizzolatti (1995): Motor facilitation during action observation. A magnetic stimulation study. *Journal of Neurophysiology*, 73: 2608–2611.

Faillenot, I., Toni, I., Decety, J., Grégoire, M. C. and Jeannerod, M. (1996): Visual pathways for object-oriented action and object identification. Functional anatomy with PET. *Cerebral Cortex*, (in press).

Farah, M. (1989): The neural basis of mental imagery. *Trends in Neuroscience*, 12: 395–399.

Faugier-Grimaud, S., Frenois, C. and Stein, D. G. (1978): Effects of posterior parietal lesions on visually guided behavior in monkeys. *Neuropsychologia*, 16: 151–168.

Faugier-Grimaud, S., Frenois, C. and Peronnet, F. (1985): Effects of posterior parietal lesions on visually guided movements in monkeys. *Experimental Brain Research*, 59: 125–138.

Fearing, F. (1930): *Reflex action. A study in the history of physiological psychology*. Williams and Wilkins. New edition, MIT Press, Cambridge, 1970.

Feinberg, I. (1978): Efference copy and corollary discharge. Implications for thinking and its disorders. *Schizophrenia Bulletin*, 4: 636–640.

Feltz, D. L. and Landers, D. M. (1983): The effects of mental practice on motor skill learning and performance. A meta-analysis. *Journal of Sport Psychology*, 5: 25–57.

Ferrier, D. (1876): *The functions of the brain*, Smith Elder, London.

Finke, R. A. (1979): The functional equivalence of mental images and errors of movement. *Cognitive Psychology*, 11: 235–264.

Fitts, P. M. (1954): The information capacity of the human motor system in controlling the amplitude of movement. *Journal of Experimental Psychology*, 47: 381–391.

Flament, D., Goldsmith, P., Buckley, C. G. and Lemon, R. N. (1993): Task dependence of responses in first dorsal interosseus muscle to magnetic brain stimulation, *Journal of Physiology*, 464: 361–378.

Flanders, M., Tillery, S. I. H. and Soechting, J. F. (1992): Early stages in a sensorimotor transformation. *Behavioral and Brain Sciences*, 15: 309–362.

Fogassi, L., Gallese, V., di Pellegrino, G., Fadiga, L., Gentilucci, M., Luppino, G., Matelli, M., Pedotti, A. and Rizzolatti, G. (1992): Space coding by premotor cortex. *Experimental Brain Research*, 89: 686–690.

Fox, P. T., Pardo, J. V., Petersen, S. E. and Raichle, M. E. (1987): Supplementary motor and premotor responses to actual and imagined hand movements with positron emission tomography. *Society for Neuroscience Abstracts*, 14: 33.

Fragaszy, D. M. (1983): Preliminary quantitative studies of prehension in squirrel monkeys (*Saimiri Sciureus*). *Brain Behaviour and Evolution*, 23: 81–92.

Fraser, C. and Wing, A. M. (1981): A case study of reaching by a user of a manually-operated artificial hand. *Prosthetics and Orthotics International*, 5: 151–156.

Freyd, J. J. (1993): Five hunches about perceptual processes and dynamic representations. In D. Meyer and S. Kornblum (Eds), *Attention and Performance XIV: Synergies in experimental psychology, artificial intelligence and cognitive neuroscience*. MIT Press, Cambridge, pp. 99–119.

Frith, C. D. (1992): *The cognitive neuropsychology of schizophrenia*. Erlbaum, Hillsdale.

Frith, C. D. (1995): Consciousness is for other people. *Behavioral and Brain Sciences*, 18: 682–683.

Frith, C. D. and Done, D. J. (1989): Experiences of alien control in schizophrenia reflect a disorder in the central monitoring of action. *Psychological Medicine*, 19: 359–363.

Frith, C. D., Friston, K., Liddle, P. F. and Frackowiak, R. S. J. (1991): Willed action and the prefrontal cortex in man. A study with PET. *Proceedings of the Royal Society*, 244: 241–246.

Funahashi, S., Bruce, C. J. and Goldman-Rakic, P. S. (1989): Mnemonic coding of visual space in the monkey's dorsolateral prefrontal cortex. *Journal of Neurophysiology*, 61: 331–349.

Funahashi, S., Bruce, C. J. and Goldman-Rakic, P. (1990): Visuospatial coding in primate prefrontal neurons revealed by oculomotor paradigms. *Journal of Neurophysiology*, 63: 814–831.

Funahashi, S., Bruce, C. J. and Goldman-Rakic, P. (1991): Neuronal activity related to saccadic eye movements in the monkey's dorsolateral prefrontal cortex. *Journal of Neurophysiology*, 65: 1464–1483.

Fuster, J. M. (1973): Unit activity in prefrontal cortex during delayed response performance. Neuronal correlates of transient memory. *Journal of Neurophysiology*, 36: 61–78.

Fuster, J. M. (1985): The prefrontal cortex, mediator of cross-temporal contigencies. *Human Neurobiology*, 4: 169–179.

Fuster, J. M. (1989): *The prefrontal cortex. Anatomy, physiology and neuropsychology of the frontal lobe*. Raven, New-York.

Gallese, V., Murata, A., Kaseda, M., Niki, N. and Sakata, H. (1994): Deficit of hand preshaping after muscimol injection in monkey parietal cortex. *Neuroreport*, 5: 1525–1529.

Galletti, C., Battaglini, P. P. and Fattori, P. (1993): Parietal neurons encoding spatial locations in craniotopic coordinates. *Experimental Brain Research*, 96: 221–229.

Gallistel, C. R. (1980): *The organization of action. A new synthesis*. Erlbaum, Hillsdale.

Gandevia, S. C. (1982): The perception of motor commands of effort during muscular paralysis. *Brain*, 105: 151–159.

Gandevia, S. C. (1987): Roles for perceived voluntary commands in motor control. *Trends in Neuroscience*, 10: 81–85.

Gandevia, S. G. and McCloskey, D. I. (1977): Changes in motor comands, as shown by changes in perceived heaviness, during partial curarization and peripheral anaesthesia in man. *Journal of Physiology*, 272: 673–689.

Gandevia, S. C. and Rothwell, J. (1987): Knowledge of motor commands and the recruitment of human motoneurons. *Brain*, 110: 1117–1130.

Gandevia, S. C., Macefield, V. G., Bigland-Ritchie, B., Gorman, R. B. and Burke, D. (1993a): Motoneuronal output and gradation of effort in attempts to contract actually paralysed leg muscles in man. *Journal of Physiology*, 470: 85–107.

Gandevia, S. C., Killian, K., McKenzie, D. K., Crawford, M., Allen, G. M., Gorman, R. B. and Hales, J. P. (1993b): Respiratory sensations, cardiovascular control, kinesthesia and transcranial stimulation during paralysis in humans. *Journal of Physiology*, 470: 85–107.

Garcin, R., Rondot, P. and de Recondo, P. (1967): Ataxie optique localisée aux deux hémichamps homonymes gauches. *Revue Neurologique*, 116: 707–714.

Gentilucci, M. and Negrotti, A. (1994): Dissociation between perception and visuomotor transformation during repoduction of remembered distances. *Journal of Neurophysiology*, 72: 2026–2030.

Gentilucci, M., Fogassi, L., Luppino, G., Matelli, M., Camarda, R. and Rizzolatti, G. (1988): Functional organization of inferior area 6 in the macaque monkey. 1. Somatotopy and the control of proximal movements. *Experimental Brain Research*, 71: 475–490.

Gentilucci, M., Castiello, U., Corradini, M. L., Scarpa, M., Ulmità, C. and Rizzolatti, G. (1991): Influence of different types of grasping on the transport component of prehension movements. *Neuropsychologia*, 29: 361–378.

Gentilucci, M., Chieffi, S., Scarpa, M. and Castiello, U. (1992): Temporal coupling between transport and grasp components during prehension movements: effects of visual perturbation. *Behavioural Brain Research*, 47: 71–82.

Gentilucci, M., Daprati, E., Toni, I., Chieffi, S. and Saetti, M. C. (1995): Unconscious updating of grasp motor program. *Experimental Brain Research*, 105: 291–303.

Georgopoulos, A. P. (1986): On reaching. *Annual Review of Neuroscience*, 9: 147–170.

Georgopoulos, A. P. and Massey, J. T. (1987): Cognitive spatial-motor processes. *Experimental Brain Research*, 65: 361–370.

Georgopoulos, A. P. and Lurito (1991): Cognitive spatial-motor processes. 6. Visuomotor memory scanning. *Experimental Brain Research*, 83: 453–458.

Georgopoulos, A. P., Kalaska, J. F. and Massey, J. T. (1981): Spatial trajectories and reaction times of aimed movements: effects of practice, uncertainty and change in target location. *Journal of Neurophysiology*, 46: 725–743.

Georgopoulos, A. P., Kalaska, J. F., Caminiti, R. and Massey, J. T. (1982): On the relations between the direction of two-dimensional arm movements and cell discharge in primate motor cortex. *Journal of Neuroscience*, 2: 1527–1537.

Georgopoulos, A. P., Schwartz, A. B. and Kettner, R. E. (1986): Neuronal population coding of movement direction. *Science*, 233: 1416–1419.

Georgopoulos, A. P., Lurito, J. T., Petrides, M., Schwartz, A. B. and Massey, J. T. (1989): Mental rotation of the neuronal population vector. *Science*, 243: 234–236.

Girard, P., Salin, P. and Bullier, J. (1991): Visual activity in areas V3A and V3 during reversible inactivation of area V1 in the macaque monkey. *Journal of Neurophysiology*, 66: 1493–1503.

Girard, P., Salin, P. and Bullier, J. (1992): Response selectivity in neurons in area MT of the macaque monkey during reversible inactivation of area V1. *Journal of Neurophysiology*, 67: 1–10.

Glendinning, D. S., Cooper, B. Y., Vierck, C. J. and Leonard, C. M. (1992): Altered precision grasping in stumptail macaques after fasciculus cuneatus lesions. *Somatosensory and Motor Research*, 9: 61–73.

Goldman-Rakic, P. S. (1987): Circuitry of primate prefrontal cortex and regulation of behavior by representational memory. In: *Handbook of Physiology. The Nervous System: Higher functions of the brain*, F. Plum (Ed.), American Physiological Society, Bethesda, Maryland, pp. 373–417.

Goldman-Rakic, P. S. (1995): Architecture of the prefrontal cortex and the central executive. In: *Structure and functions of the human prefrontal cortex*, J. Grafman, K. Hollyoak and F. Boller (Eds), Annals of the New York Academy of Sciences, 279: 71–83.

Goldman-Rakic, P. S. and Schwartz, M. (1982): Intredigitation of contralateral and ipsilateral columnar projections to frontal association cortex in primates. *Science*, 216: 755–757.

Goldman-Rakic, P. S., Chafee, M. and Friedman, H. (1993): Allocation of function in distributed circuits. In: T. Ohno, L. R. Squire and M. Fukuda (Eds), *Brain mechanisms of perception and memory. From neuron to behavior*. Oxford University Press, New York, pp. 445–456.

Goodale, M. A. (1983): Neural mechanisms of visual orientation in rodents: targets versus places. In: *Spatially oriented behaviour*, A. Hein and M. Jeannerod (Eds), Springer-Verlag, New-York, pp. 35–62.

Goodale, M. A. and Milner, A. D. (1992): Separate visual pathways for perception and action. *Trends in Neuroscience*, 15: 20–25.

Goodale, M. A., Pélisson, D. and Prablanc, C. (1986): Large adjustments in visually guided reaching do not depend on vision of the hand or perception of target displacement. *Nature*, 320: 748–750.

Goodale, M. A., Milner, A. D., Jakobson, L. S. and Carey, D. P. (1991): Perceiving the world and grasping it. A neurological dissociation. *Nature*, 349: 154–156.

Goodale, M. A., Meenan, J. P., Bülthoff, H. H., Nicolle, D. A., Murphy, K. J. and Racicot, C. I. (1994): Separate neural pathways for the visual analysis of object shape in perception and prehension. *Current Biology*, 4: 604–610.

Goodwin, G. M., McCloskey, D. I. and Mitchell, J. H. (1972): Cardiovascular and respiratory responses to changes in central command during isometric exercise at constant muscle tension. *Journal of Physiology*, 226: 173–190.

Gordon, A. M., Forssberg, H., Johansson, R. S. and Westling, G. (1991): Visual size cues in the programming of manipulative forces during precision grip. *Experimental Brain Research*, 83: 477–482.

Gottlieb, G. L., Corcos, D. M. and Argawal, G. C. (1989): Strategies for the control of voluntary movements with one mechanical degree of freedom. *Behavioral and Brain Sciences*, 12: 189–250.

Grafman, J. (1989): Plans, actions and mental sets. Managerial knowledge units in the frontal lobes. In: *Integrative theory and practice in clinical neuropsychology*, E. Perecman (Ed.), Erlbaum, Hillsdale.

Grafton, S. T., Woods, R. P., Mazziotta, J. C. and Phelps, M. E. (1991): Somatotopic mapping of the primary motor cortex in humans. Activation studies with cerebral blood flow and positron emission tomography. *Journal of Neurophysiology*, 66: 735–743.

Grafton, S. T., Mazziotta, J. C., Woods, R. P. and Phelps, M. E. (1992): Human functional anatomy of visually guided finger movements. *Brain*, 115: 565–587.

Gray, J. A. (1982): *The neuropsychology of anxiety. An enquiry into the functions of the septo-hippocampal system.* Oxford University Press, Oxford.

Gray, J. A. (1995): The contents of consciousness. A neuropsychological conjecture. *Behavioral and Brain Sciences*, 18: 659–722.

Graziano, M. S. A., Yap, G. S. and Gross, C. G. (1994): Coding of visual space by premotor neurons. *Science*, 266: 1054–1057.

Grillner, S. (1985): Neurobiological basis of rhythmic motor acts in vertebrates. *Science*, 228: 143–149.

Grunbaum, A. S. F. and Sherrington, C. S. (1903): Observations on the physiology of the cerebral cortex of the anthropoid apes. *Proceedings of the Royal Society*, 72: 62–65.

Guitton, D., Buchtel, H. A. and Douglas, R. M. (1985): Frontal lobe lesions in man cause difficulties in suppressing reflexive glances and in generating goal-directed saccades. *Experimental Brain Research*, 58: 455–472.

Haggard, P. and Wing, A. M. (1991): Remote responses to perturbation in human prehension. *Neuroscience Letters*, 122: 103–108.

Hale, B. D. (1982): The effects of internal and external imagery on muscular and ocular concomitants. *Journal of Sport Psychology*, 4: 379–387.

Halsband, U. and Passingham, R. E. (1982): The role of premotor and parietal cortex in the direction of action. *Brain Research*, 240: 368–372.

Halsband, U., Ito, N., Tanji, J. and Freund, H. J. (1993): The role of premotor cortex and the supplementary motor area in the temporal control of movement in man. *Brain*, 116: 243–266.

Halverson, H. (1931): An experimental study of prehension in infants by means of systematic cinema records. *Genetic Psychology Monographs*, 10: 110–286.

Harrington, D. L. and Haaland K. Y. (1991): Sequencing in Parkinson's disease: Abnormalities in programming and controlling movement. *Brain*, 114: 99–115.

Harris, D. V. and Robinson, W. J. (1986): The effect of skill level on EMG activity during internal and external imagery. *Journal of Sport Psychology*, 8: 105–111.

Hartje, W. and Ettlinger, G. (1973): Reaching in light and dark after unilateral posterior parietal ablations in the monkey. *Cortex*, 9: 346–354.

Hasan, Z. and Stuart, D. G. (1988): Animal solutions to problems of movement control: the role of proprioceptors. *Annual Review of Neuroscience*, 11: 199–223.

Haxby, J. V., Grady, C. L., Horwitz, B., Ungerleider, L. G., Mishkin, M. et al. (1991): Dissociation of object and spatial visual processing pathways in human extrastriate cortex. *Proceedings of the National Academy of Sciences, USA*, 88: 1621–1625.

Head, H. (1920): *Studies in neurology*, Hodder and Stoughton, London.

Heffner, R. and Masterton, B. (1975): Variation in form of the pyramidal tract and its relationship to digital dexterity. *Brain, Behavior and Evolution*, 12: 161–200.

Hécaen, H. and Albert, M. A. (1978): *Human Neuropsychology*. Wiley, New York.

Heilman, K. M., Rothi, L. J. and Valenstein, E. (1982): Two forms of ideomotor apraxia. *Neurology*, 32: 342–346.

Heilman, K. M., Bowers, D., Valenstein, E. and Watson, R. T. (1987): Hemispace and hemispatial neglect. In: *Neurophysiological and neuropsychological aspects of spatial neglect*, M. Jeannerod (Ed.), North-Holland, Amsterdam, pp. 115–150.

Hein, A. and Held, R. (1967): Dissociation of the visual placing response into elicited and guided components. *Science*, 158: 190–192.

Held, R. (1961): Exposure-history as a factor in maintaining stability of perception and coordination. *Journal of Nervous and Mental Diseases*, 132: 26–32.

Held, R. and Hein, A. (1963): Movement-produced stimulation of the development of visually-guided behavior. *Journal of Comparative Physiological Psychology*, 56: 872–876.

Hepp-Reymond, M. C., Wyss, U. R. and Anner, R. (1978): Neuronal coding of static force in the primate motor cortex. *Journal de Physiologie* (Paris), 74: 87–291.

Hepp-Reymond, M. C., Hüssler, E. J., Maier, M. A. and Qi, H. X. (1994): Force-related neuronal activity in two regions of the primate ventral premotor cortex. *Canadian Journal of Physiology and Pharmacology*, 72, 571–579.

Hess, W. R., Bürgi, S. and Bucher, V. (1946): Motorische Funktion des Tectal und Tegmentalgebietes. *Monatsschrift für psychiatrische Neurologie*, 112: 1–52.

Higgins, J. R. and Angel, R. W. (1970): Correction of tracking errors without sensory feedback. *Journal of Experimental Psychology*, 84: 412–416.

Hikosaka, O. and Wurtz, R. H. (1983): Visual and oculomotor functions of monkey substantia nigra pars reticulata. III Memory-contingent visual and saccade responses. *Journal of Neurophysiology*, 49: 1268–1284.

Hikosaka, O. and Wurtz, R. H. (1989): The basal ganglia. In: *The neurobilogy of saccadic eye movements*, R. H. Wurtz and M. E. Goldberg (Eds), Elsevier, Amsterdam, pp. 257–281.

Hinke, R. M., Xiaoping Hu, Stillman, A. E., Kim, S. G., Merkle, H., Salmi, R. and Ugurbil, K. (1993): Functional magnetic resonance imaging of Broca's area during internal speech, *Neuroreport*, 4: 675–678.

Hoff, B. and Arbib, M. A. (1993): Models of trajectory formation and temporal interaction of reach and grasp, *Journal of Motor Behavior*, 25: 175–192.

Holender, D. (1986): Semantic activation without conscious identification. *Behavioral and Brain Sciences*, 9: 1–66.

Holmes, G. (1922): The Croonian Lectures on the clinical symptoms of cerebellar disease and their interpretation. Lancet. Reprinted in: *Selected papers of Gordon Holmes*, C. G. Phillips (Ed.), Oxford University Press, Oxford, 1979, pp. 186–247.

Hoover, J. E. and Strick, P. L. (1993): Multiple output channels in the basal ganglia. *Science*, 259: 819–821.

Humphrey, N. K. and Weiskrantz, L. (1967): Vision in monkeys after removal of the striate cortex. *Nature*, 215: 595–597.

Humphreys, G. W. and Riddoch, M. J. (1987): The fractionation of visual agnosia. In: *Visual object processing. A cognitive neuropsychological approach*, G. W. Humphreys and M. J. Riddoch (Eds), Erlbaum, Hillsdale, pp. 281–306.

Hyvarinen, J. and Poranen, A. (1974): Function of the parietal associative area 7 as revealed from cellular discharges in alert monkeys. *Brain*, 97: 673–692.

Iberall, T. and Arbib, M. A. (1990): Schemas for the control of hand movements: an assay on cortical localization. In: *Vision and action. The control of grasping*. M. A. Goodale (Ed.), Ablex, Norwood, pp. 204–242.

Iberall, T., Bingham, G. and Arbib, M. A. (1986): Opposition space as a structuring concept for the analysis of skilled hand movements. In: Generation and modulation of action pattern, H. Heuer and C. Fromm (Eds), *Experimental Brain Research Series*, 15: 158–173.

Ilinsky, I. A., Jouandet, M. L. and Goldman-Rakic, P. S. (1985): Organization of the nigrothalamocortical system in the rhesus monkey. *Journal of Comparative Neurology*, 236: 315–330.

Ingvar, D. and Philipsson, L. (1977): Distribution of the cerebral blood flow in the dominant hemisphere during motor ideation and motor performance. *Annals of Neurology*, 2: 230–237.

Jacobsen, C. F., Wolfe, J. B. and Jackson, T. A. (1935): An experimental analysis of the functions of the frontal association areas in primates. *Journal of Nervous and Mental Diseases*, 82: 1–14.

Jacobson, E. (1930a): Electrical measurements of neuro-muscular states during mental activities. I. Imagination of movement involving skeletal muscle. *American Journal of Physiology*, 91: 567–608.

Jacobson, E. (1930b): Electrical measurements of neuro-muscular states during mental activities. III. Visual imagination and recollection. *American Journal of Physiology*, 95: 694–702.

Jacobson, E. (1931): Electrical measurements of neuromuscular states during mental activities. *American Journal of Physiology*, 96: 116–121.

Jahanshahi, M., Jenkins, I. H., Brown, R. G., Marsden, C. D., Passingham, R. E. and Brooks, D. J. (1995): Self-initiated versus externally triggered movements. I. An investigation using measurement of regional cerebral blood flow and movement-related potentials in normal and Parkinson's disease subjects. *Brain*, 118: 913–933.

Jakobson, L. S. and Goodale, M. A. (1991): Factors affecting higher-order movement planning: a kinematic analysis of human prehension. *Experimental Brain Research*, 86: 199–208.

Jakobson, L. S., Archibald, Y. M., Carey, D. P. and Goodale, M. A. (1991): A kinematic analysis of reaching and grasping movements in a patient recovering from optic ataxia. *Neuropsychologia*, 29: 803–809.

James, W. (1890): *Principles of Psychology*. MacMillan, London. New Edition, Dover, New York, 1950.

Jeannerod, M. (1981): Intersegmental coordination during reaching at natural visual objects. In: *Attention and Performance IX*, J. Long and A. Baddeey (Eds), Erlbaum, Hillsdale, pp. 153–168.

Jeannerod, M. (1983): *Le cerveau-machine. Physiologie de la volonté*, Paris, Fayard. English translation: *The brain-machine. The development of neurophysiological thought*, Cambridge, Mass: Harvard University Press, 1985.

Jeannerod, M. (1984): The timing of natural prehension movements. *Journal of Motor Behaviour*, 16: 235–254.

Jeannerod, M. (1986a): Mechanisms of visuomotor coordination: a study in normal and brain-damaged subjects. *Neuropsychologia*, 24: 41–78.

Jeannerod, M. (1986b): The formation of finger grip during prehension. A cortically mediated visuomotor pattern. *Behavioural Brain Research*, 19: 99–116.

Jeannerod, M. (1988): *The neural and behavioural organization of goal-directed movements*, Oxford University Press, Oxford.

Jeannerod, M. (1990): The representation of the goal of an action and its role in the control of goal-directed movements. In: *Computational neuroscience*, E. L. Schwartz (Ed.), MIT Press, Cambridge, pp. 352–368.

Jeannerod, M. (1991): The interaction of visual and proprioceptive cues in controlling reaching movements, In: *Motor control. Concepts and issues*, D. R. Humphrey and H. J. Freund (Eds), Wiley, New York, pp. 277–291.

Jeannerod, M. (1992): The where in the brain determines the when in the mind. *Behavioral and Brain Sciences*, 15: 212–213.

Jeannerod, M. (1993): Reichen und Greifen: Die parallele Spezifikation visumotorischer Kanäle. In: *Enzyklopädie der Psychologie: Psychomotorik, Kognition*, Vol. 3, chapitre 7, Hogrefe Verlag für Psychologie, pp. 509–574.

Jeannerod, M. (1994): A theory of representation-driven actions. In: *The perceived self: Ecological and interpersonal sources of self-knowledge*, U. Neisser (Ed.), Cambridge University Press, Cambridge.

Jeannerod, M. (1994): The representing brain. Neural correlates of motor intention and imagery. *Behavioral and Brain Sciences*, 17: 187–245.

Jeannerod, M. (1994): The hand and the object. The role of posterior parietal cortex in forming motor representations. *Canadian Journal of Physiology and Pharmacology*, 72: 525–534.

Jeannerod, M. (1995): Mental imagery in the motor context. *Neuropsychologia*, 33, 1419–1432.

Jeannerod, M. and Mouret, J. (1962): Etude des mouvements oculaires observés chez l'homme au cours de la veille et du sommeil. *Comptes Rendus de la Société de Biologie*, 156: 1407–1410.

Jeannerod, M. and Biguer, B. (1982): Visuomotor mechanisms in reaching within extrapersonal space. In: *Advances in the analysis of visual behavior*, D. Ingle, M. A. Goodale and R. Mansfield (Eds), MIT Press: Boston, pp. 387–409.

Jeannerod, M. and Prablanc, C. (1983): The visual control of reaching movements, In: *Motor control mechanisms in man*, J. Desmedt (Ed.), Raven, New York, pp. 13–29.

Jeannerod, M. and Decety, J. (1990): The accuracy of visuomotor transformation. An investigation into the mechanisms of visual recognition of objects. In: *Vision and action. The control of grasping*. M. Goodale (Ed.), Ablex, Norwood, pp. 33–48.

Jeannerod, M. and Rossetti, Y. (1993): Visuomotor coordination as a dissociable visual function: experimental and clinical evidences. In C. Kennard (Ed.), *Visual Perceptual Defects. Baillière's Clinical Neurology Vol. 2 No. 2* (pp. 439–460). Baillière Tindall.

Jeannerod, M., Michel, F. and Prablanc, C. (1984): The control of hand movements in a case of hemianaesthesia following a parietal lesion. *Brain*, 107: 899–920.

Jeannerod, M., Decety, J. and Michel, F. (1994): Impairement of grasping movements following a bilateral posterior parietal lesion. *Neuropsychologia*, 32: 369–380.

Jeannerod, M., Arbib, M. A., Rizzolatti, G. and Sakata, H. (1995): Grasping objects. The cortical mechanisms of visuomotor transformation. *Trends in Neuroscience*, 18: 314–320.

Jeeves, M. A. and Silver, P. H. (1988): The formation of finger grasp during prehension in an acallosal patient. *Neuropsychologia*, 26: 153–159.

Jenkins, I. H., Fernandez, W., Playford, E. D., Lees, A. J., Frackowiak, R. S. J., Passingham, R. E. and Brooks, D. J. (1992): Impaired activation of the supplementary motor area in Parkinson's disease is reversed when akinesia is treated with apomorphine. *Annals of Neurology*, 32: 750–757.

Jenkins, I. H., Brooks, D. J., Nixon, P. D., Frackowiak, R. S. J. and Passingham, R. E. (1994): Motor sequence learning. A study with positron emission tomography. *Journal of Neuroscience*, 14: 3775–3790.

Johansson, G. (1977): Studies on visual perception of locomotion. *Perception*, 6: 365–376.

Johansson, R. S. and Westling, G. (1984): Roles of glabrous skin receptors and sensorimotor memory in automatic control of precision grip when lifting rougher or more slippery objects. *Experimental Brain Research*, 56: 550–564.

Johansson, R. S. and Westling, G. (1987): Signals in tactile afferents from the fingers eliciting adaptive motor responses during precision grip. *Experimental Brain Research*, 66: 141–154.

Johansson, R. S. and Westling, G. (1988): Coordinated isometric muscle commands adequately and erroneously programmed for the weight during lifting task with precision grip. *Experimental Brain Research*, 71: 59–71.

Johnson, P. (1982): The functional equivalence of imagery and movement. *Quarterly Journal of experimental Psychology*, 34A: 349–365.

Johnson, P. B., Ferraina, S. and Caminiti, R. (1993): Cortical networks for visual reaching. *Experimental Brain Research*, 97: 361–365.

Jones, E. G. and Powell, T. P. S. (1970): An anatomical study of converging sensory pathways within the cerebral cortex of the monkey. *Brain*, 93: 793–820.

Jouffroy, F. K. (1993): Primate hands and the human hand. The tool of tools, In: *The use of tools by human and non-human primates*, A. Berthelet and J. Chavaillon (Eds), Oxford University Press, Oxford, pp. 6–33.

Kalaska, J. F. and Crammond, D. J. (1995): Deciding not to GO. Neuronal correlates of response selection in a GO/NOGO task in primate premotor and parietal cortex. *Cerebral Cortex*, 5: 410–428.

Kalaska, J. F., Caminiti, R. and Georgopoulos, A. P. (1983): Cortical mechanisms related to the direction of two dimensional arm movements. Relations in parietal area 5 and comparison with motor cortex. *Experimental Brain Research*, 51: 247–260.

Kapur, S., Rose, R., Liddle, P. F., Zipursky, R. B., Brown, G. M., Stuss, D., Houle, S. and Tulving, E. (1994): The role of the left prefrontal cortex in verbal processing. Semantic processing or willed action? *Neuroreport*, 5: 2193–2196.

Kato, M. and Tanji, J. (1972): Conscious control of motor units of human finger muscles. In: *Neurophysiology studied in man*, G. G. Samjen (Ed.), Excerpta Medica, Amsterdam.

Keele, S. W. (1968): Movement control in skilled motor performance. *Psychological Bulletin*, 70: 387–404.

Keele, S. W., Cohen, A. and Ivry, R. (1990): Motor programs. Concepts and issues, In: *Motor representations and control*, M. Jeannerod (Ed.), Attention and Performance XIII, Erlbaum, Hillsdale, pp. 77–110.

Kermadi, I. and Joseph, J. P. (1995): Activity in the caudate nucleus of monkey during spatial sequencing. *Journal of Neurophysiology*, 74: 911–933.

Kerr, N. H. (1983): The role of vision in 'visual imagery' experiments. Evidence from the congenitally blind. *Journal of Experimental Psychology. General*, 112: 265–277.

Kim, S. G., Jennings, J. E., Strupp, J. P., Andersen, P. and Ugurbil, K. (1995): Functional MRI of human motor cortices during overt and imagined finger movements. *International Journal of Imaging Systems and Technology*, 6: 271–279.

Klatzky, R. L., McCloskey, B., Doherty, S., Pellegrino, J. and Smith, T. (1987): Knowledge about hand shaping and knowledge about objects. *Journal of Motor Behaviour*, 19: 187–213.

Klatzky, R. L., Lederman, S. J. and Reed, C. (1989): Haptic integration of object properties. Texture, hardness and planar contour. *Journal of Experimental Psychology. Human Perception and Performance*, 15: 45–47.

Klatzky, R. L., Pellegrino, J., McCloskey, B. and Doherty, S. (1989): Can you squeeze a tomato? The role of motor representations in semantic sensibility judgements. *Journal of Memory and Language*, 28: 56–77.

Klatzky, R. L., Lederman, S. J. and Matula, D. E. (1993a): Haptic exploration in the presence of vision. *Journal of Experimental Psychology. Human Perception and Performance*, 19: 726–743.

Klatzky, R. L., Pellegrino, J., McCloskey, B. P. and Lederman, S. J. (1993b): Cognitive representations of functional interactions with objects. *Memory and Cognition*, 21: 294–303.

Kori, A., Miyashita, N., Kato, M., Hikosaka, O., Usui, S. and Matsumura, M. (1995): Eye movements in monkeys with local dopamine depletion in the caudate nucleus. II. Deficits in voluntary saccades. *The Journal of Neuroscience*, 15: 928–941.

Kosslyn, S. M., Flynn, R. A., Amsterdam, J. B. and Wang, G. (1990): Components of high-level vision: a cognitive neuroscience analysis and account of neurological syndromes, *Cognition*, 34: 203–277.

Kosslyn, S. M., Alpert, N. M., Thompson, W. L., Maljkovic, V., Weise, S. B., Chabris, C. F., Hamilton, S. E., Rauch, S. L. and Buonanno, F. S. (1993): Visual mental imagery activates topographically organized visual cortex. PET investigations. *Journal of Cognitive Neuroscience*, 5: 263–287.

Krogh, A. and Lindhard, J. (1913): The regulation of respiration and circulation during the initial stages of muscular work. *Journal of Physiology*, 47: 112–136.

Kurata, K. and Wise, S. P. (1988): Premotor cortex of rhesus monkey. Set-related activity during two conditional motor tasks. *Experimental Brain Research*, 69: 327–343.

Kusunoki, M., Tanaka, Y., Ohtsuka, H., Ishiyama, K. and Sakata, H. (1993): Selectivity of the parietal visual neurons in the axis orientation of objects in space. *Society for Neuroscience Abstracts*, 19: 770.

Kuypers, H. G. J. M. (1962): Corticospinal connections: postnatal development in rhesus monkey. *Science*, 138: 678–680.

Kwan, H. C., MacKay, W. A., Murphy, J. T. and Wong, Y. C. (1978): Spatial organization of precentral cortex in awake primates. II motor outputs. *Journal of Neurophysiology*, 41: 1120–1131.

Lacquaniti, F. and Soechting, J. (1982): Coordination of arm and wrist motion during a reaching task. *Journal of Neuroscience*, 2: 399–408.

Lacquaniti, F., Terzuolo, C. and Viviani, P. (1983): The law relating kinematic and figural aspects of drawing movements. *Acta Psychologica*, 54: 115–130.

Lacquaniti, F., Guigon, E., Bianchi, L., Ferraina, S. and Caminiti, R. (1995), Representing spatial information for limb movements. Role of area 5 in the monkey. *Cerebral Cortex*, 5: 391–409.

Lamotte, R. H. and Acuna, C. (1978): Defects in accuracy of reaching after removal of posterior parietal cortex in monkeys. *Brain Research*, 139: 309–326.

Landau and Jackendoff (1993): 'What' and 'Where' in spatial language and spatial cognition. *Behavioral and Brain Sciences*, 16: 217–238.

Landauer, T. K. (1962): Rate of implicit speech. *Perceptual and Motor Skills*, 15: 646.

Landsmeer, J. M. F. (1962): Power grip and precision handling. *Annals of rheumatical Diseases*, 21: 164–170.

Lang, W., Petit, L., Höllinger, P., Pietrzyk, U., Tzourio, N., Mazoyer, B. and Berthoz, A. (1994): A positron emission tomography study of oculomotor imagery. *Neuroreport*, 5: 921–924.

Laplane, D., Talairach, J., Meininger, V., Bancaud, J. and Orgogozzo, J. M. (1977): Clinical consequences of corticectomies involving the supplementary motor area in man. *Journal of Neurological Siences*, 34: 301–314.

Lashley, K. S. (1951): The problem of serial order in behavior. In L. P. Jeffress (Ed.) *Cerebral mechanisms in behavior. The Hixon Symposium*. Wiley, New York, pp. 112–136.

Laszlo, J. (1966): The performance of a simple motor task with kinaesthetic sense lost. *Journal of Experimental Psychology*, 18: 1–18.

Lawrence, D. G. and Hopkins, D. A. (1972): Development aspects of pyramidal control in the rhesus monkey. *Brain Research*, 40: 117–118.

Lawrence, D. G. and Kuypers, H. G. J. M. (1968): The functional organization of the motor system in the monkey. I. The effects of bilateral pyramidal lesions. *Brain*, 91: 1–14.

Lecas, J. C., Requin, J., Anger, C. and Vitton, N. (1986): Changes in neuronal activity in the monkey precentral cortex during preparation for movement. *Journal of Neurophysiology*, 56: 1680–1702.

Lederman, S. and Klatzky, R. L. (1987): Hand movements. A window into haptic object recognition. *Cognitive Psychology*, 19: 342–368.

Lederman, S. J. and Klatzky, R. L. (1990): Haptic classification of common objects. Knowledge-driven exploration. *Cognitive Psychology*, 22: 421–459.

Lehmkuhl, G. and Poeck, K. (1981): A disturbance in the conceptual organization of actions in patients with ideational apraxia. *Cortex*, 17: 153–158.

Lemon, R. N., Mantel, G. W. H. and Muir, R. B. (1986): Corticospinal facilitation of hand muscles during voluntary movements in the conscious monkey. *Journal of Physiology*, 381: 497–527.

Leonardo, M., Fieldman, J., Sadato, N., Campbell, G., Ibanez, V., Cohen, L., Deiber, M.-P., Jezzard, P., Pons, T., Turner, R., Le Bihan, D. and Hallett, M. (1995): A functional magnetic resonance imaging study of cortical regions associated with motor task execution and motor ideation in humans. *Human Brain Mapping*, 3: 83–92.

Lhermitte, F. (1983): 'Utilisation behaviour' and its relation to lesions of the frontal lobes. *Brain*, 106: 237–255.

Libet, B. (1985): Unconscious cerebral initiative and the role of conscious will in voluntary action. *Behavioral Brain Science*, 6: 529–566.

Libet, B., Gleason, C. A., Wright, E. W. and Perl, D. K. (1983): Time of conscious intention to act in relation to cerebral activities (readiness potential). The unconscious initiation of a freely voluntary act. *Brain*, 102: 193–224.

Loeb, G. E., Levine, W. S. and He, J. (1990): Understanding sensorimotor feedback through optimal control. *Cold Spring Harbor Symposia on Quantitative Biology*, 15: 791–803.

Luppino, G., Matelli, M., Camarda, R. and Rizzolatti, G. (1993): Corticocortical connections of area F3 (SMA-proper) and area F6 (Pre-SMA) in the Macaque monkey, *Journal of Comparative Neurology*, 335: 1–27.

Luppino, G., Matelli, M., Camarda, R. and Rizzolatti, G. (1993): Cortico-cortical connections of area F3 (SMA proper) and area F6 (pre-SMA) in the macaque monkey. *Journal of Comparative Neurology*, 338: 114–140.

Luppino, G., Matelli, M., Camarda, R. and Rizzolatti, G. (1994): Corticospinal projections from mesial frontal and cingulate areas in the monkey. *Neuroreport*, 5: 2545–2548.

Luria, A. (1966): *The higher cortical functions of man*. Basic Books, New York.

Lynch, J. C. (1980): The functional organization of posterior parietal association cortex. *Behavioral Brain Science*, 3: 485–498.

Mach, E. (1906): *Die Analyse der Empfindungen und das Verhältniss des Physichen zum Psychischen*. 5th Ed. Fischer, Jena.

MacKay, D. G. (1981): The problem of rehearsal or mental practice. *Journal of Motor Behavior*, 13: 247–285.

MacKay, W. A. (1992): Properties of reach related neuronal activity in cortical area 7a. *Journal of Neurophysiology*, 67: 1335–1345.

MacKenzie, C. L. and Iberall, T. (1994): *The grasping hand*. North Holland, Amsterdam.

MacNeilage, P. F. (1970): Motor control of serial ordering of speech. *Psychological Review*, 77: 182–196.

Macpherson, J. M., Marangoz, C., Miles, T. S. and Wiesendanger, M. (1982): Microstimulation of the supplementary motor area (SMA) in the awake monkey, *Experimental Brain Research*, 45: 410–416.

Mahoney, M. J. and Avener, M. (1987): Psychology of the elite athlete. An explorative study. *Cognitive Therapy and Research*, 1: 135–141.

Malenka, R. C., Angel, R. W., Hampton, B. and Berger, P. A. (1982): Impaired central error-correcting behaviour in schizophrenia. *Archives of General Psychiatry*, 39: 101–107.

Marcel, A. J. (1983): Conscious and unconscious perception. An approach to the relations between phenomenal experience and perceptual processes. *Cognitive Psychology*, 15: 238–300.

Marks, L. E. (1978): Multimodal perception. In: *Handbook of Perception*, C. Carterette and M. P. Freedman (Eds), Vol. VIII, Perceptual Coding, Acad. Press, New York, pp. 321–339.

Marr, D. (1982): *Vision*. Freeman, San Francisco.

Marsden, C. D. (1987): What do the basal ganglia tell the premotor cortical areas?. In *Motor areas of the cerebral cortex*, Ciba Symposium 132, Wiley, Chichester, pp. 282–300.

Marteniuk, R. G., MacKenzie, C. L., Jeannerod, M., Athenes, S. and Dugas, C. (1987): Constraints on human arm movement trajectories. *Canadian Journal of Psychology*, 41: 365–378.

Marteniuk, R. G., Leavitt, J. L., MacKenzie, C. L. and Athenes, S. (1990): Functional relationships between grasp and transport components in a prehension task. *Human Movement Science*, 9: 149–176.

Matelli, M., Luppino, G. and Rizzolatti, G. (1985): Patterns of cytochrome oxydase activity in the frontal agranular cortex of the macaque monkey. *Behavioral Brain Research*, 18: 125–136.

Matelli, M., Camarda, R., Glickstein, M. and Rizzolatti, R. (1986): Afferent and efferent projections of the inferior area 6 in the Macaque Monkey. *The Journal of Comparative Neurology*, 251: 281–298.

Matelli, M., Rizzolatti, G., Bettinardi, V., Gilardi, M. C., Perani, D., Rizzo, G. and Fazio, F. (1993): Activation of precentral and mesial motor areas during the execution of elementary proximal and distal arm movements. A PET study. *NeuroReport*, 4: 1295–1298.

Maxwell, J. C. (1867–68): On governors. *Proceedings of the Royal Society*, 16: 270–283.

McCloskey, D. I. and Torda, T. A. G. (1975): Corollary motor discharges and kinaesthesia. *Brain Research*, 100: 467–470.

McCloskey, D. I., Colebatch, J. G., Potter, E. K. and Burke, D. (1983): Judgements about onset of rapid voluntary movements in man. *Journal of Neurophysiology*, 49: 851–863.

McCloskey, D. I., Ebeling, P. and Goodwin, G. M. (1974): Estimation of weights and tensions and apparent involvement of a 'sense of effort'. *Experimental Neurology*, 42: 220–232.

McGrew, W. C. (1989): Why is ape tool-use so confusing? In: *The behavioural ecology of humans and other mammals*. V. Standen and R. A. Foley (Eds), Blackwell, Oxford.

Meeres, S. L. and Graves, R. E. (1990): Localisation of unseen visual stimuli by humans with normal vision. *Neuropsychologia*, 28: 1231–1237.

Mellah, S., Rispal-Padel, L. and Rivière, G. (1990): Changes in excitability of motor units during preparation for movement. *Experimental Brain Research*, 82: 178–186.

Meltzoff, A. N. (1995): Understanding the intentions of others. Re-enactment of intended acts by 18-month-old children. *Developmental Psychology*, 31: 838–850.

Merigan, W. H. and Maunsell, S. H. R. (1993): How parallel are the primate visual pathways? *Annual Reviews of Neuroscience*, 16: 369–402.

Meyer, D. E., Smith, J. E. K. and Wright, C. E. (1982): Models for the speed and accuracy of aimed movements. *Psychological Reviews*, 89: 449–482.

Meyer, D. E., Smith, J. E. K., Kornblum, S., Abrams, R. A. and Wright, C. E. (1990): Speed-accuracy tradeoffs in aimed movements. Toward a theory of rapid voluntary action. In: *Motor Control and representation, Attention and Performance XIII*, M. Jeannerod (Ed.), Erlbaum, Hillsdale, pp. 173–226.

Miles, F. A. and Evarts, E. V. (1979): Concepts of motor organisation. *Annual Review of Psychology*, 30: 327–362.

Miller, G. A., Galanter, E. and Pribram, K. H. (1960): *Plans and the structure of behavior*, Holt, New York.

Milner, B. (1964): Some effects of frontal lobectomy in man, In: *The frontal granular cortex and behavior*, J. M. Warren and K. Akert (Eds), McGraw-Hill, New York.

Milner, A. D., Perrett, D. I., Johnston, R. S., Benson, P. J., Jordan, T. R., Heeley, D. W., Bettucci, D., Mortara, F., Mutani, R., Terazzi, E. and Davidson, D. L. W. (1991): Perception and action in 'visual form agnosia' *Brain*, 114: 405–428.

Milner, A. D. and Goodale, M. A. (1993): Visual pathways to perception and action. In: *Progress in Brain Research*, T. P. Hicks, S. Molotchnikoff and T. Ono (Eds), Elsevier Science Publishers B.V., Amsterdam, pp. 317–337.

Mishkin, M. and Manning, F. J. (1978): Non-spatial memory after selective prefrontal lesions in monkeys. *Brain Research*, 143: 313–323.

Mishkin, M. and Ungerleider, L. G. (1982): Contribution of striate inputs to the visuospatial functions of parieto-preoccipital cortex in monkeys. *Behavioural Brain Research*, 6: 57–77.

Mishkin, M., Vest, B., Waxler, M. and Rosvold, H. E. (1969): A re-examination of the effects of frontal lesions in object alternation. *Neuropsychologia*, 7: 357–363.

Mishkin, M., Lewis, M. E. and Ungerleider, L. L. (1982): Equivalence of parieto-preoccipital subareas for visuospatial ability in monkeys. *Behavioural Brain Research*, 6: 41–56.

Mishkin, M., Ungerleider, L. G. and Macko, K. A. (1983): Object vision and spatial vision: two cortical pathways. *Trends in Neuroscience*, 6: 414–417.

Mitchell, D. B. and Richman, C. L. (1980): Confirmed reservations: mental travel. *Journal of Experimental Pychology, Human Perception and Performance*, 6: 58–66.

Mohler, C. W. and Wurtz, R. H. (1977): Role of striate cortex and superior colliculus in visual guidance of saccadic eye movements in monkeys. *Journal of Neurophysiology*, 40: 74–94.

Morel, A. and Bullier, J. (1990): Anatomical segregation of two cortical visual pathways in the macaque monkey. *Visual Neuroscience*, 4: 555–578.

Mountcastle, V. B. (1995): The parietal system and some higher brain functions. *Cerebral Cortex*, 5: 377–390.

Mountcastle, V. B., Lynch, J. C., Georgopoulos, A., Sakata, H. and Acuna, C. (1975): Posterior parietal association cortex of the monkey: command functions for operations within extra-personal space. *Journal of Neurophysiology*, 38: 871–908.

Muakkassa, K. M. and Strick, P. L. (1979): Frontal lobe inputs to primate motor cortex. Evidence for four somato-topically organized 'premotor' areas. *Brain Research*, 177: 176–182.

Muir, R. B. and Lemon, R. N. (1983): Corticospinal neurons with a special role in precision grip. *Brain Research*, 261: 312–316.

Morasso, P. (1981): Spatial control of arm movements. *Experimental Brain Research*, 42: 223–227.

Napier, J. R. (1955): Form and function of the carpo-metacarpal joint of the thumb. *Journal of Anatomy*, 89: 362–369.

Napier, J. R. (1956): The prehensile movements of the human hand. *Journal of Bone and Joint Surgery*, 38B: 902–913.

Napier, J. R. (1960): Studies of the hands of living primates. *Proceedings of the Zoological Society*, London, 134: 647–657.

Napier, J. R. (1961): Prehensility and opposability in the hands of primates. *Symp. Zool. Soc. London*, 5: 115–132.

Nashner, L. and Berthoz, A. (1978): Visual contribution to rapid motor responses during postural control. *Brain Research*, 150: 403–407.

Neisser, U. (1976): *Cognition and reality*. Freeman, San Francisco.

Nielsen, T. I. (1963): Volition: A new experimental approach. *Scandinavian Journal of Psychology*, 4: 225–230.

Niki, H. and Watanabe, M. (1979): Prefrontal and cingulate uniut activity during timing behavior in the monkey. *Brain Research*, 171: 213–224.

Norman, D. A. and Shallice, T. (1980): Attention to action: Willed and automatic control of behavior. Human Information Processing Technical Report No. 99, University of California, San Diego. Reprinted in: *Consciousness and self-regulation*, G. E. Schwartz and D. Schapiro (Eds), Plenum Press, New York (1986).

Oldfield, R. C. and Zangwill, O. L. (1942): Head's concept of the schema and its application in contemporary British psychology. *British Journal of Psychology*, 32: 267–286 and 33: 58–64.

Orgogozo, J. M. and Larsen, B. (1979): Activation of the supplementary motor area during voluntary movement in man suggests it works as a supramotor area. *Science*, 246: 847–850.

Orgogozo, J. M., Larsen, B., Roland, P. E. and Lassen, N. A. (1979): Activation de l'aire motrice supplémentaire au cours des mouvements volontaires chez l'homme. *Revue Neurologique (Paris)*, 1979, 135: 705–717.

Owen, A. M., Downes, B. J., Sahakian, B. J., Polkey, C. E. and Robbins, T. W. (1990): Planning and spatial working memory following frontal lobe lesions in man. *Neuropsychologia*, 28: 1021–1034.

Owen, A. M., James, M., Leigh, P. N., Summers, B. A., Marsden, C. D., Quinn, N. P., Lange, K. V. and Robbins, T. W. (1992): Fronto-striatal cognitive deficits at different stages of Parkinson disease. *Brain*, 115: 1727–1751.

Paillard, J. (1971): Les déterminants moteurs de l'organisation spatiale. *Cahiers de Psychologie*, 14: 261–316.

Paillard, J. and Beaubaton, D. (1974): Problèmes posés par les contrôles moteurs ipsilatéraux après déconnexion hémisphérique chez le singe. In: *Les syndromes de disconnexion calleuse chez l'homme*, Michel, F. and Schott, B. (Eds). Lyon: Hôpital Neurologique, pp. 137–171.

Paivio, A. (1986): *Mental representations. A dual coding approach*. Clarendon Press, Oxford.

Pandya, D. H., Van Hoesen, G. W. and Mesulam, M. M. (1981): Efferent connections of the cingulate gyrus in the rhesus monkey. *Experimental Brain Research*, 42: 319–330.

Parsons, L. M. (1987): Imagined spatial transformations of one's hands and feet. *Cognitive Psychology*, 19: 178–241.

Parsons, L. M. (1994): Temporal and kinematic properties of motor behavior reflected in mentally simulated action. *Journal of Experimental Psychology. Human Perception and Performance*, 20: 709–730.

Parsons, L. M., Fox, P. T., Downs, J. H., Glass, T., Hirsch, T. B., Martin, C. C., Jerabek, P. A. and Lancaster, J. L. (1995): Use of implicit motor imagery for visual shape discrimination as revealed by PET. *Nature*, 375: 54–58.

Pascual-Leone, A., Dang, N., Cohen, L. G., Brasil-Neto, J., Cammarota, A. and Hallett, M. (1995): Modulation of motor responses evoked by transcranial magnetic stimulation during the acquisition of new fine motor skills. *Journal of Neurophysiology*, 74: 1037–1045.

Passingham, R. (1975): Delayed matching after selective prefrontal lesions in monkeys. *Brain Research*, 92: 89–102.

Passingham, R. E. (1985a): Prefrontal cortex and the sequencing of movement in monkeys (Macaca Mulatta). *Neuropsychologia*, 23: 453–462.

Passingham, R. E. (1985b): Cortical mechanisms and cues for action. *Philosophical transactions of the Royal Society*. London, B308: 101–111.

Passingham, R. E., Perry, H. and Wilkinson, F. (1983a): Failure to develop a precision grip in monkeys with unilateral neocortical lesions made in infancy. *Brain Research*, 145: 410–414.

Passingham, R. E., Perry, V. H. and Wilkinson, F. (1983b): The long-term effects of removal of sensorimotor cortex in infant and adult Rhesus monkeys. *Brain*, 106: 675–705.

Paulignan, Y., MacKenzie, C., Marteniuk, R. and Jeannerod, M. (1991a): Selective perturbation of visual input during prehension movements. I. The effects of changing object position. *Experimental Brain Research*, 83: 502–512.

Paulignan, Y., Jeannerod, M., MacKenzie, C. and Marteniuk, R. (1991b): Selective perturbation of visual input during prehension movements. 2. The effects of changing object size. *Experimental Brain Research*, 87: 407–420.

Paus, T., Petrides, M., Evans, A. C. and Meyer, E. (1993): Role of human anterior cingulate cortex in the control of oculomotor, manual and speech responses: A positron emission tomography study, *Journal of Neurophysiology*, 70: 453–469.

Peele, T. L. (1944): Acute and chronic parietal lobe ablations in monkeys. *Journal of Neurophysiology*, 7: 269–286.

Pélisson, D., Prablanc, C., Goodale, M. A. and Jeannerod, M. (1986): Visual control of reaching movements without vision of the limb. II. Evidence of fast unconscious processes correcting the trajectory of the hand to the final position of a double-step stimulus. *Experimental Brain Research*, 62: 303–311.

Pellizzer, G., Sargent, P. and Georgopoulos, A. P. (1995): Motor cortical cell activity in a context-recall task. *Science*, 269: 702–705.

Penfield, W. and Boldrey, E. (1937): Somatic motor and sensory representation in the cerebral cortex of man as studied by electrical stimulation, *Brain*, 60: 389–443.

Perenin, M. T. and Jeannerod, M. (1975): Residual vision in cortically blind hemifields. *Neuropsychologia*, 13: 1–7.

Perenin, M. T. and Jeannerod, M. (1978): Visual function within the hemianopic field following early cerebral hemidecortication in man-I. Spatial localization. *Neuropsychologia*, 16: 1–13.

Perenin, M. T. and Vighetto, A. (1983): Optic ataxia. A specific disorder in visuomotor coordination. In *Spatially oriented behavior*, A. Hein and M. Jeannerod (Eds), Springer, New York, 305–326.

Perenin, M. T. and Vighetto, A. (1988): Optic ataxia: a specific disruption in visuomotor mechanisms. I. Different aspects of the deficit in reaching for objects. *Brain*, 111: 643–674.

Perenin, M. T. and Rossetti, Y. (1996): Residual grasping in an hemianopic field. A further instance of dissociation between perception and action. *Neuroreport.*

Perrett, D. I., Harris, M. H., Bevan, R., Thomas, S., Benson, P. J., Mistlin, A. J., Citty, A. J., Hietanen, J. K. and Ortega, J. E. (1989): Framework of analysis for the neural representation of animate objects and actions. *Journal of Experimental Biology,* 146: 87–113.

Petersen, S. E., Fox, P. T., Posner, M. I., Mintun, M. A. and Raichle, M. E. (1988): Positron emission tomographic studies of the processing of single words. *Nature,* 331: 585–589.

Petrides, M. and Pandya, D. N. (1984): Projections to the frontal cortex from the posterior parietal region in the rhesus monkey. *Journal of Comparative Neurology,* 228: 105–116.

Phillips, C. G. (1985): *Movements of the hand.* Liverpool University Press, Liverpool.

Pinker, S. (1984): Visual cognition: An introduction. *Cognition,* 18: 1–63.

Playford, E. D., Jenkins, I. H., Passingham, R. E., Nutt, J., Frackowiak, R. S. J. and Brooks, D. J. (1992): Impaired mesial frontal and putamen activation in Parkinson's disease. A positron emission tomographic study. *Annals of Neurology,* 32: 151–161.

Poeppel, Held, R. and Frost, D. (1973): Residual visual function after brain wounds involving the central visual pathways in man. *Nature,* 243: 295–296.

Pohl, W. (1973): Dissociation of spatial discrimination deficits following frontal and parietal lesions in monkeys. *Journal of Comparative Physiological Psychology,* 82: 227–239.

Poizner, H., Clark, M. A., Merians, A. S., Macauley, B., Rothi, L. J. G. and Heilman, K. M. (1995): Joint coordination deficits in limb apraxia. *Brain,* 118: 227–242.

Polyak, S. (1957): *The vertebrate visual system.* University of Chicago Press, Chicago.

Poppelreuter, W. (1917): *Die Störungen der niederen und höheren Schleistungen durch Verletzungen des Okzipitalhirns,* Voss, Leipzig, 1917 (Engl. transl. Oxford University Press, 1990).

Porter, R. and Lemon, R. (1993): *Corticospinal function and voluntary movement.* Clarendon Press, Oxford.

Posner, M. I., Petersen, S. E., Fox, P. T. and Raichle, M. E. (1988): Localization of cognitive operations in the human brain. *Science,* 240: 1627–1631.

Prablanc, C., Echallier, J. F., Komilis, E. and Jeannerod, M. (1979): Optimal response of eye and hand motor systems in pointing at a visual target. I. Spatio-temporal characteristics of eye and hand movements and their relationships when varying the amount of visual information. *Biological Cybernetics,* 35: 113–124.

Pribram, K. H. and Gill, M. M. (1976): *Freud's 'Project' reassessed.* Basic Books, New York.

Ptito, A., Lepore, F., Ptito, M. and Lassonde, M. (1991): Target detection and movement discrimination in the blind field of hemispherectomized patients. *Brain*, 114: 497–512.

Pylyshyn, Z. (1973): What the mind's eye tells the mind's brain. A critique of mental imagery. *Psychological Bulletin*, 80: 1–24.

Pylyshyn, Z. (1980): Computational models and empirical constraints. *Behavioral and Brain Sciences*, 1: 93–108.

Pylyshyn, Z. (1984): *Computation and Cognition*. MIT Press, Cambridge MA.

Quintana, J. and Fuster, J. M. (1993): Spatial and temporal factors in the role of prefrontal and parietal cortex in visuomotor integration. *Cerebral Cortex*, 3: 122–132.

Raichle, M. E., Fiez, J., Videen, T. O., Fox, P. T., Pardo, J. V. and Petersen, S. E. (1994): Practice-related changes in human brain functional anatomy during non-motor learning. *Cerebral Cortex*, 4: 8–26.

Ratcliff, G. and Davies-Jones, G. A. B. (1972): Defective visual localization in focal brain wounds. *Brain*, 95: 46–60.

Requin, J. (1992): From action representation to movement control. In: *Tutorials in motor behavior II*, G. E. Stelmach and J. Requin (Eds), North-Holland, Amsterdam, pp. 159–180.

Requin, J., Bonnet, M. and Semjen, A. (1977): Is there a specificity in the supraspinal control of motor structures during preparation. In: S. Dornic (Ed.) *Attention and Performance VI*, Erlbaum, Hillsdale, pp. 139–174.

Requin, J., Brener, J. and Ring, C. (1991): Preparation for action. In: J. R. Jennings and M. G. H. Coles (Eds), *Handbook of Cognitive Psychophysiology. Central and Autonomic Nervous System Approaches*. John Wiley Sons (City?).

Richman, C. L., Mitchell, D. B. and Reznick, J. S. (1979): Mental travel: some reservations. *Journal of Experimental Psychology, Human Perception and Performance*, 5: 13–18.

Riehle, A. and Requin, J. (1989): Monkey primary motor and premotor cortex. Single cell activity related to prior information about direction and extent of an intended movement. *Journal of Neurophysiology*, 61: 534–549.

Rizzolatti, G., Camarda, R., Fogassi, L., Gentilucci, M., Luppino, G. and Matelli, M. (1988): Functional organization of area 6 in the macaque monkey. II. Area F5 and the control of distal movements. *Experimental Brain Research*, 71: 491–507.

Rizzolatti, G., Fadiga, L., Gallese, V. and Fogassi, L. (1996): Premotor cortex and the recognition of motor actions. *Cognitive Brain Research*, 3: 131–141.

Robinson, D. A. (1975): Oculomotor control signals, In: *Basic mechanisms of ocular motility and their clinical implications*, G. Lennerstrand and P. Bach-Y-Rita (Eds), Pergamon Press, Oxford, pp. 337–374.

Robinson, D. L., Goldberg, M. E. and Stanton, G. B. (1978): Parietal association cortex in the primate. Sensory mechanisms and behavioural modulation. *Journal of Neurophysiology*, 41: 910–932.

Robbins, T. W., Roberts, A. C., Owen, A. M., Sahakian, B. J., Everitt, B. J., Wilkinson, L., Muir, J., De Salvia, M. and Tovée, M. (1994): Monoaminergic dependent cognitive functions of the prefrontal cortex in monkey and man.

In: *Motor and cognitive functions of the prefrontal cortal*, A. M. Thierry et al. (Eds), Berlin, Springer Verlag, pp. 93–111.

Rocha-Miranda, C. E., Bender, D. B., Gross, C. G. and Mishkin, M. (1975): Visual activation of neurons in inferotemporal cortex depends on striate cortex ans forebrain commissures. *Journal of Neurophysiology*, 38: 475–491.

Rode, G., Rossetti, Y. and Boisson, D. (1996): Inverse relationship between sensation of effort and muscular force during recovery from a pure motor hemiplegia. A single-case study. *Neuropsychologia*, 34: 87–95.

Rodman, H. R., Gross, C. G. and Albright, T. D. (1989): Afferent basis of visual response properties in area MT of the macaque. 1. Effects of striate cortex removal. *Journal of Neuroscience*, 9: 2033–2050.

Roland, P. E. (1984): Organisation of motor control by the normal human brain. *Human Neurobiology*, 2: 205–216.

Roland, P. E. and Friberg, L. (1985): Localization of cortical areas activated by thinking. *Journal of Neurophysiology*, 53: 1219–1243.

Roland, P. E., Skinhoj, E., Lassen, N. A. and Larsen, B. (1980): Different cortical areas in man in organization of voluntary movements in extrapersonal space. *Journal of Neurophysiology*, 43: 137–150.

Roll, J. P., Gilhodes, J. C., Roll, R. and Velay, J. L. (1990): Contribution of skelettal and extraocular proprioception to kinaesthetic representation. In: *Motor representation and control, Attention and Perofrmance XIII*, M. Jeannerod (Ed.), Erlbaum, Hillsdale, pp. 549–566.

Rosenbaum, D. A. (1980): Human movement initiation: specification of arm, direction and extent. *Journal of Experimental Psychology, General*, 109: 444–474.

Rosenbaum, D. A. and Jorgensen, M. J. (1992): Planning macroscopic aspects of manual control. *Human Movement Science*, 11: 61–69.

Rosenbaum, D. A., Marchak, F., Barnes, H. J., Vaughan, J., Slotta, J. D. and Jorgensen, M. J. (1990): Constraints for action selection. Overhand versus underhand grips. In: *Motor representation and control, Attention and Performance XIII*, M. Jeannerod (Ed.), Erlbaum, Hillsdale, pp. 321–342.

Rosenkilde, C. E., Bauer, R. H. and Fuster, J. M. (1981): Single cell activity in ventral prefrontal cortex of behaving monkeys. *Brain Research*, 209: 275–294.

Ross, H. E. and Bischof, K. (1981): Wundt's view on sensations of innervation: A review. *Perception*, 10: 319–329.

Roth, M., Decety, J., Raybaudi, M., Massarelli, R., Delon-Martin, C., Segebarth, C., Morand, S., Gemignani, A., Décorps, M. and Jeannerod, M. (1996): Possible involvement of primary motor cortex in mentally simulated movement. A functional magnetic resonance imaging study. *Neuroreport*, 7: 1280–1284.

Rothi, L. J. G., Heilman, K. M. and Watson, R. T. (1985): Pantomime comprehension and ideomotor apraxia. *Journal of Neurology, Neurosurgery and Psychiatry*, 48: 207–210.

Rothi, L. J. G., Ochipa, C. and Heilman, K. M. (1991): A cognitive neuropsychological model of limb apraxia. *Cognitive Neuropsychology*, 8: 443–458.

Rothwell, J. C., Traub, M. M., Day, B. L., Obeso, J. A., Thomas, P. K. and Marsden,

C. O. (1982): Manual motor performance in a deafferented man. *Brain*, 105: 515–542.

Roy, E., A. and Hall, C. (1992): Limb apraxia. A process approach. In: *Vision and motor control*, L. Proteau and D. Elliott (Eds), North-Holland, Amsterdam, pp. 261–282.

Ryding, E., Decety, J., Sjolhom, H., Stenberg, G. and Ingvar, H. (1993): Motor imagery activates the cerebellum regionally. A SPECT rCBF study with ^{99m}Tc-HMPAO. *Cognitive Brain Research*, 1: 94–99.

Sakata, H. and Kusunoki, M. (1992): Organization of space perception: neural representation of three-dimensional space in the posterior parietal cortex. *Current Opinion in Neurobiology*, 2: 170–174.

Sakata, H. and Taira, M. (1994): Parietal control of hand action. *Current Opinion in Neurobiology*, 4: 847–856.

Sakata, H., Shibutani, H., Kawano, K. and Harrington, T. L. (1985): Neural mechanisms of space vision in the parietal association cortex of the monkey. *Vision Research*, 25: 453–463.

Sakata, H., Shibutani, H., Ito, Y. and Tsurugai, K. (1986): Parietal cortical neurons responding to rotary movement of visual stimulus in space. *Experimental Brain Research*, 61: 658–663.

Sakata, H., Taira, M., Mine, S. and Murata, A. (1992): Hand-movement-related neurons of the posterior parietal cortex of the monkey: their role in the visual guidance of hand movements. In: *Control of arm movement in space: neurophysiological and computational approaches*, R. Caminiti, P. B. Johnson and Y. Burnod (Eds), Heidelberg: Springer, Berlin, pp. 185–198.

Sakata, H., Taira, M., Murata, A. and Mine, S. (1995): Neural mechanisms of visual guidance of hand action in the parietal cortex of the monkey. *Cerebral Cortex*, 5: 429–438.

Saltzman, E. (1979): Levels of sensorimotor representation. *Journal of Mathematical Psychology*, 20: 91–163.

Sanes, J. N. (1994): Neurophysiology of preparation, movement and imagery. *Behavioral and Brain Sciences*, 17: 221–223.

Scheerer, E. (1984): Motor theories of cognitive structure: a historical review. In: *Cognition and motor processes*, W. Prinz and A. F. Sanders (Eds), Springer, Berlin, pp. 77–97.

Scheerer, E. (1987): Muscle sense and innervation feelings. A chapter in the history of perception and action. In: *Perspectives on perception and action*, H. Heuer and A. F. Sanders (Eds), Erlbaum, Hillsdale, pp. 171–194.

Schieber, M. H. (1990): How might the motor cortex individuate movements. *Trends in Neuroscience*, 13: 440–445.

Schilder, P. (1935): *The image and appearance of the human body*. Routledge and Kegan Paul, London.

Schmidt, R. A. (1975): A schema theory of discrete motor skill learning. *Psychological Review*, 82: 225–2.

Schmidt, R. A. (1988): *Motor control and learning. A behavioral emphasis* (2nd ed.), Human Kinetics, Champaign, Ill.

Schneider, G. E. (1969): Two visual systems. *Science*, 163: 895–902.

Searle, J. (1983): *Intentionality. An essay in the philosophy of mind*. Cambridge University Press, Cambridge.

Seitz, R. J. and Roland, P. E. (1992): Learning of sequential finger movements in man: A combined kinematic and positron emission tomography (PET) study. *European Journal of Neuroscience*, 4: 154–165.

Sessle, B. J. and Wiesendanger, M. (1982): Structural and functional definition of the motor cortex in the monkey (Macaca Fascicularis). *Journal of Physiology*, 323: 245–265.

Shallice T. (1982): Specific impairments of planning. *Philosophical Transactions of the Royal Society*. London, 298: 199–209.

Shallice, T. (1988): *From neuropsychology to mental structure*. Cambridge University Press, Cambridge.

Shallice, T. and Burgess, P. W. (1991): Deficits in strategy application following frontal lobe damage in man. *Brain*, 114: 727–741.

Shaw, W. A. (1940): The relation of muscular action potentials to imaginal weight lifting. *Archives of Psychology*, 35: 5–50.

Shepard, R. N. and Metzler, J. (1971): Mental rotation of three-dimensional objects. *Science*, 171: 701–703.

Shepard, R. N. and Cooper, L. A. (1982): *Mental images and their transformations*. MIT Press, Cambridge.

Sherrington, C. S. (1947): *The integrative action of the nervous system*. Yale University Press, New Haven.

Shiffrar, M. and Freyd, J. J. (1990): Apparent motion of the human body. *Psychological Science*, 1: 257–264.

Shinoda, Y., Yokota, J. I. and Futami, T. (1981): Divergent projections of individual corticospinal axons to motoneurons of multiple muscles inn the monkey. *Neuroscience Letters*, 23: 7–12.

Sirigu, A., Duhamel, J. R. and Poncet, M. (1991): The role of sensorimotor experience in object recognition. *Brain*, 114: 2555–2573.

Sirigu, A., Cohen, L., Duhamel, J. R., Pillon, B., Dubois, B., Agid, Y. and Pierrot-Deseiligny, C. (1995a): Congruent unilateral impairments for real and imagined hand movements. *NeuroReport*, 6: 997–1001.

Sirigu, A., Cohen, L., Duhamel, J. R., Pillon, B., Dubois, B. and Agid, Y. (1995b): A selective impairment of hand posture for object utilization in apraxia. *Cortex*, 31: 41–56.

Sirigu, A., Zalla, T., Pillon, B., Grafman, J., Dubois, B. and Agid, Y. (1995c): Planning and script analysis following prefrontal lobe lesions. In: *Structure nd functions of the humn prefrontal cortex*, J. Grafman, K. Hollyoak and F. Boller (Eds), Annals of the New York Academy of Sciences, 279: 277–288.

Sivak, B. and MacKenzie, C. L. (1992): The contribution of peripheral vision and central vision to prehension. In: *Vision and motor control*, L. Proteau and D. Elliott (Eds), Elsevier, Amsterdam.

Sperry, R. W. (1943): Effect of 180° rotation of the retinal field in visuomotor coordination. *Journal of Experimental Zoology*, 92: 263–279.

Sperry, R. W. (1950): Neural basis of the spontaneous optokinetic response produced by visual inversion. *Journal of Comparative and Physiological Psychology*, 43: 482–489.

Sprague, J. M. (1972): The superior colliculus and pretectum in visual behavior. *Investigative Ophthalmology*, 11: 473–482.

Sprague, J. M. and Meikle, T. H. (1965): The role of the superior colliculus in visually guided behavior. *Experimental Neurology*, 11: 115–146.

Stein, J. (1978): Long-loop motor control in monkey. The effects of transient cooling of parietal cortex and of cerebellar nuclei during tracking tasks. In: J. Desmedt (Ed.), *Cerebral motor control in man. Long loop mechanisms*. Karger, Basel, pp. 107–122.

Stelmach, G. E. and Walsh, M. F. (1973): The temporal placement of interpolated movements in short-term memory. *Journal of Motor Behavior*, 5: 165–173.

Stelmach, G. E., Castiello, U. and Jeannerod, M. (1994): Orienting the finger opposition space during prehension movements. *Journal of Motor Behavior*, 26: 178–186.

Stephan, K. M., Fink, G. R., Passingham, R. E., Silbersweig, D., Ceballos-Baumann, A. O., Frith, C. D. and Frackowiak, R. S. J. (1995): Functional anatomy of the mental representation of upper extremity movements in healthy subjects. *Journal of Neurophysiology*, 73: 373–386.

Sternberg, S. (1966): High speed scanning in human memory. *Science*, 153: 652–654.

Sternberg, S., Knoll, R. L., Monsell, S. and Wright, C. E. (1988): Motor programs and hierarchical organization in the control of rapid speech. *Phonetica*, 45: 175–197.

Sternberg, S., Knoll, R. L. and Turock, D. L. (1990): Hierarchical control in the execution of action. Tests of two invariance properties. In: *Motor representation and control, Attention and Performance XIII*, M. Jeannerod (Ed.), Erlbaum, Hillsdale, pp. 3–55.

Stevens, S. S. and Guirao, M. (1963): Subjective scaling of length and area and the matching of length to loudness and brightness. *Journal of Experimental Psychology*, 66: 177–186.

Stuss, D. T., Shallice, T., Alexander, M. P. and Picton, T. W. (1995): A multidisciplinary approach to anterior attentional functions. In: *Structure and functions of the humn prefrontal cortex*, J. Grafman, K. Hollyoak and F. Boller (Eds), Annals of the New York Academy of Sciences, 279: 191–211.

Susman, R. L. (1988): Hand of *Paranthropus robustus* from member 1, Swartkrans, *Science*, 240: 781–784.

Taira, M., Mine, S., Georgopoulos, A. P., Murata, A. and Sakata, H. (1990): Parietal cortex neurons of the monkey related to the visual guidance of hand movements. *Experimental Brain Research*, 83: 29–36.

Tanji, J., Shima, K. (1994): Role for supplementary motor area cells in planning several movements ahead. *Nature*, 371: 4413–4416.

Tanné, J., Boussaoud, D., Boyer-Zeller, N. and Rouiller, E. (1995): Direct visual pathways for reaching movements in the macaque monkey. *Neuroreport*, 7: 267–272.

Taylor, J. L., McCloskey, D. I. (1990): Triggering of preprogrammed movements as reactions to masked stimuli. *Journal of Neurophysiology*, 63: 439–446.

Teghtsoonian, M. (1965): The judgement of size. *American Journal of Psychology*, 76: 392–402.

Teuber, H. L. (1960): Perception. In: Field, J., Magoun, H. W. and Hall, V. E. (Eds), *Handbook of Physiology, Section I, Neurophysiology*, American Physiological Society, Washington, pp. 89–121.

Tower, S. S. (1940): Pyramidal lesion in the monkey. *Brain*, 63: 36–90.

Trevarthen, C. B. (1968): Two mechanisms of vision in primates. *Psychologische Forschung*, 31: 299–337.

Twitchell, T. E. (1954): Sensory factors in purposive movements. *Journal of Neurophysiology*, 17: 239–252.

Twitchell, T. E. (1970): Reflex mechanisms and the development of prehension. In: Connolly, K. (Ed.), *Mechanisms of motor skill development*, Academic Press, London, 25–38.

Tyszka, J. M., Grafton, S. T., Chew, W., Woods, R. P. and Colletti, P. M. (1994): Parceling of mesial frontal motor areas during ideation and movement using functional magnetic resonance imaging at 1.5 Tesla. *Annals of Neurology*, 35: 746–749.

Tzavaras, A. and Masure, M. C. (1975): Aspects différents de l'ataxie optique selon la latéralisation hémisphérique de la lésion. *Lyon Médical*, 236: 673–683.

Ungerleider, L. and Mishkin, M. (1982): Two cortical visual systems. In: *Analysis of visual behavior*, D. J. Ingle, M. A. Goodale and R. J. W. Mansfield (Eds), MIT Press, Cambridge, pp. 549–586.

Ungerleider, L. and Haxby, J. V. (1994): 'What' and 'Where' in the human brain. *Current Opinions in Neurobiology*, 4: 157–165.

Uno, Y., Kawato, M. and Suzuki, R. (1989): Formation and control of optimal trajectory in human multijoint arm movement. Minimum torque change model. *Biological Cybernetics*, 61: 89–101.

Vallbo, A. B. (1973): Muscle spindle afferent discharge from resting and contracting muscles in normal human subjects. In: *New developments in electromyography and clinical neurophysiology, Vol. 3: Human reflexes, Pathophysiology of motor systems, Methodology of human reflexes*, J. E. Desmedt (Ed.), Karger, Basel, pp. 251–262.

Van der Heijden, A. H. C. (1992): *Selective attention in vision*. New York, Routledge.

Van der Heijden, A. H. C. and Bridgeman (1994): Action and Intention. *Behavioral and Brain Sciences*, 17: 225–226.

Van Essen, D. C. and Maunsell, J. H. R. (1983): Hierarchical organization and functional streams in the visual cortex. *Trends in Neuroscience*, 6: 370–375.

Ventre, J., Zee, D. S., Papageorgiou, H. and Reich, S. (1992): Abnormalities of predictive saccades in hemi-parkinson's disease. *Brain*, 115: 1147–1165.

Vital-Durand, F., Putkonen, P. T. S. and Jeannerod, M. (1974): Motion detection and optokinetic responses in dark reared kittens. *Vision Research*, 14: 141–142.

Viviani, P. (1990): Common factors in the control of free and constrained movements. In: *Motor representation and control, Attention and Performance XIII*. M. Jeannerod (Ed.), Erlbaum, Hillsdale, pp. 345–373.

Viviani, P. and McCollum, G. (1983): The relation between linear extent and velocity in drawing movements. *Neuroscience*, 10: 211–218.

Viviani, P. and Stucchi, N. (1992a): Biological movements look uniform. Evidence of motor-perceptual interactions. *Journal of Experimental Psychology, Human Perception and Performance*, 18: 603–623.

Viviani, P. and Stucchi, N. (1992b): Motor-perceptual interactions. In: *Tutorials in motor Behavior II*, G. E. Stelmach and J. Requin (Eds), Elsevier, Amsterdam, pp. 229–248.

Vogt, S. (1995): On relations between perceiving, imagining, and performing in the learning of cyclical movement sequences. *British Journal of Psychology*, 86: 191–216.

Von Cramon, D. and Kerkhoff, G. (1993): On the cerebral organization of elementary visuo-spatial perception. In: *Functional organization of the human visual cortex*, B. Gulyas, D. Ottoson and P. E. Roland (Eds), Oxford, Pergamon, pp. 211–231.

Von Holst, E. and Mittelstaedt, H. (1950): Das Reafferenzprinzip. Wechselwirkungen zwischen Zentralnervensystem und Peripherie. *Naturwissenschaften*, 37: 464–476.

Von Holst, E. (1954): Relations between the central nervous system and the peripheral organs. *British Journal of Animal Behavior*, 2: 89–94.

Wallace, S. A. and Weeks, D. L. (1988): Temporal constraints in the control of prehensive movements. *Journal of Motor Behavior*, 20: 81–105.

Wang, Y. and Morgan, W. P. (1992): The effects of imagery perspectives on the physiological responses to imagined exercice. *Behavioural Brain Research*, 52: 167–174.

Wannier, T. M. J., Maler, M. A. and Hepp-Reymond, M. C. (1989): *Neuroscience Letters*, 98: 63–68.

Wannier, T. M. J., Maier, M. A. and Hepp-Reymond, M. C. (1991): Contrasting properties of monkey somatosensory and motor cortex neurons activated during the control of force in precision grip. *Journal of Neurophysiology*, 65: 572–589.

Watanabe, M. (1986): Prefrontal unit activity during delayed conditional go/no-go discrimination in the monkey. 2. Relation to go and no-go responses. *Brain Research*, 382: 15–27.

Watson, J. D. G., Myers, R., Frackowiak, R. S. J., Hajnal, J. V., Woods, R. P. and Mazziotta, J. C. (1993): Area V5 of the human brain. Evidence from a combined study using positron emission tomography and magnetic resonance imaging. *Cerebral Cortex*, 3: 79–94.

Wehner, T., Vogt, S. and Stadler, M. (1984): Task-specific EMG characteristics during mental training, *Psychological Research*, 46: 389–401.

Weinrich, M. and Wise, S. P. (1982): The premotor cortex in the monkey. *Journal of Neuroscience*, 2: 1329–345.

Wiesendanger, M. (1986): Redistributive function of the motor cortex, *Trends in Neuroscience*, 9: 120–125.

Wiesendanger, M., Corboz, M., Hyland, B., Palmeri, A., Maier, V., Wicki, U. and Rouiller, E. (1992): Bimanual synergies in primates, *Experimental Brain Research Series*, 22: 45–64.

Weiskrantz, L. (1986): *Blindsight. A case study and implications*. Oxford: Oxford University Press.

Weiskrantz, L., Warrington, E. R., Sanders, M. D., Marshall, J. (1974): Visual capacity in the hemianopic field following a restricted occipital ablation. *Brain*, 97: 709–728.

Weiss, P. (1941): Self-differentition of the basic patterns of coordination. *Comparative Psychological Monographs*, 17, No. 4.

Westling, G. and Johansson, R. S. (1984): Factors influencing the force control during precision grip. *Experimental Brain Research*, 53: 277–284.

Wilson, F. A. W., O'Scalaidhe, S. P. and Goldman-Rakic, P. S. (1993): Dissociation of object and spatial processing domains in primate frontal cortex. *Science*, 260: 1955–1958.

Wing, A. M. and Fraser, C. (1983): The contribution of the thumb to reaching movements. *Quarterly Journal of Experimental Psychology*, 35A: 297–309.

Wing, A. M., Turton, A. and Fraser, C. (1986): Grasp size and accuracy of approach in reaching. *Journal of Motor Behavior*, 18: 245–260.

Wise, R., Chollet, F., Hadar, U., Friston, K., Hoffer, E. and Frackowiak R. S. J. (1991): Distribution of cortical neural networks involved in word comprehension and word retrieval. *Brain*, 114: 1803–1817.

Wishaw, I. Q. and Gorny, B. (1994): Arpeggio and fractionated digit movements used in prehension by rats. *Behavioural Brain Research*, 60: 15–24.

Wolpert, D. M., Ghahramani, Z. and Jordan, M. I. (1995): An internal model for sensorimotor integration. *Science*, 269: 1880–1882.

Wong, E. and Mack, A. (1981): Saccadic programming and perceived location. *Acta Psychologica*, 48: 123–131.

Woodworth, R. S. (1903): *Le Mouvement*. Paris, Doin.

Wuyam, B., Moosavi, S. H., Decety, J., Adams, L., Lansing, R. W. and Guz, A. (1995): Imagination of dynamic exercise produced ventilatory responses which were more apparent in competitive sportsmen. *Journal of Physiology*, 482: 713–724.

Yue, G. and Cole, K. J. (1992): Strength increases from the motor program. Comparison of training with maximal voluntary and imagined muscle contractions. *Journal of Neurophysiology*, 67: 1114–1123.

Zeki, S. (1993): *A vision of the brain*. Blackwell, Oxford.

Zeki, S., Watson, J. D. G., Lueck, C. J., Friston, K. J., Kennard, C. and Frackowiak, R. S. J. (1991): A direct demonstration of functional specialization in human visual cortex. *Journal of Neuroscience*, 11: 641–649.

Subject index

Authors' index